Latino Los Angeles in Film and Fiction

Latino Los Angeles in Film and Fiction

The Cultural Production of Social Anxiety

Ignacio López-Calvo

The University of Arizona Press   Tucson

The University of Arizona Press
© 2011 The Arizona Board of Regents
All rights reserved
First issued as a paperback edition 2013

www.uapress.arizona.edu

Library of Congress Cataloging-in-Publication Data
López-Calvo, Ignacio.
    Latino Los Angeles in film and fiction : the cultural production
of social anxiety / Ignacio López-Calvo.
        p.   cm.
    Includes bibliographical references and index.
    ISBN 978-0-8165-2926-1 (cloth : alk. paper)
    ISBN 978-0-8165-3104-2 (pbk. : alk. paper)
    1. American literature—Mexican American authors—History
and criticism—Theory, etc.   2. Mexican Americans in motion
pictures. 3. Popular culture—United States—History.
4. Mexican Americans in literature.   5. Mexican Americans—
Intellectual life.   6. Los Angeles (Calif.)—In motion pictures.
7. Culture.   8. Social phobia.   I. Title.
    PS153.M4L67   2011
    810.99928790896872—dc22   2010030215

Manufactured in the United States of America on acid-free,
archival-quality paper and processed chlorine free.

16   15   14   13   6   5   4   3   2

To my former students at California State University, Los Angeles

Contents

Figures

Foreword

Roberto Cantú

California State University, Los Angeles

In the past two decades, Chicano and Chicana literary critics have questioned the 1970s idea of the "origin" of Chicano literature, taking us back to other origins and sources to argue for alternative ways to conceptualize its history. This relatively recent theoretical break, expressed through regional variants and as yet lacking a comprehensive study, emerged in Texas, New Mexico, and California, with diverse conceptions regarding the "difference" that distinguishes Chicano from U.S. mainstream literature. In spite of the branching paths that differentiate these theoretical directions, all argue against the claim that Chicano literature was a historical possibility only after the Second World War and the civil rights era.

Ramón Saldívar's *Chicano Narrative: The Dialectics of Difference* (1990) marked the first symptom of rebellion against the 1970s idea of Chicano literary origins, pointing to the 1846–48 U.S.–Mexico war as a historical cornerstone for Chicano literature and culture. Since then, the Recovering the U.S. Hispanic Literary Heritage project, established in the University of Houston by the editors of Arte Público Press, has become the center for a study of Hispanic literature that includes writers of Latin American ancestry with connected histories to the United States, such as Puerto Ricans, Cubans, Mexicans, and Guatemalans, among others.[1]

Literary critics, such as Genaro Padilla and Erlinda Gonzales-Berry, affiliated with the Nuevomexicano Literary Heritage editorial series sponsored by the University of New Mexico, have grounded the origins of Chicano literary history in the early Spanish colonial settlements, thus spotlighting a different historical juncture: the Spanish conquest and colonization in the New World. On the other hand, critics in California have contributed with their own distinctive theoretical writings, no doubt influenced by California's "Pacific Rim" frontier. A leadership role was initiated at the UC Santa Barbara campus by literary critics such as Luis Leal, María Herrera-Sobek, and Francisco Lomelí, with an emphasis that encompasses geopolitics and world ethnic groups, led by questions concerned with historical and cultural origins (understood at the level of contending civilizations) and political conditions on a global scale.[2] The theoretical borders, however, are not strictly enforced: Chicano and Chicana critics often publish articles and books that flow in more than one new direction.[3]

In spite of internal differences in method and scope, these new critical pathways in Chicano literary theory are driven by a shared vision: Chicano literature has *origins* that are remote, manifold, and conflictive. In other words, the critical consensus—at times implicit, often categorical—tells a different story: the space and history of the Southwest have been objects of symbolic appropriation during centuries prior to the 1846–48 war between the United States and Mexico. Thus, Chicano history encompasses a heterogeneous world that has been routinely simplified and misinterpreted since the age of discovery, conquest, and colonization.

Ignacio López-Calvo's *Latino Los Angeles in Film and Fiction* is a culminating work within this generation of critics who are reconfiguring the range and scope of Chicano/Latino literary and cultural studies. This book's centralizing force gathers histories of regions, nations, and world powers—for instance, Spain and the United States—and sets the interplay of unresolved contradictions in one metropolitan area: Los Angeles. In his introduction, López-Calvo informs the reader that the book is "a story about the Los Angeles paradox . . . for some, an apocalyptic dystopia; for others . . . the promised land for a fresh start." This book is thus a study of imagined differences, of ghostly invisibilities, and of recurring dark nights in the Americas. It is a focused and extensive critique of the centuries-long blueprint that gave meaning to the power dynamics of European conquests in the New World, from the Caribbean and ancient Mexico to California, an imperial blueprint that continues to be a major subtext in most Chicano and Latino literature. The geography and historical moment that forged the template for the colonial relations between peoples of Spanish ancestry and indigenous peoples in the Americas have been traditionally set in Mexico-Tenochtitlán after the 1521 Spanish conquest. To better understand this book by López-Calvo, let us consider a previous determining contact.

Hernán Cortés's first victory in the Champotón region resulted in a symbolic ritual of territorial possession, followed by an auspicious native tribute: a translator who would later give Cortés the linguistic edge on Moctezuma's rule. According to Bernal Díaz del Castillo,

Cortés marched with his soldiers directly toward the courtyard of the Maya city of Cintla and engaged in a symbolic gesture: he declared the urban space to be the sole possession of the king of Spain and, immediately afterward—to confirm the royal ownership—he drew his sword, slashed the sign of the cross on a silk-cotton tree that stood in the middle of the courtyard (hence, Cintla's *cosmic center*), and declared that, as his king's servant, he would fight with his sword and shield against anyone who objected. No one did, not even the local rulers, who no doubt were not consulted.

After taking the city both militarily and ritually, Cortés obtained from the region's *caciques* (lords) a gift of gold and twenty maids, which included doña Marina, who would become Cortés's favorite translator, both in languages (Nahua to Spanish) and in bloodlines: she bore him a son named Martín Cortés. Declaring the native gods to be mere idols, in spite of protests from Maya rulers, Cortés ordered that an image of the Virgin Mary be set in the center of town, to be known no longer as Cintla, but as Santa María de la Victoria.[4] A new *axis mundi* was thus established based on Spanish iconography and religious discourse.

In retrospect, the Champotón battle was truly apocalyptic in the sense that it marked the beginning of the end for Mesoamerica as a flourishing civilization, opening a new historical process of European religious symbolism, different rituals of incorporation and exclusion, and dramatic but inevitable cultural mistranslations. As such, that remote battle in modern-day Tabasco was more than just a minor skirmish between the warriors of Maya lords and the soldiers of Hernán Cortés: it can be interpreted as the blueprint or template for all future European conquests in the Americas.

Novelists studied in this book by López-Calvo stem from different Latin American regions and nations, such as the U.S. Southwest, Guatemala, and, among others, Chile. The book also includes novels by non-Latino writers who have contributed to Chicano/Latino literature, among them Kate Braverman and Danny Santiago. In most of the novels studied in the book—from *Famous All Over Town* to *The Tattooed Soldier*—the history of the Spanish conquest functions as a constant narrative background that includes migrants from Mexico and Latin America who reside in the city of Los Angeles. Embedded in these narratives one finds a Mexican or Latino history of conflict that includes the United States.

The U.S. conquest of the Southwest in 1848 manifests a striking continuity in European habits of territorial incorporation and cultural appropriation. In *Memoirs of My Life,* John Charles Frémont recalls his disagreement and quarrel with José Castro, the military commander in Alta California during the 1840s. No doubt to provoke a battle that would be the pretext for an international war, Frémont engaged in a symbolic possession of Gavilán Peak, a mountain between Monterrey and the San Joaquín Valley near San Francisco. Frémont recalls raising the U.S. flag on top of the mountain and his men cheering ("it proved to be a premonitory symptom," he notes in his memoir); three days later, however, the pole and the flag fell to the ground, a chance occurrence interpreted by Frémont as a providential sign to move camp. Frémont remembers that four months after the divine sign, Commodore Sloat raised the U.S. flag in Monterrey, Yerba Buena, Sonoma, Sutter's Fort, and, soon thereafter, Los Angeles. On his way to Monterrey, Frémont and his men gave "a marching salute to the Gavilán Peak, where in March . . . we had hoisted the flag."[5] In Frémont's mind, the Californios had no likelihood of winning the war against the U.S. occupation: God was on the U.S. side.

A character trait is revealed in the memoir: Frémont did not forget his quarrel with José Castro.[6] Soon after Sloat's occupation of California, Frémont chased after the former Mexican military commander, forcing Castro and his men to find a brief sanctuary in the San Gabriel Mountains near Los Angeles. Within a few days Castro's men were captured by Frémont. Castro fled to Mexico, and Frémont marched into Los Angeles, eager to enforce the new colonial relations between Mexicans and Anglo-Americans. As a sign of national possession of place and folkways, Frémont donned Californio clothes and rode through the streets of Los Angeles on an "uncommonly beautiful sorrel horse," a gift from Juan Bandini, one of the wealthiest Californios during Mexican rule. The recollection elicited a commentary from Frémont: "little gifts nourish friendship."[7]

In such circumstances and frame of mind began the "Spanish fantasy" in California. Modeled after James Fenimore Cooper's fictional character Natty Bumppo, Anglo-Americans of the period might have dressed as Mohicans or Spaniards, but only as symbolic appropriation of Otherness. In other words, the deerskin clothes and Californio attire and sombrero are theatrical displays of land ownership, dominion, and adaptation: since then, California artists, especially those born in other parts of the United States and the world, have been dreaming and reinventing the literate culture of Los Angeles, searching for ways to settle, acclimatize, and symbolically own the region, all along perpetuating a cultural history that for the most part has not included Mexicans or Latinos.

Richard Romo and Richard Griswold del Castillo are recognized Chicano historians who rank among the first to correct the long-standing omissions by U.S. historians, securing for Chicanos and Latinos a participatory role in the history of Los Angeles and, by extension, the United States. Chicano and Chicana novelists from Helena María Viramontes to Michael Nava, Mario Acevedo, and Reyna Grande have dramatically reconfigured the city of Los Angeles with their own stories and histories, reshaping the landscape with Chicana/o characters set against a narrative background known for its satire and structural inventiveness.

To students and teachers in the field of Chicano/Latino studies, a study that bridges the work of historians, novelists, and cultural critics has been a missing research link. This book by López-Calvo marks a new direction in Chicano/Latino studies with an interdisciplinary approach that includes narratives and films and, no less important, is fully and openly engaged in the ongoing reclaiming of Los Angeles through symbolic appropriation. López-Calvo quotes David Fine, who claims that Los Angeles, very much like California itself, continues to be "the place resting dangerously on the edge of the continent, the place that forces one to look back to sources and origins." López-Calvo adds: "Fine fails to notice that when the city's Latino cultural production explores its sources and origins, it looks further back in time than its Euro-American counterpart, since it is precisely in this past where the reasons for today's marginalization often can be found."

López-Calvo's academic background is ideal for the task. As a literary and cultural critic, he has published books that study communities that include Latin Americans, Asians, and peoples of African ancestry. López-Calvo's former tenure at California State University, Los Angeles, provided him with a teaching and research experience in a campus that currently holds a student population that is more than 50 percent Mexican American/Latino, with a large percentage of these students residing in East Los Angeles. López-Calvo reminds us of the commonly held belief that Anglo-Americans had created Los Angeles ex nihilo, thus repressing a cultural past while living the Spanish colonial fantasy. The demographic statistics are facts that can no longer be repressed or ignored. As López-Calvo informs us, 35 percent of California's population is of Mexican/Latino origin, and the greater Los Angeles Metropolitan area currently lists 4.6 million people of Mexican/Latino ancestry, resulting in an impressive 46 percent of the total population in the city of Los Angeles. Despite the implications of these statistics, ninety-two different world languages constitute the new Babel in the 713 schools of the Los Angeles Unified School District. More than reclaiming a lost land or engaging in the symbolic takeover of cultural space, Chicano and Latino writers are coming to terms with an urban reality that unveils a historical truth: metropolitan areas are always transethnic and transnational in the best sense of the term. National and ethnic cultures fuse into a civilization. Under the present banner of democratic ideals and a promising political leadership, the United States has entered a new historical phase that Cortés and Frémont never imagined, much less expected, for our brave New World.

The depth of the analyses and interdisciplinary range in López-Calvo's writing guards him from the mistaken belief in teleology and the illusion of inevitable progress in narrative art or in literary criticism. Chicano and Latino cultural studies have replaced literary criticism for the most part, with a resulting atrophy in areas corresponding to close and critical reading of texts. A theoretical correlate is the long-standing argument that would explain the replacement of race and class categories by gender, as if racism and class differences were no longer conflictive and quite alive.[8] López-Calvo analyzes narratives and films by Chicano, Latino, and non-Latino writers and directors, based on theoretical sources that include Mike Davis, David Fine, and Edward Soja, to name a few. Critical acts that are realized in a post-Foucault era, these emerging critical approaches examine the flow of world capital, multipronged networks of information, labor migrations on a global scale, and complex power nodes that have reshaped the conditions of our planet. Literature, history, and culture are now being "read" in more complex ways.

The conceptual principles that give coherence to López-Calvo's book derive in part from Mike Davis's notion of "third border," defined as the policies and politics that determine the daily intercourse of two citizen communities, an interaction with much more menacing capabilities toward the noncitizen social groups. Utilizing Mikhail Bakhtin's theoretical category known as the chronotope, López-Calvo examines the manner in which time and space merge and define the nodes or organizing centers in narratives and films where relations are posited and contradictions are (sometimes) resolved. In this light, chronotopes vary: for instance, Bakhtin argues in *The Dialogic Imagination* that fundamental narrative events in Balzac's novels find their meaning in salons and parlors; in novels by Walter Scott, in castle-time; in *Madame Bovary*, in a provincial town. The chronotope of sources and origins, of dangerous continental fringes and fault lines, transforms Los Angeles into a symbolic reduction of the unresolved conflicts in the Americas. As portrayed in the film *Blade Runner* (Ridley Scott, 1982), Teotihuacán is the future of Los Angeles. One could tell a different story: Los Angeles is Cintla's fulfillment. Little gifts nourish friendship.

Los Angeles, a city of riots, fantasies, broken dreams, and renewed hope. This book offers the reader a critical glimpse at the literary and cinematic production emerging at the edge of this world city of the Americas, a place and time for reflections that once again take the reader back to origins and sources. One of this book's lessons: we think historically, therefore we are.

Acknowledgments

I would like to express my gratitude to Juan de Castro, Stephanie Fetta, Rose Johnson, Robert Rudder, José Ignacio Suárez, and Martin Towar for proofreading the manuscript. David W. Foster, Graciela Limón, Alejandro Morales, Louis Negrete, Cristián Ricci, Valerie Talavera-Bustillos, Víctor Valle, and especially my friend and colleague Roberto Cantú, were all instrumental with their insightful suggestions. I am also indebted to Paige Craig, Tonya López-Craig, and José Luis Mungaray and his daughter Gabriella, for suggesting photo locations in Los Angeles, driving me around the city, and taking some of the pictures. Kristen Buckles, the acquiring editor of the University of Arizona Press, and Arin Cumming, marketing assistant, were also very helpful throughout the manuscript review process. Likewise, Lisa Williams, the editor, did a wonderful job copyediting the manuscript. And, as always, I am especially grateful to my wife, Tonya, and to my daughter, Sofía, for all their love and support during the writing process. Finally, I wish to thank the University of North Texas and the UNT Center for Spanish Language Media Research for the grants I received in support of this book.

Parts of chapter 3 have been previously published in the article "Chicanismo Meets Zapatismo: U.S. Third World Feminism and Transnational Activism in Graciela Limón's *Erased Faces*" (*Chasqui* 33.2 [2004]: 64–74).

Latino Los Angeles in Film and Fiction

Introduction

The erasure of Chicanos from Los Angeles' literary annals is a conspicuous distortion of reality, as resident Mexicanos have long contested their displacement from both the city's cultural landscape and its historical record.
—Raúl Homero Villa, *Barrio-Logos*

Every society—and hence every mode of production with its subvariants (i.e., all those societies which exemplify the general concept)—produces a space, its own space.
—Henri Lefebvre, *The Production of Space*

When I was given my first academic job in 1997, I moved to Los Angeles, excited about the prospect of finally living in a "real" city in the United States. I had managed to overcome the warnings that some teary-eyed friends had volunteered about how an earthquake, a race war, or a drive-by shooting would inevitably bring an early end to my young life.[1] Years earlier, I had visited the metropolis as a tourist and had become fascinated by its possibilities. The first months in my new city, however, were a disappointment: I was unable to quite grasp this place that academics categorized as "postmodern" because it had more than one city center. Was Los Angeles really a city or just a scattering of small towns joined by an endless network of jammed freeways? Why was it so "racially" segregated? Why were there signs trying to prevent teen pregnancy only in East L.A.? Why were people trying to sell me a burned-down house in a questionable area of town for half a million dollars? Why did they tell me that a street looked dangerous just because "there were people walking along it"? All these questions kept lingering in my mind. On top of everything else, the super-Niño winter of 1997–98 brought constant precipitation to the Eden of eternal sunshine. During those rainy days, I would drive around the Southland, rolling my eyes every time I saw what I considered ridiculous place names, such as Mission Viejo or Playa Vista, obvious literal translations by developers who were unfamiliar with the Spanish language but were trying to evoke the romanticism of Spanish colonial days. It would take me a few more years to begin to understand the city, and even a few more to feel as though I were part of it. Reading sociological studies and literature dealing with the Latina experience in Southern California, together with listening to my students' fascinating (at times terribly sad) stories at the California State University campus in East Los Angeles, home to the biggest *barrio* in the country, I began to want to learn more about the place where I had been living for eight years.[2] Book after book, story after story, and experience after experience opened the door to a world and an urban history that finally began to make some sense! The place had little to do with the mystified city that I had naively envisioned, but I also knew that there had to be more than the Hollywood scene, the La-La Land and Tinsel Town clichés, the pollution, the traffic jams, the suburban sprawl, the "Surfurbia" described by the British architectural historian Reyner Banham, and the notorious gangs that often appeared on the news and in Hollywood films.[3] There had to be something else there, somewhere, for me to find out. This book is, in part, the result of such a journey of discovery.

Why study Latino literature and film set in Los Angeles? As the Marxist theorist Henri Lefebvre has pointed out, the representation of reality is not a mere mimetic exercise in aesthetic prowess; cultural reproduction, with all its machinery of symbolic image making, carries with it an impetus of taking possession of social space in both its territorial and political manifestations. In a way, the Latino authors and filmmakers studied in this book are symbolically appropriating this social space that, in their view, belongs to them or should at least be shared with them. There is a clear will to power in their discourse. In this sense, Julian Murphet, following Lefebvre, posits that writing is "a series of enactments of spatial appropriation by individuals (and their group affiliations)" (28) and a "tactic of territorial reclamation" (29). In the eyes of some of the Latina authors and filmmakers under discussion, rather than an appropriation of physical and sociopolitical environments, their cultural artifacts are tools for a symbolic reconquest of the territories lost in 1848, after twenty-six years of Mexican rule. As Sharon Zukin suggests, building a city also depends on the way in which people "manipulate symbolic languages of exclusion and entitlement. The look and feel of cities reflect decisions about what—and who—should be visible and what should not, on concepts of order and disorder, and on uses of aesthetic power. In this primal sense, the city has always been a symbolic economy" (138).

Often guided by ethnic pride and solidarity (sometimes also by chauvinism), Latina/o writers and filmmakers alike become flag bearers of their struggling communities and criticize through their works what they perceive as systemic injustice. With this goal in mind, their works look at the relationship between identity and the distribution and representation of urban space. By writing the city and its Latino community, Latino intellectuals provide their own representational space (to use Henri Lefebvre's term) and negotiate their interpretation of social space dynamics. In other words, they resignify and recontextualize dominant perceptions of urban space as conceived by hegemonic groups (Lefebvre's representations of space) by placing their lived experiences as well as those of their ethnic community in the middle of the (motion) picture. As a result, in the narrative deconstruction of Latino Los Angeles (which ranges from the nostalgic overtones to the reproachful diatribe and passing through the sanguine celebration of the end of Euro-American hegemony), Latinos are no longer represented just as undocumented migrant workers, gardeners, busboys, parking attendants, and domestic and sweatshop workers, but also as professionals from all fields who now venture beyond the borders of the barrio, thus remapping their sphere of influence. As we will see, the works by Latino authors and filmmakers are more easily understood when read in conjunction with the cultural production about Latinos in Los Angeles written or directed by Euro-American and Latin American authors and filmmakers.

Citing Antonio Villarreal's novel *Pocho* (1959) and Rudolfo Anaya's *Bless Me, Última* (1972), David Foster claims, "One of the very real continuities between Chicano literature and Mexican and Latin American literature had been the conviction, until at least the mid-1970s, that authentic cultural identity was to be found outside the urban context" (93). As we will see, in recent decades the massive migration of Latinos to Los Angeles has turned this late-capitalism metropolis into a privileged site for Chicano and Latino cultural production. It is no longer the Babylon where Mexican immigrants inevitably lose their "authentic" national traits and roots. From this perspective, this book is a story about the Los Angeles paradox. Whereas it is, for some, an apocalyptic dystopia, for others, as Richard Rodríguez (1944–) points out in *Days of Obligation*,[4] it has become the promised land for a fresh start: "I use the word 'comedy' as the Greeks used it, with utmost seriousness, to suggest a world where youth is not a fruitless metaphor; where it is possible to start anew; where it is possible to escape the rivalries of the Capulets and the McCoys; where young women can disprove the adages of grand-mothers" (xvi).

Latina/o Invisibility in the Pacific Rim Capital

As visitors can read on a historical marker in the Plaza Olvera, the city of Los Angeles was founded in 1781 by a mixed group of forty-four settlers, nearly half of whom were persons of African descent. The rest were Native Americans, *mestizos,* and (four) Spanish soldiers. They came from the San Gabriel Arcángel mission (founded also in 1781) and settled on the location established a few months earlier by Felipe de Neve (see fig. 1), then governor of Spanish California, near the Tongva Native American village of Yang-Na (or Yabit).[5] The original Spanish name of this settle-ment on the periphery of the colonial empire was El Pueblo de Nuestra Señora la Reina de los Ángeles de Porciúncula, and it was inspired by the name given to the local river by the 1769 Spanish expedition led by Gaspar de Portolá. Today it is one of the largest metropolitan areas in the world and, for some geographers and cultural critics, the prototype of the decentered "postmodern city."[6] Its Mexican, Salvadoran, Guate-malan, Korean, Vietnamese, Filipino, Armenian, and Jewish communi-ties are among the largest in the world, and some of them have their corresponding suburban residential and business areas or "ethnoburbs" (ethnic enclaves).[7] This "new Babel" (as some urban critics have defined it) also has the nation's largest concentration of Thais, Japanese, Cam-bodians, Iranians, Canadians, and Gypsies (or Romanies). Ninety-two languages are spoken in the 713 schools of the Los Angeles Unified School District. This extraordinary ethnocultural diversity is precisely one of the reasons the metropolis has become a highly contested territory in spatial and political terms. In the words of the geographer Edward Soja, "arguably the most segregated city in the country, . . . contemporary Los Angeles has come to resemble more than ever before a gigantic agglom-eration of theme parks, a lifespace comprised of Disneyworlds" (198–99). Competing social interests and hegemonic struggles, along with the unequal distribution of wealth, resources, and political power, have led to a multilayered polarization between social groups and spaces that was interpreted cinematically in Paul Haggis's *Crash* (2004).

Figure 1 Sculpture of Felipe de Neve, governor of Spanish California and founder of Los Angeles, in Plaza Olvera. (Photo by Paige Craig)

"They're taking over" was a complaint I kept hearing when I first moved to Los Angeles. Sometimes Latinos and Euro-Americans used this phrase to refer to the increasing presence of Asians in the San Gabriel Valley and Orange County. On other occasions, it was Euro-Americans who would utter it, with an air of resignation, to refer to the re-Latinization (represented in fig. 2) of the entire metropolis. And the most bizarre of them all: a Euro-American man, who was trying to sell me a time-share in Las Vegas, described with nostalgia his youth in the city of Alhambra, where he would eat tacos at tiny Pepe's restaurant (which he pronounced "Peppy's" and claimed as part of his own cultural heritage) in Valley Boulevard until Asians "took over" and he could no longer understand restaurant signs. It was then that I realized that the 1965 Watts riots and the 1992 Los Angeles rebellion (the so-called Rodney King riots) were only the tip of the iceberg of ongoing cultural and sociopolitical urban cold wars.

"There is no culture in L.A.!" This is another assertion that I have heard for years, particularly from people who have never visited the place. Los Angeles, of course, offers a wide range of both high and popular culture to any visitor who is not too afraid or busy to leave his or her luxury hotel. In fact, not only is there culture in this powerful megacity with a $250 billion economy, but, considering that in great measure what has been termed "globalization" is actually "Americanization," it seems safe to affirm that the ideological and cultural discourses emerging from Los Angeles have played a major part in laying down the law. Los Angeles is what geographers call "a world city," that is, one of the few major centers of control in the world's newly globalized economy. Since the Latino presence in the daily life of this Aleph (as Edward Soja, following Argentine writer Jorge Luis Borges, has metaphorically termed the city) increases by the day, it is paramount to take into account how these urban dynamics are recreated in Latino literature and film. Their collective re-creations, regardless of their fragmentary or even contradictory nature, offer an oppositional counterhistory that is the focus of this study.

In the following chapters, I shall explore Chicana and Latina chronotopes, or representations based on the unity of space and time (the 162 municipalities in the five counties of the Los Angeles metropolitan area from 1929 to the present), in several intellectual works. Together, they reconstruct, with political implications and a usually well-defined positionality, close interconnections between temporal and spatial relations, as

Figure 2 Re-Latinization of the City. Los Angeles Latino mural. (Photo by Paige Craig)

reflected in the emotional experiences of filmmakers, audiences, authors, implicit authors, narrators, characters, and readers.[8] While addressing the cognitive mapping of Latino sociopolitical, economic, and historical (dis)empowerment, the present study also examines another key and inseparable aspect: the spatial. The objective, therefore, is to incorporate the evolution of the imaging of Los Angeles in Latino cultural production as an interdependent factor that produces relations of space. This approach to spatial relations and environmental injustice goes hand in hand with the representation of social anxieties, repressed rage, and racial guilt in Latino (and non-Latino) Los Angeles's cultural production.

Why did Euro-Americans respond to Latino immigration by turning their backs on public schools, living in gated communities in the suburbs, demanding the secession of the San Fernando Valley, and even unconstitutionally deporting Mexicans and Mexican Americans in the first half of the 1930s?[9] In spite of the dependence of the region's economy on the Latino workforce, which is for the most part underpaid and nonunionized, and sometimes undocumented, the policies and practices of ethnic segregation and discrimination have continued throughout the years, taking on many faces, from racially restrictive covenants to environmental racism, gentrification, economic injustice, police brutality, bank redlining, and media misrepresentation.[10] Within the frame of these racialized class relations and the umbrella theme of the book, social and racial anxiety, I shall consider topics such as racial guilt about the marginalization of other social groups (in Boyle's *The Tortilla Curtain* and Braverman's *Palm Latitudes*) or due to double consciousness and inferiority complex (Santiago's *Famous All Over Town* and Acosta's *The Revolt of the Cockroach People*), and the apocalyptic overtones as a byproduct of authors' racial anxiety (in Rechy's *Bodies and Souls*, Braverman's *Palm Latitudes*, Acevedo's *X-Rated Bloodsuckers*, Nava's *The Burning Plain*, and Hopper's film *Colors*). Other recurrent topics in this cultural production are homelessness (in *The Tortilla Curtain* and Tobar's *The Tattooed Soldier*), the racial anxiety about the massive arrival of immigrants from a different ethnic group (in *The Tortilla Curtain*, *Palm Latitudes*, and Morales's *The Rag Doll Plagues*) or from the same ethnic group (in *The Burning Plain* and Rechy's *The Miraculous Day of Amalia Gómez*), and the anti-urban ethos of the so-called white flight, that is, the sudden withdrawal of Euro-American citizens from newly racialized urban areas (in *The Tortilla Curtain* and Fuguet's *The Movies of My Life*).

Whether motivated by xenophobia, nativism, or fear of the unknown, the re-Latinization of this global city in recent decades and the resulting changes in human and cultural landscapes (as seen in fig. 3) undoubtedly have exacerbated social anxiety among some non-Latino Angelenos as well as among some Chicanos whose families have lived in Los Angeles for several generations. While in the 1950s the Mexican American population was concentrated (or segregated), for the most part, in East Los Angeles and a few other locations, in the last decades the region has witnessed a profound expansion of Latino (now not only people of Mexican descent, but also Central Americans and, in a smaller measure, Caribbean and South American immigrants) spatial boundaries.[11] Their ever-increasing residential mobility and the new porosity of the invisible intracity borders of old (in a sense, Latinos themselves represented this invisible border within the city) have been responsible for the transformation of the old barrios and the creation of new neighborhoods with Latino majorities throughout greater Los Angeles. This "browning" of a megalopolis that in the mid-1950s was still mostly Euro-American and Protestant into the second U.S. city with the second-largest Latino population in the United States (after New York), the nation's largest Latino market in annual retail sales, and the city with the largest Mexican population outside of Mexico has not taken place without resistance.[12] As we will see, the resurgence of bigotry and nativist hysteria is reflected in much of the cultural production considered in the present work.

The evident uneasiness over the massive arrival of Latino immigrants and refugees, together with the loss of a majority status in the city, created first an identity crisis and then a fictitious common enemy that ended up strengthening white suburban identity and social agency. Their social and ideological construction of whiteness, therefore, was based on the "threat" of the Latino Other's presence. The most obvious result of this new suburban power was the passage in 1994 of the nativist California Proposition 187, which denied unauthorized immigrants and their families the benefits of health care, public education, and social services. Víctor Valle and Rodolfo Torres have denounced the connection between this proposition and the privatization of marginalization: "The law approved by electoral endorsement of Proposition 187 has no design on ending immigration or the employment of immigrants, only on ensuring that continued source of 'waged slavery' by refusing education to immigrants and cheapening the labor supply by privatizing its associated costs" (9). Two years later, Proposition 209

Figure 3 Sculpture of Francisco "Pancho" Villa in Lincoln Park. (Photo by Paige Craig)

ended the affirmative action initiative in higher education and public service contracts, and in 1998 Proposition 227 outlawed bilingual education in public schools (paradoxically, former L.A. Unified School district superintendent David L. Brewer III had his welcome message posted in both Spanish and English on the district's Web site). "This political constituency," argues Eric Ávila, referring to a white supremacist suburban consciousness, "practiced the kind of identity politics typically associated with African Americans and Chicanos, but white suburban homeowners predicated their struggle against fair housing legislation, busing, immigration, welfare, and affirmative action on the very whiteness of their communities" (18). These propositions passed against the nonwhite Other were the end result of a new racialized political activism that gave unity to the diverse groups of white suburban homeowners. In George Lipsitz's view,

> The mendacity and meanness of Governor Pete Wilson, the passage of the anti-immigrant Proposition 187 and the anti-affirmative action Proposition 209, initiatives against bilingual education, and the refusal by legally constituted authorities to enforce laws protecting the civil rights, wages, and working conditions of the people of the state made California in the 1990s the human rights equivalent of Mississippi in the 1960s. (xviii)

The Latino diaspora that gave birth to an identity crisis in the Los Angeles metropolitan area and the American Southwest is the same one that is also reshaping (albeit at a slower pace) American national identity. At the same time that Latinos north of the border have always constructed their collective identities with Euro-Americans as the hegemonic Other in mind (and in the case of Chicanos also vis-à-vis the new Latino arrivals and the African American community), the rest of the country is also adapting (more or less reluctantly) their national self-perception to the new demographic reality. In spite of the proclaimed "exceptionalism" of Los Angeles, other major American cities are undergoing similar types of urban and social developments. In fact, to the "closet Latino" category wryly mentioned in the satirical film *A Day without a Mexican* (2004), I would dare to add a new one: the "closet gringo." Indeed, it is becoming more common to meet Euro-Americans who claim to be more in tune with Mexican or Latino culture than with that of their own social group. Much to the chagrin of protesters against the "alien invasion," the "brown peril," the "takeover of the Southwest," or the "Native American reconquest," transculturation between Latino and mainstream American cultures, no matter how asymmetric it may be, is now conspicuous in American English dialects, the U.S. mass media, food, music, and everyday life in general. Despite the militarization of the U.S.–Mexico border, the construction of new walls, and the war on immigrants represented by the passing of new nativist California propositions, the uncontrolled flow of new Latino arrivals is likely to continue. Mexico's geographical proximity and alarming level of unemployment, together with political turmoil and economic crises in the rest of Latin America and the Caribbean Basin, will probably continue to be key "push and pull" factors. At the same time, the existence of NAFTA and the strength of the U.S. economy (if it manages to recover from the depression into which it has fallen since the end of 2008) will fuel the demand for cheap labor. In the case of greater Los Angeles, the insatiable demand for garment and restaurant workers as well as labor-intensive services such as agribusiness and the construction industry are still strong pull factors. At any rate, as several demographers have pointed out, even if Latino immigration stopped today, the growth of this sector of the population would remain significant. The numbers speak for themselves: 35 percent of the population in California is of Latino origin and, in the greater metropolitan Los Angeles region alone, there are currently 4.6 million Latinos (46 percent of the total population; 38 percent are foreign-born), of whom three million are between the ages of twelve and thirty-four.[13] *José,* incidentally, is now the most popular name in Los Angeles as well as in the rest of California. Although these statistics have not been automatically translated into political power, nor have Euro-American Angelenos, now from the suburbs, ceased to be the strongest political force, there has been some improvement, as evidenced by the election, on July 1, 2005, of Antonio R. Villaraigosa (1953–) as the first mayor of Los Angeles of Mexican descent since 1872. This was the Latino community's greatest political victory in Los Angeles since 1949, when Edward R. Roybal became Los Angeles's first Chicano city councilman since 1881. Paradoxically, although until recently Latinos (like Asians) were somewhat invisible in the mainstream media as well as in the discourse of local politicians, thanks to Propositions 187, 209, and 227, the "political sleeping giant" has finally awakened.

The invisibility of Latinos, suggests David Rieff in his *Los Angeles: Capital of the Third World,* has to do with the city's class segregation and its physical characteristics: "Its horizontality, and the absence of any efficient and fast system of public transportation, means that unless one is poor or chooses to go to those parts of the city where the poor live, it is easy to forget that anyone in L.A. isn't middle-class" (29).[14] Although much has changed since 1991, when Rieff's book was first published, the invisibility has been very real in Hollywood films and in the city's Anglophone mass media.[15] Until recent years, the presence of Latinos on Los Angeles's English-language television stations tended to deal with the sensationalization of gang violence and undocumented immigration. This depiction is also mirrored at the national level: other than in the situation comedy *The George López Show* (which ran from 2002 to 2007, when it was cancelled by ABC), the talk show *López Tonight* on TBS, and the television series *Ugly Betty* (an adaptation of the Colombian soap opera *Yo soy Betty, la Fea,* starring América Ferrera, which premiered on September 26, 2006, on ABC, and concluded on April 14, 2010), Chicanas and Latinas are often portrayed as maids and nannies, and men as gardeners and gangbangers.

Literary critic David Fine maintains that the narrative fiction about Los Angeles "is chiefly the work of the outsider—if not the tourist, then the newcomer" (*Los Angeles* 2). Indeed, among the authors under consideration, Danny Santiago (born Daniel James) was born in Kansas City, and four other Mexican American novelists included in this study (Mario Acevedo, Óscar Zeta Acosta, John Rechy, and Luis J. Rodríguez) were born in El Paso, Texas. However, Graciela Limón, Alejandro Morales, Héctor Tobar, and Helena María Viramontes were actually born in Los Angeles. Furthermore, Luis J. Rodríguez's family moved to Watts when he was two years old, Kate Braverman's family moved to Los Angeles when she was seven, and the Chilean Alberto Fuguet spent most of the first twelve years of his life in the Los Angeles metropolitan area. While it is true that, perhaps because many of these authors are outsiders, some of them focus on the most negative aspects of the city and tend to portray it as a schizophrenic place with no center or aesthetic standards, others, such as John Rechy and Alberto Fuguet, do celebrate its vibrant social life and exuberant urban flora.

Therefore, Fine's assertion reflects only Los Angeles's Anglo-American literature. It also sanctions the fact that anthologies of and studies about Los Angeles literature tend to ignore key contributions by Latinas and Latinos. Lionel Rolfe's *Literary L.A.* (2002), for instance, includes only Óscar Zeta Acosta among the writers studied,[16] and when John Ahouse points out important omissions in the introduction, none of them are of Latino origin. Likewise, David Fine's *Los Angeles in Fiction* (1984) and *Imagining Los Angeles* (2000), and David L. Ulin's *Writing Los Angeles: A Literary Anthology* (2002), among several other anthologies, fail to acknowledge the existence of Chicano and Latino writing in Los Angeles. A quick look at the chronological list of works at the end of this book (which, of course, covers only a small part of this cultural production) should suffice to make the reader wonder about this erasure of Chicana and Latina literature from anthologies of Los Angeles writing. Evidently, for the editors of these anthologies, Latino characters and their authors do not deserve the right of representation ascribed almost exclusively to the dominant culture. Worse than being "othered," they have been completely ignored. This book will address the exclusion and erasure of Latinas and Latinos from the urban symbolic and, therefore, from full Angelino "citizenship."

The historian and architect Dolores Hayden has pointed out the apparent "invisibility" of people of color in Los Angeles's pop culture and writing: "many influential writers have been unable to perceive the importance of the city's nonwhite population, unable to recognize that people of color occupy any significant part of the urban landscape. Such writers may go downtown, but never or rarely to East LA or South Central. The focus of their landscape becomes houses, swimming pools, cars, and pop culture" (86). Along the same lines, in 1984 Raymund A. Paredes complained about the dearth of Mexican American literary writings on Los Angeles or set in Los Angeles:

> Over the past twenty years, Mexican-American authors have quite successfully depicted the circumstances of their people in small towns of Texas and New Mexico, while in California a remarkable group of Chicano poets has emerged to portray vividly barrio life in cities such as San Jose and Fresno. But Los Angeles, despite its standing as the center of Mexican-American population and culture and despite its extraordinary recent contributions in painting, music, and film, has yet to produce a significant body of Mexican writing. Undoubtedly, the sheer vastness of Mexican-American Los Angeles has proved daunting if not simply unmanageable. (241–42)

Yet, since Paredes wrote these comments and even before, several novels by both Latino and non-Latino authors (such as Danny Santiago, Kate Braverman, and T. Coraghessan Boyle) have contributed, with varying degrees of success, to the literary representation of the Latino population of this global city. These works occupy an oppositional discursive space that transgresses the same territorial and mental urban boundaries that afflict their characters. In this sense, whereas one of the most obvious objectives of many of these novels is to raise consciousness among readers, they often aim at something that may be equally political: making sense of the city, trying to find order amid the chaotic contemporary scene through their fictional representation of urban and suburban spaces.

Although it is not easy to trace the origin of Mexican immigration literature, Nicolás Kanellos argues that Daniel Venegas's *The Adventures of Don Chipote, or, When Parrots Breast-Feed* (*Las aventuras de Don Chipote, o, cuando los pericos mamen*), written in Los Angeles and published in the Spanish-language Angelino newspaper *El heraldo de México* in 1928, is "the first 'Chicano' novel—or, at least, a precursor to the Chicano novel of the 1960s and 1970s" ("Introduction" 9).[17] Two Spanish satirical works probably informed Venegas's writing: the anonymous picaresque novel *Lazaro of Tormes* (*Lazarillo de Tormes,* 1554), whose protagonist is also the victim in a series of incidents arranged in chronological order, and, as the title suggests, Miguel de Cervantes's masterpiece *The Ingenious Hidalgo Don Quixote of La Mancha* (*Las aventuras del ingenioso hidalgo Don Quijote de La Mancha,* part 1, 1605; part 2, 1615). Other possible sources are the Mexican picaresque novels *Los infortunios de Alonso Ramírez* (1690) by Carlos de Sigüenza y Góngora (1645–1700) and *El periquillo sarniento* (1816) by José Joaquín Fernández de Lizardi (1776?–1827).

It is worth noting that some of the most obvious messages in *The Adventures of Don Chipote,* including its discouragement of pursuing "the American Dream," will later become topoi in numerous literary and filmic works produced by Latinos in Los Angeles: "We don't want to deny that a few compatriots may have made something of themselves in the United States, but they, like a needle in a haystack, are the minority. But the majority go to the United States only to waste all their energy, get abused by the foremen and humiliated by that country's citizens" (Venegas 28).[18] By the same token, beyond the devastation caused by the Mexican Revolution, the author considers the emigrants' habit of lying to their compatriots about their experiences in the North one of the main factors in the massive migration of Mexicans to the United States during the third decade of the century. This is also the case with Don Chipote de Jesús María Domínguez, the illiterate protagonist who believes all the exaggerations that his friend Pitacio tells him. Other traits, such as the reflection of linguistic changes (anglicisms, code-switching, and language borrowing), the process of cultural hybridization in Los Angeles, the contestatory tone, and, of course, the nostalgia for the homeland are already present in this immigration story: "Those big bells, which mean nothing to those who have lived for a while in Los Angeles, are very significant for new arrivals, who still have the smell of their native land in their nostrils" (Venegas 95).

One of the main targets of criticism in *The Adventures of Don Chipote* is the unscrupulous Americanized Mexicans and Mexican Americans who, having themselves suffered numerous humiliations at the hands of both Euro-Americans and African Americans, now take advantage of the new arrivals' naïveté:

> Can there be any greater wickedness than that of these bastards who, passing themselves off as *gringos,* refuse to speak their own language, denying even the country in which they were born? I think not.
>
> From these renegades—who are neither fish nor fowl, who speak neither Spanish nor English, who are, in a word, ignorant—is where the harshest epithets about us have come. (51)

Drawing from his own experiences as a Mexican worker in the United States, Venegas also exposes the indolence of U.S. authorities who ignore the discrimination against and exploitation of newly arrived Mexican immigrant workers (an exploitation that Venegas compares to slavery) when these, also known as braceros (Venegas calls them "Chicanos"), try to seek justice.

Latino Los Angeles's Writing and Film

Although I could have included many other cultural texts and films in this study, I have selected a few that I deem representative of the evolving imaging of Latino Los Angeles and that attest to the existence of Latino writing and filmmaking in Los Angeles. While most of them deal, in one way or another, with the previously mentioned topics (as well as with many others, including urban alienation, hopelessness, family dysfunction, and unemployment), they do not posit a monolithic position regarding their approach to them; on the contrary, they vary dramatically according to the work, and sometimes within the same text. Conceptualizations of the barrio, for instance, range from the nostalgic idealization of a comforting refuge from "the other side" (meaning the ever-changing Euro-American megacity that surrounds it—although some may argue that one is progressively becoming the other) to overt anti-urbanist images that conceive it as a haven for drug dealers, gang-bangers, violent husbands, and unscrupulous developers. But, as we will see, barrio fictions ultimately yield to transnational and even post-nationalist narratives where more open categories, such as liminality, heterogeneity, hybridity, transculturation, and *mestizaje* take center stage, displacing the notion of ethnic identity, usually determined by the territoriality and imagined homogeneity of the nation-state. In any case, these authors' and filmmakers' speaking positions are usually situated within the boundaries of a collective, contestatory project: creating a new conceptual landscape that works as a strategy for entering and leaving predetermined concepts of *latinidad* as needed according to the circumstances, in order to metaphorically relocate Latinas and Latinos from the periphery to the center, and to provide them with a heightened sense of place. In a way, their writing, which is based on the harsh realities of everyday life in Latino Los Angeles, presents itself as an alternative to the idyllic "theme parks" and simulated environments promoted by developers as well as the powerful entertainment industry. The exception, as we will see, is Alberto Fuguet's *The Movies of My Life* (2003), a novel in which these postmodern virtual milieus pose no threat to his own cognitive cartography of the city and its suburbs.

Rob Shields has defined social spatialization as "the ongoing social construction of the spatial at the level of the social imaginary (collective mythologies, presuppositions) as well as interventions in the landscape (for example, the built environment)" (188). Following Henri Lefeb-vre, he explains that physical space is "produced"; that is, we perceive geographical space "via classification schemes with various (ideological) divisions as good and bad areas (for example, the 'redlining' effect on urban districts when banks and mortgage companies refuse to lend money to high-crime or high-bankruptcy areas)" (192). Inevitably, this production of space may determine who inhabits a certain area; it also has repercussions at the levels of social and cultural reproduction. I shall trace these levels in this book as they relate to social tensions among ethnic groups. Surprisingly, as urban theorist and historian Mike Davis has pointed out, despite the success of border studies, little attention "has been focused on the historical geography of Latino settlement patterns in nonborder cities, although in at least one case (metropolitan Los Angeles) the reality is unparalleled" (*Magical* 49). Davis has termed this urban phenomenon the "third border": "Whereas the second border nominally reinforces the international border, the third border polices daily intercourse between two citizen communities: its outrageousness is redoubled by the hypocrisy and cant used to justify its existence. Invisible to most Anglos, it slaps Latinos across the face" (*Magical* 71).

The present study will attempt to fill this lacuna in academic scholarship. Echoing Mike Davis's remarks, in this cultural production the politics of place are marked by some sort of third border that signals areas of marginalization within the metropolis, be it artificial (freeways, railroad tracks) or topographical ("from the other side of the river"). In *The Revolt of the Cockroach People* (1989), for instance, Óscar Zeta Acosta (1935–1974[?]) refers to his own social group as those "from the wrong side of the tracks" (29). As stated, the borderline can also be mental. In this regard, Genaro Padilla provides the example of Alejandro Morales's (1944–) first novel, *Barrio on the Edge* (*Caras viejas y vino nuevo*, 1998), where the narrator, Mateo, considers Julián's demise his own fault and "refuses to shift all responsibility when he tells his mother that Julián, a wino-junkie friend, is not simply a victim of social determinism. . . . He realizes that the people of the barrio are ultimately responsible for maintaining their own humanity" (164). The same type of self-criticism is also prevalent in Yxta Maya Murray's novel *What It Takes to Get to Vegas* (1999), as we will see.

Part of this production also challenges the official history of Los Angeles: the idea that Anglo-Saxon forefathers, promoters, and speculators such as William Mulholland, Henry Huntington, and the *Los Angeles Times*' General Harrison Gray Otis and Harry Chandler created Los Angeles ex nihilo. Alejandro Morales's novel *The Brick People* (1988), for example, reveals the contributions of Mexican labor to the construction of the Southern Californian dream. At the same time, it condemns the marginalization and oppression of this community that, for some time, was virtually replaced by the new Euro-American conquerors. Dolores Hayden underscores this historical manipulation by citing a 1986 study by Gail Dubrow in which it was revealed that 97.7 percent of the city's cultural-historic landmarks were Anglo-American: "So three-quarters of the current population must find its public, collective past in a small fraction of the city's monuments, or live with someone else's choices about the city's history" (86). On the same note, just as the California grizzly bear that was brought to extinction now paradoxically represents the state in its official flag, the displaced downtown Mexicans (who were either deported or sent east of the Los Angeles River) were replaced by a "Spanish fantasy" of faux Mediterranean, Mission, and Moorish facades with red-tiled roofs, which was supposed to camouflage what had actually been a history of usurpation of Mexican territories. The "historic preservation" of "Mexican" tourist spots such as Olvera Street ended up supplanting the longtime Mexican and Mexican American residents of the area.

For several decades now, there has been an ongoing cultural war about the reinstatement of *latinidad* as an intrinsic part of the city's image making. After all, as Sharon Zukin posits, "As a source of images and memories, it [culture] symbolizes 'who belongs' in specific places" (137). Reflecting this spatial consciousness, the new Latino majority now demands museums of Hispanic (Latin American and Latina) art (such as the Museum of Latin American Art [MOLAA] in Long Beach, which was founded in 1996 by Dr. Robert Gumbiner),[19] as well as the inclusion of these artists in other museums. Also part of the city's symbolic economy is the creation of the Bilingual Foundation of the Arts by Mexican American actor Carmen Zapata, Cuban-born actor-director Margarita Galbán, and Argentinean-born artist Estela Scarlata. Since 1973, it has been fulfilling its mission of serving the community by bringing Spanish, Latin American, and Latino plays to Los Angeles theaters, thereby celebrating Hispanic culture and bringing awareness of its diversity.[20] Furthermore, the true democratization of public spaces is another contested territory in current cultural and ethnic struggles over the right to the city and the right to difference. In this context, who should have access to a public park is determined by certain regulations, such as charging a certain amount on weekends (as they do at San Marino's Lacy Park) or forbidding soccer games. In this sense, Héctor Tobar points out, "At Griffith Park, where I played as a child, the city's Department of Parks and Recreation has placed enormous boulders in the center of the lawns to discourage the most popular pastime, the playing of soccer" (*Translation* 7).

It is against this background of ethnic politics, gentrification, and institutionalized urban fears that the works discussed in this book rewrite (beyond the mythical birthplace of Aztlán as a political metaphor) the lost history of the past Spanish (last quarter of the eighteenth century through 1820) and Mexican (1821–46) presence in the region and vindicate today's new Latino visibility. As we will see, on the other side of the spectrum some Euro-American authors considered in this book participate, with their writing, in the same cultural wars and urban fears when they fall into the trap of "multiculturalism as racial anxiety" (Kyung-Jin Lee xxv). In this sense, James Kyung-Jin Lee posits that although multiculturalism proposes as its axiomatic principle to imagine a new fantasy by crossing the metaphoric color line, it is not so easy to combat the legacy of racism in real life: "Multiculturalism imagines anew how to reorganize the heretofore unequal representation of American life; its more difficult task lies in its capacity or even its willingness to redistribute uneven resources in American communities. The fantasy of multiculturalism's practitioners depends on this parallel movement of more equitable representation and resources" (xiv). As we will see in the following chapters, this type of multiculturalism, which is intricately linked to racial anxiety and guilt, is apparent in several of the works under study.

There are numerous points in common between the cultural manifestations about Los Angeles (or set in this city) created by Latinos and those produced by non-Latinos. Not surprisingly, all the topoi and clichés in Los Angeles writing that Murphet (quoting Michael Sorkin) enumerates are often shared by Los Angeles's Latino cultural production: "the weather . . . , Disney . . . , death . . . , the Movies; banality; America *in extremis;* cars on freeways; the artist in a strange land; the beach; the antithetical trope of 'back east'; the future; and of course above all of these and somehow subsuming and orchestrating them all, the master trope of apocalypse" (Murphet 31). David Fine also points out that the "city built by its founders on the promise of a utopian future took its essential literary identity in the decades since the 1930s—in hard-boiled crime and tough-guy detective stories, Hollywood novels, and apocalyptic fictions—as the place resting dangerously on the edge of the continent, the place that forces one to look back to sources and origins" (*Imagining* 257). This assertion, like so many others in anthologies of and criticism on (Euro-American) Los Angeles writing, attests to the blatant disregard for Los Angeles's Latino writing that characterizes these types of studies and collections. Fine fails to notice that when the city's Latino cultural production explores its sources and origins, it looks further back in time than its Euro-American counterpart, since it is precisely in this past that the reasons for today's marginalization often can be found.

The Book and Its Organization

The book's three chapters reflect the main topics chosen to analyze the representation of racial tension and anxieties in Latino (and non-Latino)

Los Angeles's cultural production: environmental injustice (in chapter 1), the marginalization of Latino urban youth (in chapter 2), and women's space and postnationalist discourse (in chapter 3). The first chapter of this study examines Latino (and some non-Latino) cultural production from an ecocritical perspective as it relates to urban interethnic relations. Thus, the first subchapter looks at the consequences of the white flight and the ensuing "middle-class flight." The three texts analyzed situate Latinos within the racialization of Los Angeles's landscape. The first one focuses on a novel by T. Coraghessan Boyle, one of the three non-Latino authors included in this study (along with Danny Santiago and Kate Braverman) to contrast the interpretations of the same social issues from "both sides of the tracks." His social satire *The Tortilla Curtain* reveals the hypocrisy of the Angelino suburbs' take on the impact of unauthorized Latino immigration on local ecologies. *The Movies of My Life,* a novel by the Chilean author Alberto Fuguet, complements this depiction of the "civilized" suburbs and their relationship with the new Latino presence. By contrast, in the second subchapter, the city of Los Angeles, particularly through the description of homelessness in its downtown, becomes a symbol of barbarism in *The Tattooed Soldier,* a novel by the Guatemalan American Héctor Tobar. The third subchapter studies the effect of urban redevelopment projects on the Chicano community as echoed first in the novel by a Euro-American author, Danny Santiago's *Famous All Over Town,* and then in the works by three Mexican American writers: Luis J. Rodríguez's *The Republic of East L.A.,* Helena María Viramontes's *The Moths and Other Stories* and *Their Dogs Came with Them,* and Mario Acevedo's *X-Rated Bloodsuckers.* The fourth subchapter, which closes chapter 1, deals with environmental racism and ecocritical views of the metropolis in the narratives of two Chicano authors: John Rechy and Alejandro Morales.

Chapter 2 concentrates on the representation of daily life in the barrio and the marginalization of Latino urban youth, with a particular emphasis on the figures of the *pachuco* and his successor, the contemporary *cholo* (Latino gang member). While the first subchapter explores the spectacularization of Latino gang life in films and television, the second one looks at the visualization of the gang and the barrio as independent "counternations" in Miguel Durán's *Don't Spit on My Corner* and other texts and films. In turn, the third subchapter concentrates on the Los Angeles school system as a starting point of disenfranchisement. The fourth and last subchapter concentrates on the representation of the LAPD as a camouflaged gang in competition with minority youth gangs, as seen in Michael Nava's *The Burning Plain*, Óscar Zeta Acosta's *The Revolt of the Cockroach People*, and Mona Ruiz and Geoff Boucher's *Two Badges*.

Moving on to the first section of the third chapter, Kate Braverman's take on Latino machismo in her novel *Palm Latitudes* is interpreted as an example of multiculturalism as racial anxiety. The second subchapter continues the study of women's third space within their male peers' social struggles, with a focus on the female gangbanger as represented in Rodríguez's *Always Running, Two Badges*, Laura del Fuego's *Maravilla*, Yxta Maya Murray's *Locas* and *What It Takes To Get To Vegas*, and Allison Anders's film *Mi Vida Loca*. Before the conclusion, the third subchapter examines the transnational and postnationalist links in Graciela Limón's narrative and in Michael Nava's novel *The Burning Plain*. This final broadening of perspectives and "de-barrioization" (i.e., an expansion of spatial perceptions from the barrio to the rest of the city, the nation, and the world) completes this study of the relation between social spatializations and anxieties in Latino (and non-Latino) cultural production.

1

Environmental Racism and the Politics of Nature

Recent explorations in the history of white racial formation
describe the process by which ethnic and racial identities
change over time, but how such identities change across
space remains relatively unknown.
—Eric Ávila, *Popular Culture in the Age of the White Flight*

Metropolitan Los Angeles—with its estimated 500 gated
subdivisions, 2,000 street gangs, 4,000 minimalls, 20,000
sweatshops, and 100,000 homeless residents—is a dystopian
symbol of Dickensian inequalities and intractable racial
contradictions. The deepest anxieties of a postliberal era—
above all, the collapse of the American belief in a utopian
national destiny—are translated into a demonic image of
a region where the future has already turned rancid.
—Mike Davis, *Ecology of Fear*

In contrast with nineteenth-century debates on the dichotomy civilization (the city/European influence) versus barbarism (the country-
side/the American autochthonous) led by Argentine writers Domingo
Sarmiento and Esteban Echeverría, among other Latin American
thinkers, subsequent representations of the city have leaned toward
images that evoke a disturbing lack of cohesion and order. "In the last
three decades of the twentieth century," as Amanda Holmes posits,
"representations of Spanish American urban centers repeatedly evoke
similarly disquieting analogies. For these authors, urban space is seen
as equivalent to ruptured phrases or incomplete bodies" (Holmes 13).
This fictional approach to the city in Latin America, which, in Holmes's
view, is a response to authoritarianism, class struggle, and sociopolitical and economic upheavals, is echoed north of the U.S.–Mexico
border. Thus, several of the works considered in the present study
conceive of the Los Angeles inner city as the epitome of barbarism:

a disreputable space where chaos, depravity, and danger reign. In this chapter, I shall look at the spatiality of social life in the metropolis, taking into consideration three different fictional approaches to the representation of urban and suburban spaces. As the epigraph by the historian Eric Ávila suggests, the historical approach to Latina presence and cultural production in Los Angeles, which has traditionally focused on issues dealing with time, could be refocused to incorporate the category of space in a prominent position. In this context, the common denominator among the three novels analyzed in this chapter is the spatial and mental movement from the urban center to the suburban periphery.

Several urban theorists, including Mike Davis and Eric Ávila, have studied the proliferation of suburbs and "edge cities" as a reaction to the presence of black and brown people in American inner cities. As suggested in the mural in figure 4, the suburbs represent, according to them, the locus of white fear in the urban political economy. Dreaming of a suburban utopia (or "autopia," to use Reyner Banham's neologism) far from pollution, traffic congestion, a deteriorated school system, and the criminality associated with ghettos and barrios, many Euro-American and white ethnic families segregated themselves into gated and walled housing subdivisions in the San Fernando Valley, Orange County, and other areas in the outskirts of Los Angeles.[1] In this regard, Ávila has pointed out that the post–World War II suburbanization of Euro-American culture was based on a long tradition of "racial" segregation: "an expanding generation of Americans exercised their preference for a landscape that epitomized homogeneity, containment, and predictability, one that marked a safe contrast to the heterosocial, unpredictable, and often dangerous cultural experiences of industrial urbanism" (6). The increased presence of nonwhite Angelenos in urban public spaces, continues Ávila, brought about a new type of mass culture in the suburban periphery that suggested an illusion of classlessness as well as a new sociospatial order determined by a number of "spatial fantasies": "Movies, theme parks, freeways, ballparks, television, shopping malls highlighted the cultural landscape of chocolate city and vanilla suburbs and shaped the development of a racialized political culture in a period of intense social change" (6). In his view, this new model of community encouraged traditional gender divisions, promoted isolation, and precluded the creation of the communal haven it had promised. To borrow from Henri Lefebvre's terminology, this "representation of space" at once demonized the "blighted" and racialized inner city and fomented the flight of the Euro-American

DEVELOPMENT OF SUBURBIA

Figure 4 Illustration depicting the "White Flight" from the inner city. Great Wall of L.A. (Photo by Tonya López-Craig)

middle class to a utopian space of isolation from all the purported evils of city life.

Inevitably, some time later it became apparent that the hope that a homogeneous Euro-American middle class would manage to insulate itself from the lower classes and people of color had failed. By way of example, Mike Davis has noted that the San Fernando Valley "now has a slight non-Anglo majority of Latino, black, Middle Eastern, and Asian residents, including more than 500,000 recent immigrants. There are more people of Mexican descent in Ozzie-and-Harriet land than in East L.A." (*Ecology* 405).[2] He also points out how their efforts to escape from the dangers of the inner city were also in vain:

> In the [San Fernando] Valley as a whole (population 1.2 million), one in six residents now lives below the poverty line, and one in ten collected an unemployment check in 1995. Gang violence has relentlessly kept pace with the new immiseration. The "most dangerous street in Los Angeles," according to the LAPD, is not in South Central or East Los Angeles; it is Blythe Street in the Valley. (*Ecology* 401)

Given that there are now numerous suburban gangs as well, the common use of the term *urban street gangs* has become obsolete.[3] In this

regard, David R. Díaz has described the three-tiered urbanization system of Southwest Chicana/o urbanism: "The expansion of traditional
barrios due to immigration and population growth was the cornerstone
of historic urban settlement patterns. This was followed by the expansion of smaller barrios interspersed throughout the urban area. The third
phase, occurring mainly in the past twenty years, has been the migration
to suburban zones by middle-class Chicanas/os" (27). Because of this
new reality, many Euro-Americans in Southern California are now in
the middle of a neo–white flight from older suburbs (Orange County,
the San Fernando Valley) to edge cities in beach and foothill areas, and
to other states.

Suburbs, Edge Cities, and Privatopia

The novels *The Movies of My Life* (*Las películas de mi vida*, 2003), by
the Chilean Alberto Fuguet (1964–), and *The Tortilla Curtain* (1996),
by the Euro-American T. Coraghessan Boyle (1948–), present contrasting cartographies of these suburban spaces and desires.[4] Set against the
background of the white flight (i.e., the stampede of middle-class Euro-
Americans leaving the inner city, which became increasingly visible after
the 1965 Watts riots), the latter book explores suburban perceptions of
the impact of Latino migration on Los Angeles's ecology. This satire,
where echoes of John Steinbeck's *The Grapes of Wrath* (1939) and Tom
Wolfe's *Bonfire of the Vanities* (1989) can be found, narrates how a car
accident (Delaney Mossbacher hits an unauthorized Mexican immigrant named Cándido Rincón) unveils the ostensibly progressive driver
as a bigot, a racist, and a xenophobe. Delaney is initially presented as a
liberal humanist and a firm defender of nature (the ecosystem of the
nearby Topanga Canyon in particular), but after the fortuitous encounter with his "Other," he begins to show his true colors.[5] In reality, as is
later revealed, he worries only about his own self-interest, a white privilege that he perceives as threatened by massive Latino immigration. The
pseudoprogressive life philosophy of this wealthy nature writer ends up
sounding like mere snobbery once his indifference toward the suffering
of underprivileged groups becomes apparent. In accord with the stereotypical superficiality of Angelenos, the Mossbachers' lifestyle (their pas-
sion for fitness and recycling, their expensive diet and pets) is unmasked
as a fad, just like the numerous Buddha statues that a Latina character
has to scrub at someone else's house.[6]

Throughout the plot, Delaney struggles with an ethical dilemma about unauthorized immigration. He constantly problematizes his own mixed feelings in a sort of tour de force between compassion and selfishness: "Because he'd just left the poor son of a bitch there alongside the road, abandoned him, and because he'd been glad of it, relieved to buy him off with his twenty dollars' blood money. And how did that square with his liberal-humanist ideals?" (13). Yet, to his own surprise, Delaney's first concern immediately after hitting Cándido is not for the human being, but for the car. After considering fleeing the scene, he eventually unburdens his conscience by giving the injured man a twenty-dollar bill. Delaney questions his own feelings of rejection toward these immigrants, but, in the end, he acts as if blinded by hatred and, like several of his neighbors in the exclusive community, uses racist epithets and tries every means to rid Latinos from his life: he destroys evidence proving that Cándido was not the vandal at Arroyo Blanco Estates, harasses a Latino man who was innocuously delivering flyers, and accuses two unassuming Mexican men of being arsonists. Mike Davis has noticed this tendency among Los Angeles suburbanites:

> The homeless also cast demonic shadows in Southern California's social imaginary. The Eaton Canyon fire, accidentally triggered by a transient, seemed to confirm the worst fears of mountain and canyon homeowners: that an invisible army of careless, embittered strangers was lurking in the brush. Clandestine hobo encampments, like those in Tuna Canyon along the Malibu coast, were singled out as intolerable fire hazards. Blazes of indeterminate origin were routinely ascribed to the homeless. (*Ecology* 131)

It seems, therefore, that Boyle has bought into this way of thinking since in *The Tortilla Curtain* it is the homeless man, Cándido, who inadvertently causes the wildfire.

At one point, the naturalist becomes so obsessed with hatred for the Mexican man he hit that (at least, according to the latter) he tries to hit him with his car again. In the last chapter, a paranoid Delaney with a gun in his hand becomes the flag-bearer of white racial anxiety in contemporary Los Angeles. Leaving behind his liberal conscience, he now embraces the wall around Arroyo Blanco and even tries to alleviate his rage against Latino immigration by attacking Cándido's dwelling in the canyon. Ironically, after the Mossbachers' long discussion about the privatization of space and the right to defend themselves from an alien invasion into their white middle-class haven, Delaney is the one who ends up trespassing at someone else's home, no matter how humble or unauthorized it may be. In his worldview, the safeguarding of privacy, security, and order does not apply when dealing with the dwelling of the Other. Therefore, urban and suburban spaces become racialized: the worlds of civilization (understood as white supremacy/privilege and the resulting privatization/suburbanization of space) and barbarism (the racialized inner city and the presumed nonwhite invasion of white property) take a drastic turn in the denouement of the story. Delaney, always so fearful of mingling with the Other, has now "descended" into the hell of immigrant destitution at the bottom of the canyon, purportedly in self-defense. In his determination to protect white privilege, panic ultimately turns into racial paranoia and historical amnesia. Rather than considering the deliberate structural destruction of Los Angeles's black and Chicano communities by city authorities, he rationalizes (an emblem of what Mike Davis, in *City of Quartz,* termed "ideology of protective siege") that white Angelenos have been expelled from the inner city by people of color.

Now, all the dammed rage overflows. Yet Delaney, who was determined to prevent these "undesirables" from displacing his social group from the suburbs, sees his crusade interrupted when a mudslide (yet another of the natural disasters repeatedly recreated in Los Angeles literature) ends the encounter and the life of the immigrants' son.[7] In the open-ended plot, Cándido offers Delaney a helping hand that saves this sociopolitical novel from a completely pessimistic outlook. This generous gesture also demonstrates that Delaney has unfairly criminalized the Latino immigrant and projected an image of aggression and provocation that is far from real. Whereas Cándido and América Rincón are examples of resistance from the bottom of the social scale, their tactics are nonviolent. Mike Davis has studied the type of mentality embodied by Delaney in *City of Quartz:*

> The social perception of threat becomes a function of the security mobilization itself, not crime rates. Where there is an actual rising arc of street violence, as in South Central Los Angeles or Downtown Washington D.C., most of the carnage is self-contained within ethnic or class boundaries. Yet white middle-class imagination, absent from any firsthand knowledge of inner-city conditions, magnifies the perceived threat through a demonological lens. (224)

The denouement of the story exposes how Delaney and his peers have used the role of the nonwhite Other to create a coherent sense of hegemonic, white, suburban identity out of a heterogeneous social group. This new imagined identity emerges ex nihilo from the forces of exclusion that, according to Michael J. Dear, define these "security-obsessed" communities that have been termed "privatopias": "a private housing development based in common-interest developments (CIDs) and administered by homeowners' associations. . . . privatopia has been fueled by a large dose of privatization, and promoted by an ideology of 'hostile privativism.' It has provoked a culture of non-participation" (144). On the other hand, it proves that the wall and all the other measures of physical and mental fortification taken by his community to avoid contact with the "invaders" have been in vain. The cognitive map of racial prejudice and fear finally comes to a point of closure: social insulation through interdictory spaces has become an unattainable fantasy. Therefore, there is no symbolic redemption for Delaney. Through his unforgiving satire, Boyle condemns his bigotry as well as that of the suburban community obsessed with security that he emblematizes. They are, paradoxically, the ultimate cause of social disorder.

As we have seen, alternating between the narrative perspectives of the two couples, the Mossbachers and the Rincóns, the plot offers a dialogical interpretation of the undocumented immigration conundrum (and, by extension, of "the American Dream"). However, although, following James Kyung-Jin Lee's notion of multiculturalism as racial anxiety, one may wonder whether there is some degree of authorial racial guilt, the narrative voice hardly hides his sympathy for the Rincón family's plight. The satire is clearly aimed at exposing the Mossbachers' hypocrisy. Their values—especially their environmental concerns—seem ludicrous once they are contextualized with the suffering of Cándido and his seventeen-year-old pregnant partner, América, who were beaten and robbed while crossing the international border and who are now trying to survive in a ravine at the bottom of Topanga Canyon while accepting exploitative jobs. Notably, in a foreshadowing passage, Delaney expresses his anxiety over the impact of undocumented immigrants' camping in the canyon:

Making the trees and bushes and the natural habitat of Topanga State Park into his own private domicile, crapping in the chaparral, dumping his trash behind the rocks, polluting the stream and ruining it for everyone else. That was state property down there, rescued from the developers and their bulldozers and set aside for the use of the public, for nature, not for some outdoor ghetto. And what about fire danger? (11)

Again, his lack of compassion for the immigrants' trials makes his complaints sound hollow and suspicious. Delaney's true fear becomes a reality when he encounters in "his backyard" the very thing he had been fleeing: people from minority groups, whom he associates directly with drive-by shootings, gangbanging, tagging, and carjacking. The dialectic between private and public use of space ultimately becomes entangled with veiled expressions of white supremacy and racial power.

In his monthly column for a naturalist magazine, Delaney exposes the ambivalence of his ecologist discourse when he unconsciously makes analogies between coyotes (the animals; not the smugglers of undocumented immigrants) and immigrant Latinos in Southern California: "The coyote is not to blame—he is only trying to survive, to make a living, to take advantage of the opportunities available to him. . . . The coyotes keep coming, breeding up to fill in the gaps, moving in where the living is easy. They are cunning, versatile, hungry and unstoppable" (214–15). Two years after the publication of *The Tortilla Curtain*, Mike Davis comes to the same conclusion, noticing how often natural history and social history are read intertwined: "in the minds of most suburbanites, the unruliness in the center of the metropolis is figuratively recapitulated in the periphery. It is not surprising that predators are criminalized as trespassers and discursively assimilated to 'serial killers' or 'gangbangers.' Reciprocally, the urban underclass is incessantly bestialized as 'predators,' 'wilding youth,' and 'wolf packs' in an urban 'wilderness'" (*Ecology* 208).[8] By the same token, Delaney unintentionally reminds his readers about his selective amnesia; he fails to remember that California used to be Mexican territory: "(after all, the coyote roamed these hills long before *Homo sapiens* made his first shaggy appearance on this continent). . . . If we invade his territory, then why indeed should we be surprised when he invades ours?" (212). When a coyote circumvents the new eight-foot wall around his house and devours the Mossbachers' second dog (he had previously eaten one before the building of the wall), the allegoric parallelism seems to convey the message that no wall will stop desperate immigrants from crossing the international border.

Delaney does not notice the paradox of writing about ecological balance when he chooses to live in a gated community in the canyon.

Neither does he realize that the Tongva (or Gabrieleño) Native American place-name of the canyon, Topanga, is a reminder that neither Spaniards, nor Mexicans, nor Euro-Americans were its first inhabitants. Following in his footsteps, his wife, Kyra Menaker-Mossbacher, an unscrupulous, "workaholic" real estate agent who believes that the presence of "too many" Mexicans may scare potential clients away, calls the immigration services to prevent Latino immigrants from gathering in the nearby labor exchange site. She also supports the construction of the wall around their private community in order to protect her family from the perceived threat of immigrants and minorities. Ironically, not only does she employ Mexican workers to build the wall, but she also increases her sales in the suburbs thanks to the white flight.

Overall, *The Tortilla Curtain* portrays Los Angeles as an inhospitable place. Cándido, who had previously lived in Echo Park, takes América to the canyon precisely to avoid exposing her to those Los Angeles mean streets, full of gangs, graffiti, trash, and immigration agents. When the Rincóns finally venture into the city, they end up eating garbage after being robbed by a Mexican American who had promised to help them out (another commonplace present in Daniel Venegas's novel *The Adventures of Don Chipote, or, When Parrots Breast-Feed,* the film *El Norte,* and many other works).[9] This feeling of distrust spills into the suburbs: Delaney is afraid of checking on the person he has hit, because he has read about inner-city gangs using these tactics to prey on unsuspecting drivers.

From Topanga Canyon, we move on to another suburb, the San Fernando Valley, as described by Chilean author Alberto Fuguet in his semiautobiographical *The Movies of My Life.* Although Fuguet refuses to consider this novel autobiographical (he insists that he was trying to make his readers believe that everything in the story is true), it does recreate, from a nostalgic viewpoint, at least part of his childhood in Inglewood and the San Fernando Valley. In January 2001, the thirty-seven-year-old semiautobiographical protagonist, the seismologist Beltrán Soler Niemeyer, stops at the Los Angeles International Airport (LAX) on his way to Japan, but then decides to spend some time in the city of his childhood memories. Time has transformed most of the neighborhoods he once knew, but he still recognizes the hot Santa Ana winds,[10] the Hollywood sign, the huge plaster doughnut on Manchester Avenue, and other landmarks from his cherished childhood days. Despite some soft criticism, his overall representation of the metropolis is, undoubtedly, the most positive one of all the works analyzed in this book. According to a Salvadoran taxi driver, for example, Los Angeles turns thieves into law-abiding citizens: "Everyone in El Salvador is a thief, but here Salvadorans are hard workers and completely devoted to paying what they owe. It just goes to prove that it's the environment that's bad and not the people" (153–54).

Belying the common criticism of the soulless environment of the suburbs plagued by "alienation, anomie, and isolation" (Ávila 224) that stifle the feeling of community, the novel depicts the city of Encino, the protagonist's symbolic affective center, as an idyllic and family-friendly town in the San Fernando Valley where he spent the best years of his life, playing all day in the streets without fear. His family, fed up with gang warfare and urban decline, had fled Inglewood, never to return. A light-complected Latin American family, therefore, decides to pursue the dream of a peaceful and utopian suburban life that was originally off-limits to blacks and Latinos. To put it in the narrator's words: "In those days, the Valley breathed with a new, less industrial air. It was like some sort of sociological experiment: the suburbs as an autonomous city, with the mall as its temple and the teenager as king" (84). The anti-urban *ethos* of this mostly middle- and upper-class community that had moved to the Valley to escape Los Angeles is emphasized in several passages: "Almost everyone, even those who earned just enough to get by, like our neighbors, was linked in one way or another to the television and film industry. This wasn't by chance. Encino was simultaneously located sufficiently close to and yet comfortably apart from L.A.'s two centers of film production" (84–85).

As a "user" of space, Fuguet's narrative voice sees no conflict between his own "representational space" (a subjective and appropriated *lived* space with its associated images, symbols, dreams, and memories) and the "representation of space" (in Lefebvre's sense of the verbal signs of an abstract space) *conceived* by "producers" of space such as architects and urban planners. Neither does he object to Hollywood's visualizations of the city and its suburbs. On the contrary, he voices his pride in the fact that Encino had been used in the past as a movie set for westerns and gangster films. In his elaborated eulogy of life in the suburbs, he even chooses to reconstruct its romanticized origins, obviously forgetting (or rejecting the fact) that, like Chile, California was also colonized by the Spanish Empire:

Years later, in a history class at McArthur English School, they explained to me that Santiago was founded by the Spanish conquistador Pedro de Valdivia, and I felt myself extremely fortunate to have lived the first years of my life in a place colonized by Frank Capra and Jimmy Stewart and not by a group of stinking, resentful Spaniards who escaped their native land to kill Indians and rob them of their riches at the other edge of the world. (86)

While, admittedly, not much of importance happened in Encino, there were scattered moments of Hollywood glamour: Yul Brynner ate dinner at Beltrán Soler's house once, and one of his neighbors was the actor Edward Everett Horton, who, incidentally, had the same contempt for Los Angeles County (eighty-eight cities) that one can see today in the San Fernando Valley's and Hollywood's secessionist movements. Thus, by recreating an ideal childhood in the suburbs of the early 1970s, the author turns the supposedly utopian suburban way of life into a lived reality. Not even earthquakes dim the brightness of this lost childhood paradise: Beltrán used to daydream about being one of the few survivors of an earthquake in Los Angeles.

In Encino, explains the first-person narrator, everyone knew each other and there was a true sense of community. Children and teenagers would play happily in the many peaceful streets, pools, and parks bathed by sprinklers and the sun. Alternatively, they enjoyed the sanitized and disciplined environments of shopping malls or the family entertainment provided by movie theaters, amusement parks, and "manicured" theme parks such as Disneyland, Lion Country Safari, Sea World, Japanese Village, and Knott's Berry Farm. The protagonist, therefore, has interiorized these virtual environments and sees no conflict between the preestablished homogeneous connotations of these consumer-oriented milieus and his own representational space of cherished memories and affective "lived situations." As Lefebvre postulates, "all 'subjects' are situated in a space in which they must either recognize themselves or lose themselves, a space they may both enjoy and modify" (35). In the case of Fuguet's narrative voice, it is clear that he recognizes himself in the suburban social space described in the novel. The virtual "theme park" of the suburbs becomes very real in the representational spaces created by his memory, particularly in contrast with the grim reality of the Chile he encounters after moving to his parents' homeland. In Chile, this lost North American paradise acquires quasi-mythological connotations: he constantly compares California, with its mass culture and consumer economy "in Technicolor," to what he perceives as a backward and small country where everything turns black-and-white.

While the protagonist never criticizes directly the so-called American way of life, his author, it must be noticed, is aware of the fact that he is going against the grain. Thus, Fuguet wryly confesses, in an interview with literary critic Guillermo García-Corales, "The problem is that for me, it is difficult to hate the United States, which here in Latin America is a dirty little secret."[11] For the protagonist, the spatial reconfiguration emblematized by white-flight suburbanization (together with the concomitant construction of freeways for commuters at the expense of inner-city communities) and the proliferation of consumer-oriented, enclosed, and privatized milieus such as shopping malls, ballparks, and theme parks represent "home." They are a distant memory of a happy childhood and the paradise he lost when his family moved back to Chile. Consequently, he sees no reason to criticize the way in which these built environments have arguably ruined heterosocial interaction in public open-air spaces in American cities; communal life, in *The Movies of My Life,* persists in shopping malls, private pools, and city parks. Neither is Fuguet inclined to point out how freeways, that quintessential symbol of Southern California's progress and of the way of life in the suburbs, has been resignified in Latino Los Angeles's imaginary. "By the 1980s," as Raúl Homero Villa has explained, "freeway construction had consumed 12 percent of the land in East Los Angeles while displacing approximately 10 percent of its residential population, thereby adding to the chronic shortage of decent and affordable housing on the Eastside" (82). Likewise, Víctor Valle and Rodolfo Torres have argued that freeways "represent not only communication and speed but containment and territorialization" (9).

Thus, with the avowed influence of Mario Vargas Llosa's *Aunt Julia and the Scriptwriter* (*La tía Julia y el escribidor,* 1977) and Manuel Puig's novels, this reader-friendly novel embraces American popular culture, including its films, television programs, Hollywood actors, commercial products, and advertisements. Even the giant plaster doughnut on Inglewood's Manchester Avenue is remembered with nostalgia and presented on the cover of the original Spanish version of *The Movies of My Life.* In this context, Juan de Castro perceptively notes,

This wholesale, though not fully uncritical, adoption of the forms of mass media and communication is an attempt at representing the life experiences of McOndo, that is, of middle- and upper-class Latin

Americans. This group, like Beltrán and Fuguet, if not necessarily beneficiaries, have at least managed to adapt to the cultural and economic changes promoted by neoliberal economic reforms, of which Chile has been the paradigmatic example. (117)

Curiously, Fuguet, in an interview with Ernesto Escobar Ulloa, has explained how he connects his notion of McOndo with the city of Los Angeles: "McOndo, for me, is what you feel when you are in Downtown, Los Angeles."[12] Yet there is also room for a polyphonic discourse, as we see when a Mapuche Indian character named Tyrone Acosta Acosta briefly condemns the social values fomented by the Walt Disney Corporation:

> Tyrone didn't like the movie at all; to him it seemed "reactionary" and "more Disney than necessary." Years later I found out that Tyrone had been a student and disciple of Ariel Dorfman; his thesis was on Dorfman and Armand Mattelart's seminal "How to Read Donald Duck: Imperialist Ideology in the Disney Comic." Then I understood why he preferred cursing parrots to Scrooge McDuck, and why he never took us to Disneyland. (122)

While Beltrán's lack of response to these perceptions seems to imply skepticism (if not denial), Eric Ávila agrees with Tyrone's assessment when he points out Disneyland's commendation of consumerism, patriotism, patriarchy, and small-town Midwestern whiteness:

> Walt Disney, meanwhile, strongly identified himself with the countersubversive tradition of the 1950s America and built Disneyland as a reinstatement of traditional social values that seemed threatened by the hegemony of the New Deal and its brand of liberal modernism. Disneyland modeled a privatized, consumer-oriented subjectivity, predicated on notions of white supremacy and patriarchy and upheld by a new generation of political leaders who would come to constitute the New Right. (228)

Although the Solers occasionally interact with Chilean families exiled from Augusto Pinochet's dictatorship, they do not consider themselves exiles; on the contrary, they seem to be completely assimilated to American values and an American way of life. Later, however, they grasp the spatial dynamics of Los Angeles's racialized political culture and turn this feeling into a more radical one, de-ethnification: "Being left without a social class, without a circle of friends, the Solers had to invent new

hatreds, angers, and fears to mitigate the fact that they had found themselves so far removed from the place that they once belonged to. . . . The
solution was as simple as it was drastic: stop being Latino" (113). As Beltrán explains, his family defines their whiteness in relation to the indigenous blood of others, since their main fear is to be identified with people
they describe as uneducated and starving Latin Americans. Changes in
space have brought with them new racial geographies that inspire different sociopolitical choices and alliances. Ostensibly, at the same time that
they abandon the violent and racialized inner city to join the postwar
movement toward the suburbs (a space of utopian social order originally created for Euro-American Angelenos), the Soler family acquires
a new self-perception that awakens them to the privileges of suburban
whiteness. The same family that had become déclassé by moving from
the middle-/upper-class commune of Ñuñoa, in the Santiago metropolitan region, to Inglewood, a decaying, semi-industrial neighborhood
populated by Latin Americans and lower-class Euro-Americans, and
contaminated by industrial smog and terrible noise from airplanes and
trains, has now adopted a new set of social identities anchored in the site
of residence. Suburban home ownership, however, is not an automatic
green card to white racial identity; their self-perception is also informed
by the way in which they are perceived by others. In the end, this claim
to whiteness will alienate them from both groups, Latinos and Euro-
Americans. The young Beltrán, in turn, rebels against his family's new
aspirations for white identity (he associates this desire with classism and
racism) with yet another ethnocultural fantasy: identifying with the culture of most of his friends, he claims himself Jewish. This self-perception
survives his family's decision to return to Santiago de Chile in 1974: once
there, his first (and, for a while, only) friend is also Jewish.

The Inner City: Homeless Capital of the USA

> Homelessness confronts urban societies at the beginning of the
> twenty-first century with fundamental questions about the nature
> of the social contract and the relationships between institutions,
> the society of citizens, and the poor.
> —Madeleine R. Stoner, in *From Chicago to L.A.*

With the introduction, in figures 5 and 6, of downtown scenes, we now
leave behind the dreamscapes of suburbs, edge cities, and the utopian

Figure 5 Life in the inner city: Fortune-telling store in downtown's 7th Street. (Photo by Tonya López-Craig)

private space that Mike Davis has termed "privatopia," to enter the "production" of the inner city. If suburbs are developed for the pursuit of safety, order and homogeneity, the inner city embodies the opposite characteristics: it is a barely livable space.[13] Within this economically depressed physical space, we find a new level of immiseration, the carceral city, which Michael J. Dear describes as "the 'new incendiary urban geography' brought about by the amalgam of violence and police surveillance" (148). As Jennifer Wolch has explained, with the shift to post-Fordism in the 1980s, Los Angeles became the homeless capital of the United States.[14] A number of systemic forces, including the apathy of local politicians, exacerbated the problem: "These forces, operating at spatial scales ranging from global to local, led to a re-structuring of the regional economy, loss of critical welfare state supports, and a shrinking supply of low-cost housing" (Wolch 390).[15] According to the Los Angeles

Figure 6 Life in the inner city: Spanish-language church in downtown's 648 South Broadway Street. (Photo by Paige Craig)

Homeless Services Authorities (LAHSA) 2007 count in greater Los Angeles, on any given day there were 68,608 homeless persons throughout Los Angeles County (40,144 in the city of Los Angeles, with the biggest concentration, 5,131 persons, in Skid Row).[16] Fifteen percent of these people (10,100) are children under the age of eighteen. An additional 5,094 homeless, in the adjacent cities of cities of Pasadena, Glendale, and Long Beach, bring the total to 73,702. Another shocking statistic claims that 141,737 persons (1.5 percent of Los Angeles County's total population) experience homelessness at some point during the year (LAHSA n.p.).

These views of the inner city carry with them implications dealing with social and cultural reproduction. In contrast with the story of the protagonist's family in Fuguet's *The Movies of My Life*, many fictional works reveal that when Latin American and Latino immigrants move to Los Angeles, they immediately acquire a series of spatial and conceptual assumptions: they unconsciously deduce that they do not "belong" in the suburbs or other privileged urban and suburban spaces, but in the mean streets of the inner city or in the Latino barrios. Similarly, homeless and destitute citizens, "knowing their place" in the social field, find temporary residence on Skid Row or in other neglected areas of Los Angeles until the police forcibly remove then. They have all internalized social norms and structures through what Pierre Bourdieu has termed *habitus:*

> The work of inculcation through which the lasting imposition of the arbitrary limit is achieved can seek to naturalize the decisive breaks that constitute an arbitrary cultural limit—those expressed in fundamental oppositions like masculine/feminine, etc.—in the form of a *sense of limits,* which inclines some people to maintain their rank and distance and others to know their place and be happy with what they are, to be what they have to be, thus depriving them of the very sense of deprivation. It can also tend to inculcate durable dispositions like class tastes. (123)

Bourdieu argues that subjects acquire lasting cognitive dispositions, beliefs, and patterns of thought, perception, and behavior in response to a number of social structures and objective conditions they experience. Therefore, with no need for established rules, cultural hegemony inculcates a set of supposedly universal beliefs into the subjective mental experience of these subaltern characters that must be observed (123).

From this perspective, the struggle between the acquired habitus of a homeless person and the possibility of recovering personal agency becomes a matter of survival for the Guatemalan refugee Antonio Bernal, one of the two protagonists in *The Tattooed Soldier* (1998), the first novel by the Guatemalan American Héctor Tobar (1963–).[17] Tobar incorporates into Latino Los Angeles's writing the tragedy of homelessness for migrant laborers, an inner-city reality that has been, for the most part, overlooked. His novel also adds new nuances to the notion of invisibility often ascribed to Latino subaltern populations in this cycle of novels and films.[18] Bernal is well aware that when Latinos move to the United States, they often end up moving down the social ladder. Because he is traumatized by the political assassination of his wife and two-year-old son in a Guatemalan village, however, he drops further than expected when he becomes undocumented and homeless. His new life on the margins of society progressively takes a toll on his self-perception, as he is now suffering new levels of "invisibility": "He was used to being unseen. There was the invisibility of being a busboy, walking between the tables unnoticed, a shadow rolling the cart, clearing the dishes. However, this was another kind of invisibility. People now made a point of turning away from him" (9–10). Against the stereotype, his homelessness is not the result of mental unbalance, alcoholism, laziness, or immorality, but of a socioeconomic misfortune that is intimately related to global forces. In fact, it epitomizes urban ills in an inner city that is also plagued with widespread violence, poverty, and political neglect.

The plot of the novel is relatively simple: a refugee from Guatemala's dictatorship, after unexpectedly identifying in MacArthur Park his wife's and son's killer thanks to a tattoo on his forearm, prepares his revenge. In the last pages of the novel, his personal rage blends into the collective outcry and violence of the Los Angeles riots that lasted from April 30 through May 2, 1992. Many other characters decide, as he does, to settle their personal revenge at that historic moment. At a more metaphoric level, the United States is paying for its flawed foreign policy by now having to accept in its city streets both the victims and the victimizers of the Central American military dictatorships it supported for many years. This narrative is eventually linked to the 1992 Los Angeles uprising, where, despite the national media's obsession with presenting it as a black vs. white confrontation, more Latinos than African Americans were arrested. The story opens with a scene in which Bernal and his Mexican friend, José Juan Grijalva, are being evicted by their Korean landlord. Earlier, Bernal, who had reluctantly joined the revolution out of love for his then-girlfriend, had to flee his native country to avoid execution. Traumatized, he fails to apply for refugee status, and his life turns into a downward spiral: "I can't get any lower than this. This is the lowest. Where did I go wrong?" (51). In an implied national allegory, Bernal's seemingly irreparable downfall runs parallel to that of his country, Guatemala. In contrast, José Juan manages to find his way out of homelessness, and it is suggested that he will help Bernal begin a new life as well.

Trying to come to grips with the fact that he has become homeless, even though he is an educated man, Bernal also realizes, after seeing the police bulldoze the homeless camp on a Crown Hill hillside, that he is now part of the criminalized poor.[19] Therefore, in this novel the homeless, rather than Latino immigrants, are the ones perceived as trespassers who are "taking over." Their marginalization is intimately connected with the topic of environmental injustice that gives the title to this chapter: the scene with the bulldozers is reminiscent of the strategy of spatial containment of the homeless in Skid Row used in real life by Los Angeles authorities as part of the proliferation of microprisons that Mike Davis and others have termed "carceral cities." Madeleine R. Stoner has also exposed this homeless containment policy as a scheme that isolates the poor and prevents their mobility, hence blocking their access to rehabilitation:

> The containment of homeless people on Skid Row raises the possibility of viewing the area as a microprison. Moreover, its proximity to the central jail serves as a reminder that the jail is an integral component of the multiservice arrangement of containment. Many persons on Skid Row frequent the jail, and its presence reinforces the threat of criminal charges against homeless people. (225)

Crown Hill, a neighborhood near the imposing skyscrapers of Los Angeles's financial district, where Bernal is camping, becomes emblematic of the other Los Angeles: the failed one. In this area, where some years earlier greedy developers had turned beautiful Victorian mansions into vacant lots, the American Dream has become the American Nightmare for Central American refugees. Paradoxically, in contrast to the rest of the city, these homeless men of different nationalities and ethnic groups (some suffering from mental illness or drug addiction) live together in relative harmony and even protect one another when needed. This inner-city heterogeneity represents the only real example of the officially proclaimed "mosaic of cultures" one may find in the metropolis: "it was the nature of Los Angeles that the many races stayed separate, everyone on their own turf, Latinos with Latinos, blacks with blacks, whites with whites. It was only in the little camp in the tunnel that Antonio had seen the races mixing, all thrown together because they had no place else to go" (256). It is, in fact, an African American homeless man known as The Major who helps Bernal purchase a gun to kill his victimizer.

This world of undocumented and homeless immigrants in Westlake and Crown Hill is politically interconnected and then metaphorically blended with the Guatemala that the two protagonists are fleeing. Although both Bernal and the retired sergeant of the Guatemalan army who killed his family, Guillermo Longoria, hope to escape their past by moving to Los Angeles, once there they are surprised to find a mirror image of their war-torn country. Not surprisingly, the Los Angeles that Bernal had envisioned has little to do with the city where he is living: "In Antonio's homeland, the words 'Los Angeles' sparkled, like sunlight glimmering off a mountain lake. And now this. Skinny question-mark men with dirty bodies and unshaven faces, hanging clothes on a line strung between palm trees, in a lot in the center of the city" (41). What

Bernal finds instead are similarities: MacArthur Park reminds him of the Guatemalan park where he saw Longoria for the last time; likewise, the demonstration of garbage workers that he joined, along with his then-girlfriend, Elena, back in his country, now metamorphoses into a demonstration of nannies in Los Angeles. Yet these mean streets, a few weeks before the 1992 riots, provide Bernal with the courage to carry out his revenge, seven years after the assassination of his family.

In the same vein, Longoria, who, inspired by the exemplary behavior and orderly atmosphere he had enjoyed in the military training camps in Fort Bragg, North Carolina, and in the School of the Americas, had hoped to help build a new Guatemala, sees his role model vanish once he discovers that drug addiction, gang warfare, and riots are common in Los Angeles. Until then, he had believed that order and discipline were the norm throughout the United States. His ethnic pride is also damaged upon finding the streets full of impoverished Spanish-speaking immigrants and refugees. His frustration deepens when he comes upon a political meeting with the red flags of the Farabundo Martí National Liberation Front (Frente Farabundo Martí para la Liberación Nacional; FMLN), the Salvadoran political party that was formerly a revolutionary guerrilla organization.[20] Although in Los Angeles, all the power to combat militant leftists that he had as a member of the Guatemalan army has vanished, there are persons, such as his boss, the Salvadoran nationalist and member of the right-wing Arena Party, William Duarte, who continue the confrontation beyond national borders: "We monitor their activities. Once in a great while we organize a little action to let them know we're here. A little letter, a little phone call, sometimes something more serious. The newspapers get all excited and call us a 'death squad,' but it's nothing like that" (29).

Besides hearing about death squads in Los Angeles, during the 1992 riots Longoria also sees in the looting gang members a reflection of the Guatemalan guerrilla's activities. Later, he realizes that his own jaguar tattoo is a mirror image of the homegirl tattoo on the forearm of one of the gang members in his neighborhood. In a sense, adverse social circumstances have driven both of them into different but parallel violent paths. At any rate, Latino gangbangers are, in his view, the new "infection" that should be extricated, the American version of Guatemala's communists. Drawing from his experience as a soldier, he analyzes the tactics used by gangs as well as the LAPD in military terms: "As far as he could tell, the cholos were engaged in what his instructors at Fort Bragg called 'conventional warfare.' Their game was to claim a position—in this case, the front steps of the Westlake Arms—and then hold it against an enemy that could be counted on to ambush them" (200). Overall, Tobar describes life in the inner city as a sort of dystopian nightmare akin to and interconnected with Central American civil wars.[21]

Thus, following the path opened by Gregory Nava's 1983 film *El Norte* and Graciela Limón's first novel, *In Search of Bernabé* (1993), Tobar continues the exploration of the plight of Central American political refugees in Los Angeles. This time, however, he places additional emphasis on the direct consequences of Washington's imperialistic policies on the saddest face of the global city. As the author makes explicit, "I had grown up in Los Angeles, but the L.A. of the late twentieth century bore little resemblance to the optimistic, gleaming metropolis I remembered from my youth. Instead, I came to see Los Angeles as an imperial capital whose central core had been abandoned, left to the refugees of the empire's wars, the detritus of the empire's failures" (Tobar's home page). Raymond A. Rocco concurs with this perception of Central American civil wars as a "push" factor for immigration: "in the case of many immigrants from El Salvador, Nicaragua, and Guatemala, war, and the economic and other kinds of dislocations it caused, was a primary reason for leaving. Based on our interviews and ethnographic work, it appears that the economic and political motivations were often intertwined" (372). Hamilton and Stoltz Chinchilla have also pointed out how the repression carried out by the military dictatorship over the years led to the massive exodus to Southern California in the 1980s:

> During the 1980s, forced recruitment into the military or guerrilla armies also prompted many young men to flee the region. Military attacks in rural zones in both countries [Guatemala and El Salvador], including the highland regions of Guatemala, led to the internal displacement of large numbers of refugees, who fled to the cities and, in the case of indigenous communities of Guatemala, to the Petén area. Population movement across borders escalated, with Salvadorans fleeing to Honduras and Guatemalans, especially from the western highlands, escaping into Mexico. International migration also accelerated; Salvadorans as well as Guatemalans went to Mexico and in many cases from there to the United States. (33)

The Tattooed Soldier, therefore, exposes Central American immigration to Los Angeles as a result of Washington's key role in destabilizing democratic governments in the region and then replacing them with military dictatorships, in hopes of stopping the advance of Marxism during the cold war.[22] Indeed, this involvement in Guatemalan politics culminated with the CIA-sponsored overthrow of a freely elected government led by President Jacobo Arbenz (1913–71; president 1951–54) in 1954. After Arbenz nationalized land owned by the United Fruit Company and distributed it among 100,000 peasant families, the U.S. government began to regard him as a communist and planned his overthrow with the support of Guatemala's oligarchy (Weaver 135–41). The subsequent appointment of Colonel Carlos Castillo Armas (1914–57) as president (1954–57) constituted the beginning of several decades of military dictatorship. Pressed by the CIA, Castillo Armas created the National Committee of Defense against Communism, which is widely considered the first modern death squad in Latin America. U.S. economic and military support to the Guatemalan army would continue through the 1990s until, after thirty-five years of bloody conflict and genocide, the civil war ended in 1996. Three years later, President Bill Clinton acknowledged and apologized for Washington's role in this sordid history:

> "It is important that I state clearly that support for military forces or intelligence units which engaged in violent and widespread repression of the kind described in the report [released by the Guatemala Truth Commission] was wrong," President Clinton said. "And the United States must not repeat that mistake. We must and we will instead continue to support the peace and reconciliation process in Guatemala." (Kettle n.p.)

Together with his criticism of U.S. international policy and the discussion of this local–global dialectic, Tobar also condemns the role of Central American officials and their supporters. In this sense, Longoria and his Salvadoran boss add a new dimension to the traditional presence of victimized immigrants and minorities in the United States. Instead of demonizing the Guatemalan death squads, however, the author avoids Manichaean overtones by explaining Longoria's downfall as a human being: he has been the victim of different social forces and historical events, including the Guatemalan civil war and the cold war. First, the author takes us to the Guatemala of the military dictatorship, where he introduces Longoria as an innocent indigenous teenager who is kidnapped from a movie theater by the Guatemalan army. He evolves into a product of the U.S. training of Latin American military personnel,

and by the time he assassinates Bernal's family, he has unproblemati-
cally accepted a leadership position in a government death squad, the
Jaguar Battalion, whose assignment is to assassinate student activists.
Even when he exterminates an entire village of his own ethnic group, he
sincerely believes that it is his patriotic duty. Longoria, now a sociopath
trained in U.S. military camps, will eventually bring his personality dis-
orders to Los Angeles. Again, by linking Bernal's personal vendetta with
the 1992 riots, Tobar implies that Washington is paying its dues for its
political interventionism in Central America. Los Angeles then becomes
"a global city" in the worst sense of the term.

This subchapter thus traces a movement from relative harmony, the
comforting environment of the peripheral suburban space, to the disquieting setting of postindustrial city centers. Several of these novels
envision the suburbs and edge cities as a sort of haven under siege by
menacing inner-city dwellers. By extension, decrepit urban settings bring
along a rupture of identities that were previously constructed by suburban characters as settled and homogeneous. Inevitably, the crisis in the
citizens' identitarian self-perceptions sparks a feeling of loss. Whereas
disoriented characters struggle to make sense of an unwelcoming urban
setting full of indecipherable signs, the suburbs appear as an easily leg-
ible space where one can follow predictable daily routines. Impoverished
and hyperviolent inner-city neighborhoods find their antithetical image
in the livable spaces of the suburbs. This dichotomy, uncanny inner city
versus cozy and orderly suburbs, becomes a metaphor for the fragmen-
tation and disintegration of an increasingly decentered Los Angeles.
Both stages, however, are interconnected as they form a site of violent
power struggles where race (a social construct with very real effects),
ethnicity, class, homelessness, and citizenship play significant roles. In
similar fashion, whether urban or suburban, characters share their dis-
satisfaction and disillusionment with the experience of living in a contemporary city that is no longer a "civilized" space, but a return to the
places whence they fled, be it the inner city, a war-torn region, or an
economically underdeveloped country. In the case of *The Tattooed Soldier,* it also signifies a loss of faith in the American model of modern
citizenship. In sum, Fuguet, Boyle, and Tobar perceive, conceive, and
imagine the postmodern urban model of Los Angeles, with its seemingly
unstoppable urban growth, as the result of this rejection of the urban
experience and the subsequent embrace of suburban living. The next
subchapter focuses on the fictional representation of the ugliest face of

urban redevelopment projects: the forced displacement of Latino communities in Los Angeles.

Tales of "Urban Renewal"

> "Barrio" is a generic term denoting a Chicano neighborhood.
> Chicanos use it to complement their bilingual and bicultural
> history. The Homeboy element, however, gives it a heavy
> symbolic meaning synonymous to an extended Chicano
> family. . . . El Barrio is looked upon as a positive entity that
> nourishes and reenergizes the Homeboys' true love and affection.
> —Gus Frías, *Barrio Warriors*

In the western tradition, locations and spatial relations have been metaphorically associated with moral hierarchies. Dante's *Divine Comedy* (*Divina Commedia,* completed 1321), for example, offers an allegorical gradation of blessedness and wickedness in terms of celestial spheres and the nine circles of Hell beneath the earth. From this perspective, if we consider contemporary urban social relations in the United States, the collective unconscious of mainstream society would place the Mexican American barrio (like the African American ghetto) not far from the center of the earth, where Dante's Satan was held in bondage. In this context, David R. Díaz argues:

> During the most influential period of redevelopment, from 1950 to
> the early 1970s, barrios absorbed the worst abuses of the practices
> associated with urban reconstruction. Numerous communities were
> destroyed, partially dismantled, and/or excluded from the benefits of
> redevelopment. In fact, the logic of redevelopment served to desta-
> bilize rather than reinvigorate the economy of the barrio. In con-
> junction with regressive transportation policy that targeted minority
> communities, redevelopment policy as practiced in Southwestern
> cities treated barrios as expendable areas in relation to regional eco-
> nomic development. (23)

Indeed, as we will see in this subchapter, the barrio was sometimes perceived as a cultural void, a tabula rasa that needed to be filled through urban renewal.

Several works considered in this subchapter explore, at times from a first-person narrative perspective, the subjective experiences and

Figure 7 Effects of freeway and Dodger stadium construction on the barrios. Great Wall of L.A. (Photo by Tonya López-Craig)

the spatial perceptions of both regular residents of Mexican American barrios and urban gang members, who are often derogatively called *pachucos, vatos locos,* or *cholos* (or their feminine versions).[23] The latter characters are inseparable from the space that they often consider their legitimate domain, the barrio. As we see in Gus Frías's epigraph to his essay *Barrio Warriors* (1982), this word, which in standard Spanish simply means "neighborhood," has very different connotations in a Mexican American context.

Urban theorists as well as novelists have revealed the hypocritical ways in which Los Angeles's city authorities have repeatedly victimized East Los Angeles, Bunker Hill, Chávez Ravine, and other Chicano communities (as depicted in fig. 7). As they explain, the prospect of increasing tax revenue through corporate investment in office buildings, commercial malls, sports stadiums, and hotels, while uprooting minority communities that were considered eyesores and slums, seemed enticing to local politicos. Historically, industrial decentralization, political disenfranchisement, and the right of eminent domain, along with deficient housing and public services, have impaired the economy and the quality of life in the barrio. In fact, Los Angeles's high-rises often hide a palimpsest of immoral displacements, as they were built on the bulldozed land of formerly thriving Chicano, African American, and Native American communities. David R. Díaz has condemned these fraudulent policies:

> While the dialectical conceptualization of the term "revitalization" is a mantra professed solemnly by the urban cartel and the planning professions, the bald manipulation of this word constitutes an open question in relation to the moral and technical validity of the entire policy. The abject failure of the urban cartel and the planning profession to substantially address the urban crises of barrio spatial relations, when given the advantage of four decades of hundreds of millions of local, state, and federal funds, is mismanagement at best and fraud at worst. (188)

Henri Lefebvre, in his *The Production of Space* (*La production de l'espace*, 1991), introduces the notion of "social space," an environment designed for economic production and social reproduction that is based on the social creation of meanings and values. At the same time, he adds, space reproduces, mediates, and transforms social relations. Through representational practices, hegemonic groups are able to produce social spaces that influence society's perceptions and spatial practices. These spatial metaphors are a key element for the reproduction of their dominance. Likewise, Edward Soja has postulated that "the organization of space is a social product filled with politics and ideology, contradiction and struggle, comparable to the making of history" (198). Lefebvre's and Soja's theoretical approaches are useful in the study of one of the most recurrent topics in the cultural production about Latino Los Angeles: the programmatic environmental racism that has crumbled the hopes of Chicano youth through eradication programs disguised as "redevelopment" or "urban revival," which included gentrification and the construction of stadiums, freeways, toxic waste sites, and prisons. This orchestrated "barrioization" of Chicano communities offers a telling contrast with the fact that, as Mike Davis notes, Los Angeles is the third-largest metropolitan economy in the world, after Tokyo and New York (*Magical* 2). Therefore, the wealthy Los Angeles region, having close ties to the dynamic Pacific Basin region, plenty of petroleum, tourism, and agriculture, and all sorts of industry, including entertainment, is blemished by shameful pockets of misery. As we will see in this subchapter, the cheap labor that sustains this powerful economy comes with a price.

Symbolic and Spatial Erasures

The erasure of communities of Mexican origin in Los Angeles has been not only physical but also symbolic, a reality that has been echoed on both sides of the international border by canonical as well as noncanonical authors. Half a century after Octavio Paz (1914–98) recreated the pachuco in *The Labyrinth of Solitude* (*El laberinto de la soledad*, 1950), Carlos Fuentes (1928–), a celebrated Mexican writer of the Latin American Boom who grew up in Washington D.C., sees again a touch of Mexico in the Los Angeles cityscape of the year 2000. Through the eyes of one of his characters in the novel *The Years with Laura Díaz* (*Los años con Laura Díaz,* 1999), he conceives both cultural traditions blending in the city; he also envisions the Mexican world superimposed on the American one. Thus, after the protagonist, Laura Díaz's great-grandchild, and his girlfriend drive by a gigantic mural (probably the Great Wall of Los Angeles designed by Judith Baca and located on the eastern edge of the Valley College Campus in the San Fernando Valley) with such Mexican icons as the Virgin of Guadalupe, Emiliano Zapata, the Catrina skull, Subcomandante Marcos, Joaquín Murrieta, and Fray Junípero Serra, he visualizes a Mexican tropical landscape taking over the metropolis.[24]

While Laura Díaz's great-grandchild drives along the congested Los Angeles freeways of the year 2000 toward Olvera Street, where he plans to photograph the restoration of David Alfaro Siqueiros's 1930 mural *América tropical,* seventy years after the scandalized owner decided to erase its subversive message, he ponders the repeated American attempts at erasing Mexicans from sight.[25] He has discovered a common denominator during his preparation of a book on Mexican muralists in the United States (including José Clemente Orozcos's in Pomona College): "What caught my attention was the consistency with which the Mexican murals in the United States had been objects of censure, controversy, and obliteration" (510).[26] Likewise, his Chicana girlfriend, Enedina Pliego, who sees in the rebirth of the mural a restoration of herself, criticizes the "Spanish fantasy" with which the city's promoters and boosters have romanticized and Europeanized the Mexican past of the city. All these schemes, however, have been in vain. In contrast with Paz's pessimism in the 1950s, now that the sheer number of people of Mexican descent in Los Angeles makes it no longer possible to completely negate their physical presence, artistic heritage, and contributions to the city's economy, the couple celebrates the Mexican comeback.

Of course, beyond the symbolic and iconic invisibility of Los Angeles's Mexican American community, there is a history of actual dislocation. Urban historian and architect Dolores Hayden concurs with Carlos Fuentes's fictional approach when she avers, "One of the consistent ways to limit the economic and political rights of groups has been to constrain social reproduction by limiting access to space" (22). Besides canonical Mexican authors such as Carlos Fuentes, noncanonical novelists have reflected on this erasure of Mexican American communities from the physical geography of Los Angeles as well as from collective memory. Thus, Danny Santiago's novel, *Famous All Over Town* (1984), explores the spatial injustice caused by the privatized projects for regenerative "urban renewal" that, using the right of eminent domain, systematically uprooted entire Chicano communities. The protagonist's barrio goes from relative harmony (despite the warfare between Chicano gangs) to the obliteration and virtual oblivion that will inevitably shape his psychological and moral development.

Eric Ávila's study *Popular Culture in the Age of White Flight* (2004) provides a historical background to this process of forced relocation. He argues that in the aftermath of the 1943 Zoot Suit Riots (depicted in fig. 8) that heightened racial anxieties in Los Angeles, these areas, officially identified as "blighted" and unsightly "pachuco zones," became the target of so-called revitalization or redevelopment strategies aimed at gentrifying the downtown and increasing the cultural visibility of the city: "Centering Los Angeles through the placement of hefty cultural institutions such as opera houses and museums within the vicinity of the downtown became a key tactic by which downtown elites sought to reinforce the economic vitality and political significance of the central business district" (157). Eventually, the groups that sponsored the initiative to rebuild the downtown (city officials along with national and international corporations mostly from the finance, insurance, and real estate sectors) managed to evict local Chicano families with a promise of progress anchored in public housing projects subsidized by the government, which would later be ignored and deemed "socialistic" (Ávila 57, 163). While city authorities achieved their goal of eliminating the "eyesore" of ethnic diversity in the downtown districts, the evicted residents, like the protagonist of *Famous All Over Town,* felt betrayed by the new spatial order. Just as freeways were used to preclude or replace ethnic neighborhoods, now someone had decided that in Los Angeles's downtown the vertical was to replace the horizontal.[27]

Figure 8 Illustration about the so-called Zoot Suit Riots. Great Wall of L.A. (Photo by Tonya López-Craig)

In *Famous All Over Town,* a former neighbor of the protagonist shows her awareness of the racialization of space as well as of the existence of a "third border" (to use Mike Davis's term) in Los Angeles's geography: "'We should Americaníze ourself, compadre,' Virgie announced. 'Just because we're Mexicans by blood is that any reason for us to crowd up together on the wrong side of the tracks? We discrimináte ourself, and you should think about it" (124–25).[28] Incidentally, as is now widely known, the author of this novel was from "the right side of the tracks": the seventy-three-year-old Euro-American Daniel James, who chose the Chicano-sounding pen name Danny Santiago for this novel, was born to a wealthy family from the eastern United States.[29] Therefore, not only Mexican and Mexican American novelists, but also Euro-American writers, have denounced this historical injustice.

As to the fictional rendering of Los Angeles, spatial perceptions vary drastically according to the protagonist's mood. While Rudy "Chato" Medina is in the hospital, he still looks, with naive and innocent eyes, at the city he loves and considers his own: "The whole city stretched out under me and there was no end to it, my L.A. which I was once almost marbles champion of. It made me proud and I pitied guys from poor little Oxnard and El Centro and all those towns they have to keep apologizing for" (34). As expressed by the use of the possessive, at this point in the novel there is still a sense of belonging to the city where he was born. The same affectionate use of the possessive applies when he refers to his beloved barrio: "Shamrock, my Shamrock. Familiar cozy little homes drifted past my window, so close together they seemed to be holding hands. Well-known doors and windows made smiling faces at me and I was welcome in every one of them, excepting two or three" (38). He even deems the neighborhood's flaws—it is admittedly a little rugged—positive for young men's development: they make them street-wise. After Rudy and his family return from their trip to Mexico, he is so happy to be back in Los Angeles that he actually enjoys the Santa Ana winds and the polluted air. By contrast, once he feels betrayed by both the city authorities and his own father (who sells their house and then moves in with his pregnant lover), the familiar smog ceases to be so appealing: "Outside was all smog now, only not smog exactly, more like some kind of yellow, gray, brown wetness that came up out of the ground" (281).

"Decades of 'urban renewal' and 'redevelopment' of a savage kind," Dolores Hayden points out, "have taught many communities that when the urban landscape is battered, important collective memories are obliterated" (9). Yet even in the aftermath of the power struggles of urban renewal, when Rudy's neighborhood has vanished by a joint decision of city authorities and the Southern Pacific Railroad Company, the psychological process of place attachment survives. *Famous All Over Town* begins with the twenty-eight-year-old, inebriated protagonist and first-person narrator driving to the place where Shamrock used to be located while he plans his revenge. Once there, he nostalgically reminisces about a world (his own) that was destroyed in a clear act of environmental and institutional racism.[30] After daydreaming alone for an hour, hearing the echoes of his former neighbors' laughter and code-switching between English and Spanish, Rudy takes revenge on the Southern Pacific Rail-road Company by setting its trailers on fire. This cathartic scene had been foretold by Mr. Pilger, his school's principal, after learning that the police officer who killed Rudy's friend was only suspended for two weeks: "Rudy, God love you, try not to hate. Hate will poison you" (192).

Most of the plot takes place in East Los Angeles's Shamrock Street, presumably a pseudonym for the real-life Clover Street in Lincoln

Heights. Immediately after the scene of the protagonist's revenge against the railway company, a long flashback takes us back to the daily life in the streetscape of a humble Mexican American barrio, where assimilated Chicano children confront the more traditional worldview of their proud Mexican parents. Seemingly oblivious to life in the rest of the metropolis, the barrio thrives with social interaction. Danny Santiago chooses a neo-*costumbrista*[31] approach when he presents, with a refined sense of humor, the peculiarities of Chicano culture and traditions, including the language used, the rituals held at the cemetery, "the Mexicatessen" they ate, and even the different ways in which they killed chickens. In fact, in several passages the narrator turns into a cultural translator for non-Chicano readers, teaching them about the meaning of the word *menudo* (which is, obviously, an unnecessary explanation for readers of Mexican origin) and the term *con safos* sprayed on the walls.[32]

This rich social interaction among families in the doomed neighborhood is often interrupted by the urban warfare waged by gangbangers, who have been marking their meager turf for several generations in search of self-preservation and self-affirmation. At the young age of fourteen, Rudy, the antihero of the novel, steals merchandise and participates in other antisocial activities with his peers, Los Jesters de Shamrock (the self-proclaimed "Kings of Eastside"). Although the members of this gang and those of rival ones are all of Mexican descent, they refuse to see one another as brothers; rather, they are enemies caught in a never-ending chain of aggression and revenge. The fact that their violence makes the headlines on local television channels and newspapers is actually a source of pride for these boys obsessed with leaving a mark and becoming "famous," as the title of the novel suggests. Incidentally, this anecdote seems to conform to reality. Gang scholars Cheryl L. Maxson and Malcolm W. Klein have identified "the diffusion of gang culture through the media" (241) as one of the most important factors in the spread of gangs.[33]

Unbeknownst to the Chicano boys in the novel, the menacing presence of this antisocial subculture will be used by city planners as an excuse for the annihilation of their beloved barrio. When at the end of the story an angry Rudy, abandoned by his parents and betrayed by mainstream society, sprays graffiti with his *placa*, or moniker, "Chato de Shamrock," all over the district, the reader cannot help but sympathize with his subversive spirit.[34] His choice of emblematic buildings such as the one owned by Bank of America carries a profound semiotic meaning and suggests that his "tagging" is directed against a hegemonic ideology that has failed to subsume and absorb him. Since society has prevented him from fulfilling his dream of leaving a mark in the world by becoming a physician, he now leaves his imprint everywhere. Now Rudy has nothing to lose. With his antisocial stance and his provocations against the rival Sierra gang, he tries to destabilize the same mainstream cultural standards that have displaced his family. His quest for "fame" represents a desperate attempt to delay his enemies' objective of erasing him from the city's map.

The epigraph by the Spanish chronicler and conquistador Bernal Díaz del Castillo that opens the novel foretells the ensuing denunciation of the marginalization and enforced displacement of Chicano communities. This passage points at the beginning of a long process of colonization that, as the novel suggests, continues today; that is, it presents the deterritorialization of Rudy's community as the last chapter in a continuum that began in Tenochtitlán several centuries before. From this perspective, in a deceitful attempt to convince Shamrock Street's residents, city planners—who conceive of all Chicano families as broken homes with welfare parents and criminal children—condescendingly assure in a public presentation that building a "more up-to-date L.A." is for their own good and that they are "paying them to trade up into the American Standard of Living" (137). Although Rudy briefly considers the possibility that relocation may be the best way to avoid imprisonment or a premature death in Los Angeles's mean streets, he realizes that it is all part of a shameless ploy: "Was I deprived and disadvantaged like this man said, or destitúted? My father worked steady. I had never been sorry for myself before, except maybe two Christmases back. And here I was living in The Slums and never knew it, because by the time Mr. Cockburn added it all up, even a cucaracha would be ashamed to admit Shamrock Street was his home address" (136). Yet, despite blaming the city developers, the novel suggests that Rudy's father and other *vendido* (sellout) neighbors are also to blame, since, instead of standing united (as Rudy had envisioned in his heroic dreams of resistance), they betray their principles by selling their houses to employees of Southern Pacific Railroad.

Gayatri Spivak, in a lecture titled "The Trajectory of the Subaltern in My Work," which she gave at the University of California, Santa Barbara, defined the subaltern as a person without access to social mobility and then introduced the idea of an international civil society in opposition to the nation-state. Within this framework, she considers the subaltern's intuition of and insertion into the public sphere of the nation. For this process to take place, she argues, citizens must metonymize themselves; they must become the nation, make themselves synecdoches to claim the idea that the state belongs to them. One may reasonably argue, however, that this same process occurs within the city, as we have seen with the narratives and films about Latino Los Angeles. For instance, Rudy, in *Famous All Over Town,* initially locates the part by which he feels connected to both his barrio and "his L.A." The young boy relates to a city that he considers his own and actually feels sorry for those who come from smaller cities or other countries. In contrast, some time later, this self-abstraction or metonymization process described by Spivak is interrupted by one of the so-called projects of urban renewal that opens his eyes to a reality that catches him off guard: he has suddenly been robbed of his agency and left outside the public sphere. Rudy is no longer part of the whole, be it Los Angeles or the United States of America, since he feels that both entities have betrayed his loyalty. He then chooses to confront his new enemies with an antisocial behavior that will inevitably ruin his young life, but that will, at least, allow him to be heard. With his "nation" first invaded and then obliterated, now the petty turf battles between Chicano gangs seem insignificant in comparison with the real turf war that had been looming behind his back, perhaps for years.

The Struggle against Oblivion from the "Wrong" Side of the Tracks

Whereas in his novel Danny Santiago offered a Euro-American interpretation of the Los Angeles barrio, Luis J. Rodríguez (1954–) and Helena María Viramontes (1954–), like Mario Acevedo but in a more realistic approach, represent the Chicano self-image from the "wrong" side of the tracks.[35] The topics of environmental racism and the forced displacement of Mexican Americans in Los Angeles continues in the short story "Oiga," included in Rodríguez's *The Republic of East L.A.,* where the protagonist claims to be a direct descendant of the wealthy Californios who once owned the ranch where Griffith Park is located today. Perhaps romanticizing the Californio oligarchy, he laments the generalized historical amnesia. The United States, he reminds us, took over the lands of the handsome and brave dons who "had fancy clothes, stiff-brimmed hats, sashes, swords" (136) and then betrayed them with treaties that were never honored. His great-great-uncle, he bemoans, went from being the owner of the ranch to cleaning the place: "at the very end was an old stick of a man, *oiga,* beaten down, roaming the park, picking up trash" (137). But land takeovers are not a thing of the past; history repeats itself when the narrator's neighborhood, Kern Mara, is destroyed to make way for the construction of a new freeway. Once again, discriminatory environmental politics end up deepening the marginalizion of Mexican Americans.

Likewise, in "Pigeons," another short story from the same collection, Miguel condemns the destruction of Aliso Village, the demolition of the Chávez Ravine area, and the construction of freeways in the western section of East L.A.: "Miguel conceded that something had to change, that barrio warfare had claimed too many lives and that the poverty in the area was only getting worse. But 'change from the heart of the people,' as he called it, is different from urban planners, city officials, and major developers meeting in plush offices to carve up the barrio so they can profit on the renovations" (171–72). Later, he describes the elimination of housing projects in Boyle Heights as another step toward the eventual dislocation of Mexicans from real state that has become too valuable. Tellingly, in his study of the impact of these urban development projects in the Chicano community, Homero Villa uses the term "turf war," which is more commonly associated with gang warfare: "The evisceration of residential places in Chávez Ravine and Bunker Hill—to respectively make room for the jewel projects of building the Dodger Stadium and raising a corporate-cultural citadel in the massive Bunker Hill Urban Renewal Project—and the loss of nearly 12 percent of the land in East Los Angeles to freeway construction are signal instances of this protracted turf war" (115). The construction of corridors for five different freeway systems in East Los Angeles was, according to David R. Díaz, "the most intense level of community destruction by transportation policy in the history of the United States" (212).

The origins of this process of marginalization go even further back in time in another short story of the same collection, "My Ride, My Revolution," where the protagonist, Cruz, describes the downfall of his own people, the Purépecha Indians from Michoacán (called *Tarascos*— brothers-in-law in the Purépecha language—by the Spanish conquistadores), from the proud warriors they were before the Spanish conquest to the destitute situation in which they find themselves today. The Purépechas were never conquered by the Aztecs and continued to be their main enemies in the western border of their empire until Hernán

Cortés's arrival. Once again, contemporary forced displacement is directly connected to a long history of European and then Euro-American colonialism.

As we have seen, Latino and Latina writers in Los Angeles have consistently denounced this strategy for the disenfranchisement of Chicano neighborhoods. Among them, Helena María Viramontes has also tried to keep the memory alive by criticizing the heinous effects of freeway construction. Thus, in her short story "Neighbors," included in the collection *The Moths and Other Stories* (1995), a character named Fierro recalls:

> Then the government letter arrived and everyone was forced to uproot, one by one, leaving behind rows and rows of wooden houses that creaked with swollen age. He remembered, realizing as he watched the carelessness with which the company men tore into the shabby homes with clawing efficiency, that it was easy for them to demolish some twenty, thirty, forty years of memories within a matter of months. As if that weren't enough, huge pits were dug to make sure that no roots were left. The endless freeway paved over his sacred ruins, his secrets, his graves, his fertile soil in which all memories were seeded. (113)

In the same vein, Viramontes has explained that her 2007 novel *Their Dogs Came with Them* (2007) was inspired by the construction of the Pomona Freeway that severed her neighborhood in East Los Angeles from the rest of the metropolis during the 1960s. Moreover, she has compared the Los Angeles freeway intersections to the nonlinear structure and the intercalated stories of her own novel: "I realized that the structure of the novel began to resemble the freeway intersections. . . . And like the freeways upheld by pillars, I realized I had four pillars in four characters of which most other characters orbited around" (Olivas n.p). Near her house, she recalls, there were four cemeteries, and she did not want the cement poured on those souls to erase them from collective memory. As a continuation of Fierro's plight in "Neighbors," the lives of four young Chicanas—Ermila, Tranquilina, Ana, and Turtle—end up intersecting, as they feel disenfranchised and impotent to stop the destruction of their world by the new freeway.

As we will see in chapter 2, the idea of defending one's "nation" (be it the gang, the barrio, or both of them) is a commonplace in much of Los Angeles's Latino writing. In this tradition, the bulldozers and other earth-moving machinery that are brought to the barrio for the construction of the new freeway metaphorically become an invading foreign army that will occupy and destroy the national territory. This is explicitly expressed in the passage in which Luis, Turtle's younger brother, is practicing his tough homeboy demeanor: "the downward three-finger signal meaning *M* for McBride-Marijuana-Muerte, Que Rifa; the confident badass walk protecting a nation of city blocks claimed by McBride" (158). Although the uprooting of this "nation" comes in the name of progress, the main characters are well aware that the city developers did not plan the freeway construction for their benefit. The destruction that precedes freeway construction is comparable only, according to a character named Chavela, to the one caused by earthquakes: "Nothing was left, I tell you. Nada" (89). For this reason, Chavela tells a child that "it was important not to forget" (14). To the seclusion caused by these new conquerors, the freeways, the author adds a fictional Quarantine Authority that further isolates the population of East Los Angeles through helicopter supervision, identity card checks, barricades, and city roadblocks. Then they segregate barrio residents with an aggressive police curfew, using the excuse that it will save them from rabies: "Ten years later the child becomes a young woman who will recognize the invading engines of the Quarantine Authority helicopters because their whir of blades above the roof of her home, their earth-rattling explosive motors, will surpass in volume the combustion of engines driving the bulldozer tractors, slowly, methodically unspooling the six freeways" (12).

As the title of the novel suggests, Viramontes, like Luis J. Rodríguez, Danny Santiago, Kate Braverman, and several other authors included in this study, finds a historical precedent of this event—which, in her characters' view, should reach mythical proportions one day—in the Spanish conquest of the Americas. Using Aztec imagery to connect both historical periods, the comparison evokes images of destruction as well as of survival in times of upheaval: "And under the rubble, under all that swallowed earth, the ruins of the pyramid waited" (8). In this context, Jennifer Harris states that this novel is not "merely a portrait of one family, *Their Dogs Came with Them* is both a requiem for, and celebration of, a community on the verge of eradication and dispersal" (n.p.). After the impending devastation has become a reality, the androgynous Turtle (a homeless girl who "passes" as a boy and is a member of the McBride Boys gang) tries to survive wandering alone in the streets without the protection of her barrio. Hungry, sleep-deprived and in fear

of rival gangs, she looks for a new identity after her old one has been shattered by the Other's "progress." Her city's authorities have destroyed her
barrio, and her government has sent her beloved younger brother, Luis
Lil Lizard, to fight in Vietnam: "someone pulled out Luis Lil Lizard's
draft number, someone stole him away to another war" (23). In these
last two words, we have again the implicit idea of the barrio and the gang
as nation: like the Vietnam War, the tragic events in her barrio are also
a different type of war between nations. Likewise, it is her gang and not
her government that provides protection for her: "The boys all vowed
to be there for each other, always and por vida, hasta la muerte, because
that's what it's all about. About loyalty. About tightness" (25). Only a
sudden death, presumably at the hands of the Quarantine Authority, at
the end of the novel frees her from her suffering.

Mario Acevedo (1955–), also a Mexican American author, has found
alternative ways to denounce the environmental injustice originating
from various fraudulent redevelopment projects that have displaced
entire Chicano communities in Los Angeles. In his gothic detective story
entitled *X-Rated Bloodsuckers* (2007),[36] the sequel to the best-selling *The
Nymphos of Rocky Flats* (2006), he continues with the adventures of Félix
Gómez, a Chicano detective and vampire who returns to his native Los
Angeles to conduct a double investigation: into the conspiracy behind
the assassination of a surgeon turned erotic film actor, and the vampire/
human collusion that threatens to unveil the true existence of vampires.
Along with the witticism and sarcasm that characterizes this social satire
and original take on the vampire genre, Acevedo explores the corrupt
world of a different group of "vampires": Los Angeles's politicians and
redevelopers who make immense profits from the fraudulent displacement of Latino communities. The victim, Freya Krieger, known in the
porn industry as Roxy Bronze, had invested her time and savings to
support her friend Verónica Torres and the local community in their
collective effort to defeat Project Eleven, an "urban renewal" plan in
the city of Pacoima. Thanks to their efforts, the local press found out
about the developers' scheme: "'Independent' consultants not disclos-
ing that they worked for the developers. Contracts let out ahead of time.
Silent partners who were not so silent. Off-the-record meetings between
elected officials and lobbyists" (96). As a result, the city council had to
withdraw its plan of building a corporate office park and hotel, much to
the chagrin of the real estate developer Lucius "Lucky" Rosario and his

associates, councilwoman Patale Venin and a corrupt vampire and porn mogul named Cragnow Vissom.

Verónica Torres also discloses that in a separate case the city authorities had planned to bulldoze an entire neighborhood along Altadena's Loma Alta Drive (including the newly built library and Barrios Unidos, the center where Verónica worked) for commercial development. Using the excuse of eminent domain, Lucky Rosario accused Verónica's organization of trespassing: "I was told Project Eleven would bring jobs. . . . Oh yeah. Replace family-owned businesses with dead-end service work. Project Eleven was a scam, a huge bag of stinking pork. Know what made it worse? The project was to be paid for by a special tax levied against us, the community. In other words, we were to pay Project Eleven to screw us" (96). This time, however, no one was able to stop them. After demolishing the residential neighborhood, the development trust, as planned by Reverend Dale Journey, went bankrupt and the land became vacant. Only then was he finally able to build his evangelical church in the area where they were supposed to build the giant mall that would increase the city's tax revenue. As Verónica's organization and the rest of the local community later found out, all this construction was paid by the state of California, using a grant for community development with the support of the state's two senators.

In a new twist to the apocalyptic or postapocalyptic leitmotif (perhaps again a reflection of the racial anxiety that can be sensed in Rechy's and Braverman's writings), Acevedo's Los Angeles sports a *nidus* (or community) of vampires that is considered the largest in the world. Approximately two thousand vampires fill the ranks of the LAPD as well as California's political class, and their leader, Cragnow Vissom, plans to create a new social order in Southern California through their collusion with humans.[37] Whereas some of these humans, like Councilwoman Venin, are in a position of power, many others are "chalices" who voluntarily allow vampires to suck their blood. Certain scenes and events are, of course, not verisimilar, but characters find a simple explanation in the fact that they have taken place in Los Angeles, the eccentric city par excellence. Thus, when Félix Gómez asks Councilwoman Venin if she is not afraid of collaborating with bloodsucking vampires, she answers that in the land of fad diets, the way in which her constituents gain their sustenance is not her concern. Other clichés about shallowness in "the land of make-believe and cosmetic anything" (233) are also present: "In L.A., everything, even the government buildings, led double lives for the camera, and this art deco structure [the city hall] had once served as the Daily Planet in the *Superman* TV show" (215).

In direct contrast with the epigraph from Gus Frías's *Barrio Warriors* that opens this subchapter, in *X-Rated Bloodsuckers* the Latino barrio is portrayed, without qualms, as a place whence one must flee as soon as possible. In this regard, Félix, a Pacoima native, is surprised that his new lover, the Panamanian Verónica, has chosen to leave aside several lucrative offers in order to work for this blue-collar and run-down Latino community on the north side of the San Fernando Valley: "Verónica didn't see Pacoima the same way I did. For me, it was a dump to escape as soon as I could. For her, this was a place where she could fight injustice and bring hope" (92). Incidentally, the main representative of the barrio in the novel is not Félix, but Coyote, a vampire with a thick Chicano accent who acts as the protagonist's cohort. Although he uses contemporary slang (*ése, vato, simón, carnal*), he is actually the son of a Jewish Spanish soldier and doña Marina "La Malinche," Hernán Cortés's interpreter, adviser, and mistress.

In all, Euro-American and Latina authors join their voices to protest against the historical injustice against Chicano communities in Los Angeles. Economic underdevelopment and social failures such as the persistence of gang warfare are studied here in the context of the invasion and annihilation of this group's social space. In many cases, Los Angeles's mainstream preconception of the barrio as a "blighted" eyesore and as a collection of dysfunctional families that depend on government welfare has impaired its social reproduction. City authorities and developers have influenced these false perceptions by misrepresenting the barrio through the creation of meanings that do not correspond to real-life social relations. Their representational practices, which ultimately respond to power struggles between ethnic groups, have been used, according to these authors, to justify the immoral destruction of urban habitats under the pretext of progress. However, these works succeed in elucidating that the spatial metaphors of the barrio fabricated by these hegemonic groups have little to do with their authors' lived experiences and representational spaces. Instead, they prove that the social space dynamics of the barrio go well beyond urban gang warfare and other stereotypes such as the widespread dependence on welfare. The next subchapter explores ecocritical renderings of Latino Los Angeles and the importance of urban vegetation as a buffer against racial tension and repressed rage.

Ecocriticism of an Urban Dystopia

> The social construction of "natural" disaster is largely hidden
> from view by a way of thinking that simultaneously imposes false
> expectations on the environment and then explains the inevitable
> disappointments as proof of a malign and hostile nature.
> —Mike Davis, *Ecology of Fear*

In Ursula K. Heise's words, "Ecocriticism analyzes the ways in which literature represents the human relation to nature at particular moments of history, what values are assigned to nature and why, and how perceptions of the natural shape literary tropes and genres. In turn, it examines how such literary figures contribute to shaping social and cultural attitudes toward the environment" (1097). Considering the long tradition of environmental fiascos that have afflicted the city, this approach opens new ways to understand the cultural production of both Latino and non-Latino authors and filmmakers in Los Angeles. David R. Díaz, for example, has noted one of the legacies of environmental racism and regressive land use in the metropolis: "in Los Angeles, some elementary and middle schools have had inordinately high levels of cancer-related illnesses and death. Cancer-related deaths have been attributed to the siting of schools on former manufacturing sites or next to industrial zones" (211). Díaz also cites the protests of Las Madres del Este de Los Ángeles (Mothers of East Los Angeles) against the construction of a major state prison near the barrio in the late 1980s and the way in which Chicanas/os in Wilmington (near the Los Angeles harbor), "a community located in the middle of the most intensive oil refining and petrochemical manufacturing zones in Southern California, began fighting the Southern California Air Quality Management District (AQMD) over the complete lack of attention paid to public health relating to discharges of toxic emissions, fires, and petrochemical disasters in the area" (213).[38]

As figure 9 suggests, this subchapter explores ecocritical approaches to the fictional recreation of Los Angeles, dealing with topics such as the intersection between ecology and racism, the sexualization of landscapes, ecophobia, and ecological commitment. It also studies the use of allegory, prosopopeia (or personification), and pathetic fallacy (Rechy attributes human emotions to nature to reflect his own feelings or those of his characters) as well as ruptures of the traditional barrio setting and various topoi in the narratives of John Rechy and Alejandro Morales. I have selected the works by these two authors because I consider them

Figure 9 Los Angeles skyline and palm trees. (Photo by Tonya López-Craig)

representative of an area of Chicana/o literature that has been somewhat overlooked: the concern for the relationship between human beings (U.S. Latinos in particular) and their physical environment. This approach goes hand in hand with a denunciation of the detrimental effects of contemporary civilization on the natural environment (particularly on urban flora), together with an appeal for conservation and prevention of additional ecophobic acts in the future. In the case of Morales, the satirical commentary of his science fiction novel also brings an original take on racism in the Latino social environment.

Latino Los Angeles's Science Fiction and Ecocriticism

Switching now to a more futuristic approach that is somewhat reminiscent of the previously mentioned *Blade Runner* and *Strange Days* (Kathryn Bigelow, 1996), Alejandro Morales's science fiction novel *The Rag Doll Plagues* (1992) speculates about the future appearance of macro-environmental catastrophes that would cut across today's North American international borders.[39] Using a first-person narrative perspective, its three sections take place in colonial Mexico, contemporary Los Angeles, and LAMEX (a future Triple Alliance or confederation of Mexico, the United States, and Canada). In a sort of eternal return, they suggest that the connection between racism, pandemic diseases (which are themselves an allegorical take on racism in the United States), and environmental concerns is not new; human beings have been repeating the same mistakes for centuries. In this sense, Marc Priewe has addressed the allegorical meanings and the criticism of bio-political regimes in this novel: "my term contamiNation refers not only to epidemic infections of a single body, but also connotes a process of making impure, by contact or mixture, on a collective, cultural level" (400).

The plot opens when King Charles IV of Spain is ordering the first-person narrator, a physician named don Gregorio, to travel to the New Spain of 1788 to help eradicate a plague called La Mona, which is invigorating the fledging independence movement. Following the wishes of the crown and the church, he quickly forbids the work of *curanderos* (folk healers), which he discredits as witchcraft. Later, however, a Catholic priest realizes that this work had been a great resource in prolonging the life of the patients and asks don Gregorio to convince the Inquisition to allow the practice of the native medicine again. In reality, Priewe explains, "The main objective of Gregorio's quest is to implement a bio-political regime by disseminating a medical discourse and practice based on Western rationality, scientific discoveries, and the will to truth" (402). At any rate, what the Spanish physician finds on the other side of the Atlantic is a hellish underworld of decadence, corruption, and unsanitary conditions, three factors that, as we will learn, are neatly interconnected. Feces and dead bodies have contaminated the city, and moral depravity has aggravated the problem with the spread of sexually transmitted diseases. After three years, don Gregorio's efforts bring about the first results: he has been able to slow down the havoc by asking the viceroy and the king to fund medical services and to improve sanitary conditions in the city. Environmental awareness, therefore, has been crucial for the well-being of the population and, at the same time, has slowed down the revolutionary fervor in the colony. With time, however, the physician begins to empathize with the cause of Mexican independence and even considers Mexico his new home.

In the next two parts, La Mona is replicated first in the 1980s AIDS pandemic and then in a futuristic lung disease that causes cancer. The second section takes place in a barrio in Santa Ana, California, during the 1970s. The individual experience of a Jewish American hemophiliac actor named Sandra Spears serves as a vehicle to expose the widespread hysteria and intolerance against AIDS patients, who are being marginalized and even massacred. Eventually, she travels to Mexico with her lover, Gregory Revueltas, to find alternative healing practices for the disease, and there she learns to conceive of death as a positive transformation. In turn, Gregory, a descendant of the first-person narrator of the first part, reads his ancestor's historical chronicle and, like him, has a spirit guide called Damián.

In the third part of the novel, Gregory, yet another descendant of the Spanish physician, who works as medical director for the LAMEX Coastal Region of the Triple Alliance, is conducting research on severe pulmonary cases in the extremely polluted Mexico City. While there, he finds out that a huge accumulation of toxic waste in the Pacific Ocean has caused an outbreak of cancer in what is today's Southern California. In a satirical commentary on recent nativist propositions passed in California, the historical apprehension against the Mexican presence in the region disappears in the mid-twenty-first century, once their blood turns out to be in great demand for medical purposes. Gregory has accidentally discovered that after living in conditions of extreme environmental contamination for over a century, Mexico City's inhabitants have become immune to the hypercancer that is killing thousands of people in Southern California. Although the so-called MCMs (Mexico City Mexicans) and, in particular, the *pepenadores* who live off the city's garbage have a severe leukemic blood count, their health does not deteriorate; their blood has mutated and a radical change in their immune systems has made them resistant. Now, Mexican soldiers willing to donate their blood are hailed as heroes in Los Angeles. "The projected fear that alien elements infect and ultimately destroy the ostensible unity of the national body through racial and cultural difference," as Priewe puts it, has disappeared at this point in the novel (401). The novel enhances its postcolonial critique with incidental comments such as the one in which we are informed that these soldiers were stationed in "the Philippine Islands, one of those countries whose territories we rented for military use and synchronously converted into a waste dump" (143). This passage brings to mind the high cancer rates (27 percent higher than for mainland Puerto Rico), infant mortality, vibroacoustic disease, and radiation contamination that have affected the people of Vieques, Puerto Rico, after the sixty-two-year use of the island for naval training and testing (from 1941 to 2003).[40]

In yet another satirical commentary, this time on late capitalism, workers, such as Gregory's girlfriend, Gabi Chung, lose their basic human dignity when they have to amputate one of their arms to insert a cyborgnetic-computerized device that makes them more efficient at work. By the same token, corporations take over and the MCM blood business becomes a multimillion-dollar industry. Obviously implying that nothing is off-limits for today's unscrupulous corporations, the author includes pharmaceutical companies that build luxurious "breeder communities" on the outskirts of Los Angeles and begin to commercialize Mexican blood. With time, it becomes a status symbol for Euro-American families to maintain a couple of Mexicans living in residence "as expensive pets": "Euroanglos always wanted to be photographed with their Mexican at their side. People took their Mexicans everywhere, fearing that friends or relatives would steal them. Millions of MCMs signed contracts of blood enslavement. Here again, the Mexican population became the backbone of the LAMEX corridor" (195). Soon, Mexican blood metaphorically regains control of the land that was lost in the 1848 Treaty of Guadalupe Hidalgo and the 1853 Gadsden Purchase.[41] Moreover, the fact that, in contrast with the local Mexican and Asian populations, people in the Higher Life Existence (where most Euro-Americans live) have almost no offspring seems to imply that they will eventually disappear from the LAMEX confederation. At one point in the plot, Morales cannot resist the temptation to explain the message of his allegorical novel; thus, Gregory Revueltas ponders:

> For thousands of years, on authorities' terms, whether by a high Aztec priest or a United States or Mexican president, Mexicans have offered their blood to the world and to the sun only to be exploited and manipulated. Mexican blood paid the price: human sacrifice, physical or psychological. The Mexicans suffered the abuse but because of their extreme spiritual strength, they have survived like the delicate butterfly or hummingbird or like the repugnant insects of the earth. (181)

In spite of the allegorical evocation of colonial exploitation of Mexican people throughout the centuries, the last pages of *The Rag Doll Plagues* become more optimistic about interethnic social relations in the Southern California of the future. Asian immigrants and longtime Mexican immigrants coexist peacefully, intermarry, and collaborate in all areas of economic, political, and cultural life. Yet one can still sense that, just as some novels portray Euro-American racial anxiety about the massive arrival of Latino immigrants, others, like *The Rag Doll Plagues*, hint at the same sensitivities toward the massive waves of Asian immigrants. Thus, just a few lines before the aforementioned optimistic comments about racial integration, we read:

> Monterey Park/East Los Angeles was a center for Mexican/Asian culture. Chinese, Japanese, Koreans and Southeast Asians had migrated in great numbers at the turn of the century. The Chinese had become the dominant force in sheer numbers.
>
> After 1996, as I understood the novels of history, hundreds of thousands of mainland Chinese went to Taiwan, an island which became a transition center to the United States. In a few decades, millions of Chinese arrived in California. At one time there existed boat colonies consisting of hundreds of thousands of immigrants waiting to enter the United States. As the Chinese arrived, they settled next to Middle Life Existence areas made up of earlier Asian immigrants and long-time Mexican immigrants. (148)

Urban Vegetation: A Remedy against Racial Tension and Repressed Rage

Ecocriticism, which brings literary studies closer to the natural world and our interaction with it, provides useful tools for the interpretation of the works of John Rechy (1934–). Through the use of pathetic fallacy, in his 1983 novel *Bodies and Souls*, the detailed and ornate descriptions of all sorts of different urban plants allegorize human interactions against a collage of ethnic, cultural, sexual, or religious backgrounds.[42] The combination of disparate urban landscapes reaches a point of coherence precisely in a lack of harmony that is emphasized by the recurrent use of the adjective "incongruous." Like plants, asphalt and other artificial components of the cityscape echo the trials of its inhabitants and remind us of the human condition in this last frontier where bodies and souls navigate adrift: "all its freeways or their extensions connect into a twisted concrete star connecting all the parts of the city, its varied lives and destinations" (1).

Besides the topos of the America in extremis, in *Bodies and Souls* we have another commonplace in Los Angeles writing: the image of the metropolis as the American mecca for human rebirth. Characters leave behind their uneventful lives in moribund midwestern towns and, after crossing a lifeless desert where one can hear only religious radio stations, they arrive in this oasis of simultaneous hope and hopelessness in search of one last chance in life. These dreamers, according to David Foster, are part of the paradigmatic Los Angeles denizens of Rechy's "Gothic dirty realism": "the homeless, violent racist police, oppressed people of color, agents of transcendence through religion and popular culture (especially, of course, the movies), and other tourists, each seeking the fulfillment of a personal vision of the city" (92).

Although born in El Paso, Texas, this Mexican American author has often declared his unconditional love for his adopted city. Undoubtedly echoing their author's admiration, Rechy's characters constantly praise the beauty of the urban vegetation, which has learned to live together in harmony with tacky plastic flowers (the same ones that become one of the paramount symbols in another of his novels, *The Miraculous Day of Amalia Gómez* [1991]) and even corpses:

> Los Angeles is a city of scarred beauty. But for miles and miles throughout its stretching horizon, its flowered, verdant beauty, as grand as that of any other city in the world, is unmarred. In this city of grass and trees perennially green, layered in shades of amber green, rusted green, silver green; of flowers that flash out of shrubs in crimson and gold flames; a city overlooked by palm trees that transform long streets into corridors to distant hills; a city where blood-red bougainvillea pours over walls, balconies, sidewalks, streets, even the edges of freeways; a city in which giant hibiscuses open into sparklers, scarlet orangy leaves form proud paradisaical birds, and Joshua trees clutch torches of white blossoms . . . in such a city, the young sheik filled his concrete urns with plastic yellow and white flowers and waxy artificial leaves. (6)[43]

Yet Rechy does not hide his disappointment with other idiosyncrasies of Los Angeles that he sees as irrefutable proof of collective negligence and failure. In this sense, in an interview with Debra Castillo, he explains a sentence in *City of Night*, his first novel: "'It's possible to hate the filthy world and yet to love it with an abstract, pitying love.' I increasingly view life as a trap, shaped by all the meanness and ugliness that human beings (especially in the guise of religion and morality!) are capable of" (116). This sort of *chiaroscuro* composed of two colliding worlds, one of extreme beauty and the other one of utter ugliness, continues in *Bodies and Souls:* light confronts darkness; order faces chaos; innocence (Lisa and her doll) opposes decadence (prostitution, crime, police brutality, and drugs); the artificial (wax museum and stars of the planetary) relives authenticity and lost nature (the starry sky); and flowers challenge the six hundred miles of freeways in the Los Angeles area. Occasionally, one leads to the other, just like the narrow, curvy, and inadequate Pasadena Freeway leads to Pasadena, a city adorned by beautiful, flowery trees.[44]

Still within this contrapuntal conceptualization of Los Angeles, the exotic vegetation of the smoggy and tawdry Hollywood streets conjures an explosion of life and acts again as a remedy against latent social and racial tension. Personified plants struggle side by side with humans to survive in an ominous environment that connotes death: "Many still alive, brave trees, just beginning to mourn, surrendered enormous white and red blossoms to the blemished ground. Farther ahead, an urgent crush of bougainvillea splashed dazzling color into the desolation. The long, wide street ended in a field of dirt, wind-shoved dried vines entangled like tumbleweeds and huge clumps of concrete like overturned tombstones" (48–49). The theme of death is also evoked through the description of advertisements for mortuaries and billboards (another commonplace in Los Angeles literature) announcing the daily reenactment of the destruction of Los Angeles at Universal Studios and the Movieland Wax Museum.[45] Yet this apocalyptic take on the city, which in *Bodies and Souls* culminates in the freeway shoot-out, is another cliché of Los Angeles literature and film apparent in cyberpunk films such as *Blade Runner* and *Strange Days.* The two epigraphs that open the novel seem to convey that everything about Los Angeles, including the weather, with its lack of seasons and its long summers, ultimately evokes the inevitability of death or the imminent advent of the Apocalypse. After all, as we see in the epilogue, death (this time on the freeway) is one of the main unifying agents for this wide range of apparently unrelated characters.[46] John Rechy, like Kate Braverman, is a clear exponent of the fictional obsession of authors and filmmakers with the apocalyptic destruction of Los Angeles, which Mike Davis considers a byproduct of their racial anxiety. Could their social anxieties be leading them subconsciously to those fictional dreams of destruction?

Rechy represents most of these sporadic scenes of rage, violence, and death (which contribute to remove the label of superficiality often ascribed to Los Angeles) in an indirect and impressionistic manner.

The city's anger and fears are reflected mostly in people's makeup and scars, as well as in the ironwork that protects windows. In fact, the entire city is a visual fallacy that hides a rarefied subtext: "The facade of passivity, of ease—of life flowing effortlessly to congregate at the beaches—a city of bodies adoring and being adored by the sun—is deceptive. Under the tanned facade are constant intimations of massive violence. In one moment's shrug, earthquakes, fire, flood, murder may ravage" (87). Mike Davis seems to coincide with Rechy in this view of Los Angeles as a city that is exceptionally prone to major natural and social disasters. While other big cities in the United States are known for their frequent natural disasters, he argues, "none bear Los Angeles's heavy burdens of mass poverty and racial violence. What is most distinctive about Los Angeles is not simply its conjugation of earthquakes, wildfires, and floods, but its uniquely explosive mixture of natural hazards and social contradictions" (*Ecology* 54).

In this panoramic view, characterized, in David Foster's words, by its "postmodern decentering for individual and cultural meaning" (99), it is not until the second subchapter of the first part that the Mexican American space of East Los Angeles begins to take shape. Challenging the decrepit physical appearance of the barrio, the personified urban flora strives, alongside murals exalting ethnic pride, to preserve beauty and contain rage in a world of misery, gangs, sweatshops, freeways, and corrupt cops: "Even the poorest sections of East Los Angeles have an impressionistic prettiness that camouflages the poverty. Flowers seem pasted on crumbling walls; vines splash color on rotting porches. In wrecked-automobile yards—which are everywhere—enormous yellow-leafed sunflowers with brown velvet centers peer at twisted chrome veins on mangled metal bodies. And green, green trees are everywhere" (58). Environmental racism and repressed rage are also rampant in Watts, a predominantly African American district of Los Angeles (at the time in which the novel was written) where one can still touch the scars of the racial tension and violence epitomized by the civil unrest of the 1965 riots. In this area, the flora is not as ubiquitous and exuberant as in other sections of the metropolis, but it still manages to embellish the depressed district at the same time that it mirrors human misery: "Even the flowers here grow more desperate, in splashed colors, and die more quickly—with one exception, giant-headed, ordinary sunflowers. It is always hotter in Watts, because the houses are shoved together, miles from a soothing ocean breeze" (101). Throughout *Bodies and Souls,* the deterioration of the vegetation is a warning sign of the impending decay and seediness of formerly elegant districts. The encroaching waste that affects local parks on Wilshire Boulevard, for example, foretells the replacement of aging houses and theaters by more parking lots.

Rechy has expressed pride in his use of metaphoric language: "In all my novels, I extend 'realism' into metaphor for deeper meaning" (Castillo 118). Along these lines, in *Bodies and Souls* the flora (in spite of being, for the most part, exogenous to California) is a measuring device, a powerful metaphor whose representative value ranges from a status symbol in Bel Air to a last resort for survival in Watts and East Los Angeles. In one of the chapters, for instance, Hester Washington, a domestic worker from Watts, takes the longer route on her bus drive to Bel Air just to enjoy the abundant colors of the flowers in the area. Once in Bel Air, however, she transposes her anger against her rich employers onto their pampered plants. Moreover, the orange bird-of-paradise flowers in their lush gardens remind her of the widespread fire during the Watts riots, which, perhaps subconsciously, she wishes to export to these exclusive neighborhoods as a sort of mental revenge. The symbol resurfaces in the ninth subchapter, where an indigent woman's only prized possession is a paper bag with the ashes of long-dried roses. Again underscoring the woeful contrasts of the city, the woman, who lives surrounded by the high-rises of powerful multinational corporations, has not eaten in days and struggles to find a safe place to sleep. In a heartless environment in which other indigents have been stabbed and burned alive, several people try to take the bag away from her, but she defends it as if it were her own life; in fact, when asked what she keeps in it, she answers with the words, "My life" (292). The memory of the flowers, an obvious metaphor for survival in an inhospitable urban environment, is the only beautiful thing that she has left. Finally, the novel's three protagonists, Lisa, "Jesse James," and the mysterious Orin, drive from East Los Angeles and Watts to West Hollywood, the gay district of Los Angeles, where, after various scenes of prostitution and depravity, the positive side appears again with Lisa's amazement at the sight of a beautiful oasis of flowers, trees, and light.

Rechy's sexualization of urban space adds a new twist to the formation of individual subjectivities in a city setting. Simon C. Estok has equated sexualized landscapes with rape, violence, and "ecophobia," which he defines as an "irrational and groundless hatred of the natural world, or aspects of it": "Sexualization of landscapes has more to do with visualizing power and indifference than with allegorizing sexuality or desire.... The mentality that sees women as environmental commodities is one that does not blanch at prospects of violence to either the natural world or the women who live in it. As rape implies misogyny, sexualized landscapes imply ecophobia" (n.p.). Yet, as we see in Rechy's novel, this is not always the case. Deep in the heart of this cluster of cities interconnected by freeways, the three protagonists discover Griffith Park, a huge green area where trees, birds, caves, cliffs, coves, and rare wildflowers hide from the sea of cement and asphalt.[47] When a gay character named Dave Clinton uses the park to gather sexual energy for his performances, the connotations of power and violence usually ascribed to descriptions of land conquest in historical texts are nowhere to be found: "He always showered before going to the park, but not after—to preserve the sexual connections" (141). Here land is certainly not equated with the female human body, and the scene does not generate from a feeling of ecophobia, since no violence against the natural environment is committed.

Bodies and Souls, therefore, proposes a transformation of our environmental consciousness. In fact, characters are often judged by their capacity to respect nature. This is the case in the fifth subchapter, where the judge's inability to appreciate the beauty of flowers becomes a way for his wife to measure his inhumanity. Similarly, we get to know better the personality of another character, Mandy Lang-Jones, through his relationship with plants: he lives in a cul-de-sac where there are no flowers, since "[Mandy] didn't like to be 'owned by things,' especially anything living, like flowers. Grass was different—it was mowed down regularly" (342).

In spite of Rechy's love for his adopted city, at times the novel seems to play along with the contempt that part of the country feels for Los Angeles by emphasizing the ostentatious pretense of some city sights and the snobbishness of its inhabitants. In the city of Encino, for example, we see "determinedly *imitation* Spanish, *imitation* colonial, imitations of imitations" (240). Among many others, Mexican American author Richard Rodríguez seems to coincide with this perception: "Of course L.A. is shallow. Lips that are ten feet long and faces that are forty feet high! But such faces magnify our lives, reassure us that single lives matter" (*Days of Obligation* 154).[48] Yet Rechy's overall recreation of Los Angeles has little to do with the clichés of a superficial city that, enthralled in its narcissistic ego, sunbathes to the music of the Beach Boys. On the contrary, the metropolis emerges as a sophisticated intersection of culture and nature where people and plants share their joy to be alive. The lecture of a character named James Huston allows the author to explain his own novel: "He did not consider it the flippant land of the inherited clichés. To him it was the most spiritual and physical of cities, a profound city which drew to it the various bright and dark energies of the country. All its strains, of decay and rebirth, repression and profligacy, gathered here in exaggeration—as exaggerated as actors in Greek tragedies" (202).

Lawrence Buell has argued that, besides studying the relationship between literature and nature in an age of environmental crisis, ecocritics must have a true "commitment to environmentalist praxis" (430). From this perspective, Rechy not only praises the natural beauty of Los Angeles but also demands an environmentally sustainable culture for the preservation of its remaining natural resources. Against the background of Pasadena's success story, *Bodies and Souls* denounces several cases of faulty urbanism. The narrator recalls, for example, how, long ago, city authorities decided to remove all the houses and vegetation from a neighborhood to build a freeway, only to abandon the project a few days later; as a result, today the area is a dark wasteland with shattered streetlights. Yet his environmental concerns have been, for the most part, overlooked. The fact that much of the criticism about his novels has dealt with the topic of homosexuality may have contributed to ghettoizing his opus. Accordingly, Ilan Stavans points out that his work has been the victim of labels: "John Rechy, whose 1963 novel *City of Night*, a book about hustlers, whores, drugs, and urban criminality, garnered him accolades and a reputation as one of the most promising Chicano writers of his generation. Shortly thereafter Rechy's book was categorized as 'gay novel,' a stigma that tarred the book for Hispanic readers in the United States" (58).[49]

All things considered, while the main topic of *Bodies and Souls* may well be neither the Chicano condition nor the aforementioned ecological preoccupation, but rather topics such as homoeroticism, death, decadence, and the clichés about Los Angeles, Rechy succeeds in bringing attention to this dilemma by condemning faulty urban planning and the city's failure to preserve its natural environment.[50] In fact, the omniscient narrator's consciousness about the natural surroundings throughout the chapters creates a sense of coherence in this fragmentary plot. At the same time, Rechy's description of the urban vegetation contributes to the novel's more ample attempt to psychoanalyze a city with multiple personalities. In Foster's view, Los Angeles in this novel is a nightmarish mixture of corruption and injustice, which "teeters precariously somewhere between a very fleshy Garden of Eden and a compost heap of decaying nature. Yet Rechy's purple prose is not just an exercise in overwriting. Rather, it is an objective correlative of the intense sensuality that the city offers as the promise of a new life to the millions that have flooded into it in this century" (107–8).

Moving on to a novel published several years earlier, in *Numbers* (1967) Rechy resorts to a similar approach to the representation of nature within an urban setting. This time, however, the semiautobiographical protagonist's mention of a Mexican mother in Laredo, Texas, and of a dreary, fatherless Mexican and Catholic childhood are the only references to the Chicano world per se. Haunted by the same feelings of guilt and loss that affected the protagonist of *City of Night* (1963) and by the omnipresence of death also characteristic of *Bodies and Souls,* Johnny Río speeds along the freeway until he sees, from one hundred miles away, the smog cloud that hovers over Los Angeles. At first, the Mexican American protagonist wonders why he is returning to a city that, fed up, he had left three years earlier but later realizes his need to prove to himself that he can still hustle. Obsessed with the symbolic goal of "scoring numbers," that is, of having vagrant sex with as many partners as possible, he embarks into a ten-day sexual adventure that turns him into a sort of gay version of Don Juan. After Johnny meets his challenge of achieving thirty "numbers," he remains in Los Angeles but cannot rationally understand the reason. This behavior may be better understood in the context of Rechy's oeuvre, since, according to Stanton Hoffman's analysis of *City of Night,* his characters are moved by a feeling of guilt about their own homosexuality: "as characters they are ultimately unable to love, thus reflecting the culture which surrounds them and creates and destroys them" (196).

This plot about hustling and "sex hunters," occasionally taking on pornographic overtones, is intertwined with reflective segments that criticize, again from an ecocritical viewpoint, the progressive physical deterioration of Los Angeles. This approach begins with an ironic epigraph that analogizes the smog that contaminates the metropolis with the biblical cloud and fire that represent the presence of God in the covenant. In line with Rechy's recurrent use of pathetic fallacy, for Johnny, the best way to escape the pollution is by taking refuge in Griffith Park, where, surrounded by beautiful flowers, he finds cathartic moments of serenity and inner harmony. In fact, whereas one could reasonably argue that the city of Los Angeles is the protagonist of *Bodies and Souls,* in *Numbers* it is Griffith Park that takes center stage. Although this urban oasis of nature becomes his symbolic antagonist and challenger, he still uses it as a shelter for his narcissistic (he is obsessed with feeling wanted and adored) and almost compulsive sexual escapades. While he spends some time in other city parks such as Westlake, MacArthur, and Lafayette, his craving for Griffith Park is such that he compares it to a narcotics addict's withdrawal. In this sense, Ricardo L. Ortiz contends that "Rechy's text offers us a post-modern inversion of both picaresque and pastoral forms. . . . a post-modern, apocalyptic landscape, which is, if anything, pastoral in its emphasis on secret places in public parks, leafy grottoes and caves where the 'phallic' hero both exposes and hides himself" ("Sexuality" 116).

As we have seen, Rechy's novels challenge the traditional barrio setting, as he sees no need to make a distinction between writing about Mexican Americans and writing about Los Angeles. His Chicano characters are no longer isolated and marginalized in the space typically ascribed to them in both reality and fiction; instead, he portrays their daily interactions with the rest of the city. His recreation of a Mexican American chronotope (an essential correlation between inseparable temporal and spatial relationships) is, therefore, intimately related to the liberating formation of individual as well as collective identities. In this sense, Mary Pat Brady argues that the processes of producing space "have an enormous effect on subject formation—on the choices people can make and how they conceptualize themselves, each other, and the world" (7–8). Brady has also emphasized the importance of sexuality in the highly social process of producing space: "Taking the performativity of space seriously also means understanding that categories such as gender, race, and sexuality are not only discursively constructed but spatially enacted and created as well" (8). From this perspective, *Numbers,* like *City of Night,* resignifies the eroticization of landscapes, city parks, and nature in general. In the first chapter, for instance, the omniscient narrator describes the protagonist's communion with the sun: "When he lies stretched under the stark gaze of the sun—and he does so religiously each summer—he feels that the heat is making love to him, licking his body with a golden tongue" (18).[51] For other Angelenos, the natural world is also the only available shelter in a city that is rapidly deteriorating before their eyes: the downtown is described as "trashy and ugly" (25), Hollywood Boulevard has become "unbelievably trashy and shabby" (150), and Selma Avenue is like "a skimpy movie set" (150). By the same token, Johnny cannot cope with the feeling of loss when he notices how much Los Angeles's beaches and theaters have deteriorated:[52]

The blame for all this dilapidation falls time and again on city authorities:

> Johnny sees the enemy's weapon—the hideous machines that have already swallowed, digested, and thrust out as dust so many familiar places. It's Saturday, and even the machines rest now; but they sit there like monstrous dinosaurs, heads bent but ready to resume their fatal devastation, giant claws ready to scoop up the earth. Jagged outlines of demolished buildings create gutted craters. That portion of the city—a part of Santa Monica, a part of Venice West—looks as though it had been ravaged by bombs. (59)

In their zeal to stop the seedy activities of hustlers, sex hunters, and other "undesirables," the narrator contends, city authorities closed down theaters and changed the human landscape of Venice and Laguna beaches, traditionally composed of hippies, bodybuilders, squatters, dark old Jews, and the gay crowd. The same social anxieties made them replace old beach houses and bars with identically rectangular glassed apartment buildings and then ruin the benches, trees, and ledges of Pacific Ocean Park and Pershing Square. Stanton Hoffman has examined the symbolic importance of these disappearing Los Angeles landmarks in Rechy's writing: "Rechy's Pershing Square (in his Los Angeles section [of *City of Night*]) is also a 'Hybrid of all the tarnished fugitives of America.' For his Pershing Square is inhabited by pensioners, revivalists, their listeners, as well as by hustlers, 'queens,' 'scores,' and cops. It is a place where all the lonely come, and a place which is meant to bring together all kinds of incongruities into an image of despair" (201).

The flora continues to be a crucial metaphor in Rechy's *The Miraculous Day of Amalia Gómez* (1991), a novel about a day in the life of an impoverished Mexican American woman. This time, however, the author turns to artificial flowers to convey the characters' efforts to cope with the ugliness of daily life among male chauvinist Latinos in East Los Angeles and Hollywood.[53] The Mexican American protagonist, Amalia Gómez, flees impoverished barrios in Texas and East Los Angeles only to end up in the supposedly glamorous Hollywood that, as it turns out, is becoming yet another gang-infested area. To combat the acoustic pollution from the nearby Hollywood freeway, she imagines it is the sound of the ocean. Likewise, to hide the destitution made apparent by her worn-out furniture, Amalia uses the only type of plants she can afford: plastic ones. In the last scene of the novel, she enters a luxurious shopping mall and notices that there are natural plants, exotic flowers and even a real tree inside, which symbolize everything she cannot afford to own. Although there are no explicit signs preventing her from entering the mall, she immediately reads the uninviting semiotics of the place. In Mike Davis's view, this type of reaction from underprivileged social groups is precisely the one that some architects are seeking:

> Today's upscale, pseudo-public spaces—sumptuary malls, office centers, culture acropolises, and so on—are full of invisible signs warning off the underclass "Other." Although architectural critics are usually oblivious to how the built environment contributes to segregation, pariah groups—whether poor Latino families, young Black men, or elderly homeless white females—read the meaning immediately. (*City* 226)[54]

Like so many other characters in these works, Amalia had arrived in Los Angeles with a glamorous image of the metropolis in mind that has little to do with the gloomy reality she encounters. Again following another commonplace in Los Angeles writing, the author, upon her arrival, has nature foreshadow the hard times ahead: "she would also come to fear the ominous winds and the scorched odor that permeated the city during the season of fires, the floods she heard about that swept distant cliffs into the ocean—and she would come to hate and fear the prospect of earthquakes—and the presence of gangs" (41). Throughout the plot, the protagonist chronicles the progressive decay of her new neighborhood: weeds and dirt are taking over the lawn; discarded cars are left around; windows are boarded up or protected with iron bars; the ubiquitous graffiti announces the arrival of gangs; and homeless people wander around at night . . . yet she finds an unexpected symbol of hope and resurrection in a rosebush that has managed to survive in her yard. In spite of the devastation caused by faulty urban planning and environmental racism, the biological processes of nature (a symbol of hope) remain at work everywhere the characters go. In other poor sections of Hollywood, this metaphoric struggle between the resilient flora (splashes of bougainvillea, lavender blossoms, white oleanders) and man-made urban decay continues to mirror social relations between multiethnic Angelenos. Rechy's fictional Los Angeles is, after all, a site for reflection in which environmental issues and ethical commitment to cultural change intersect.

Wolch, Pincetl, and Pulido have complained about urban theory's disregard for urban ecology, which reinforces a false nature/culture divide:

> Nature is treated as synonymous with wilderness, a place beyond the city and the realm of human habitation. Fights about nature in urban theory are thus often characterized as disputes about changes in the city–country boundary. But the relevant nature is not "out there" but within every human and throughout every city, however thoroughly manipulated and reordered, as well as far beyond the city. (396)

In this context, while Rechy is certainly not the only Chicano author to deal with environmental issues, his fictional study of urban social relations has contributed to the thematic expansion of Chicano literature by extending the denunciation of social injustice related to race, class, gender, and sexuality to the realm of spatiality and the concern for nonhuman beings, such as the Los Angeles flora.[55] In his novels, which tend to advocate the mutual benefits of a peaceful coexistence between humans and nature, he incorporates the natural world (a type of nature that either threatens human life or struggles for survival against human encroachment and pollution) not as wilderness, but as an intrinsic aspect of urban life and social relations.

As we have seen, Morales and Rechy tie their ecological concerns for the ecosystems and Latino habitats of the Los Angeles metropolitan area with issues dealing with racism, white supremacy, and intolerance. Even though they use two very different literary approaches (Rechy's direct denunciation of the abuses committed by city authorities gives way to a futuristic social satire in Morales's science-fiction novel), they share their social commitment and denunciatory spirit.

The next chapter studies fictional and cinematic renderings of the marginalization of Latino urban youth as seen by Latino and non-Latino authors.

2

The Marginalization of Latino Urban Youth

Together with environmental injustice, another crucial factor in the creation of new social anxieties and "racial" animosities in Los Angeles has been the disenfranchisement of Latino and African American youth in the inner city and, for some time now, in suburban areas as well. This chapter examines the literary and cinematic representations of Latino youth's experiences in their barrios, with an emphasis on the structures of subjectivity and consciousness. Still within this framework, it explores the spectacularization of Latino gang life and the self-stereotypification of Latinos in film and television. Combining the self-perceptions of gang members and regular young citizens alike, I shall analyze these Latino characters' conception of gangs and barrios as independent counternations modeled after American nationalistic discourse. The last two subchapters study these works' denunciation of the adverse effects of Los Angeles law enforcement agencies on Latino communities and Latino characters' negative self-perceptions as a result of systematic discrimination in the city's schools. According to the works included in this chapter, the racial anxieties that affect institutions such as police departments, public schools, mass media, and the entertainment industry account for certain practices that negatively affect the self-esteem of Latino urban youth. In turn, their symbolic exclusion from the discourse of nation makes some young Chicanas and Latinos develop new social anxieties that lead them to seek alternative ways to become socially accepted. Eventually, behavioral patterns such as those of street gangs, which they created in an attempt to recover their dignity and to take possession of what they deem is their territory (the barrio), end up paving the way for their own physical and civic self-destruction.

Although Los Angeles has several Latino barrios and incorporated cities, the quintessential barrio is still East Los Angeles.[1] Consequently, most texts and films address this "city-within-a-city" (to use Davis's term) as the hearth of everything Chicano. Some of the works set in the barrio focus on the marginal figure of the pachuco. To provide a historical context for these characters, it is useful to keep in mind the hostile climate of the 1930s. The historians Francisco E. Balderrama and Raymond Rodríguez summarize, in *Decade of Betrayal*, these adverse conditions:

> Americans, reeling from the economic disorientation of the depression, sought a convenient scapegoat. They found it in the Mexican community. In a frenzy of anti-Mexican hysteria, wholesale punitive measures were proposed and undertaken by government officials at the federal, state, and local levels. Laws were passed depriving Mexicans of jobs in the public and private sectors. Immigration and deportation laws were enacted to restrict emigration and hasten the departure of those already here. Contributing to the brutalizing experience were the mass deportation roundups and repatriation drives. Violence and "scare-head" tactics were utilized to get rid of the burdensome and unwanted horde. (1)[2]

In some cases, literary portrayals of barrio dwellers are a continuation of, or perhaps a reaction to, the much-maligned (at least in Chicano studies) chapter "The Pachuco and Other Extremes" ("El pachuco y otros extremos"), included in Octavio Paz's *The Labyrinth of Solitude*. There, the author elaborates upon the surprise of finding a distorted self-image in Los Angeles's Mexican Americans and, more specifically, in the pachucos. Taking the role of an ethnologist, he opens his argument by comparing Los Angeles's inability to blend its Mexican and Euro-American atmospheres with the pachuco's insistence on flaunting his difference from both cultures. A number of descriptors jump from the pages of this book. Paz's pachuco represents exaggeration, enigma, and contradiction; he is uprooted, hybrid, disturbing, defenseless, and suicidal; he is both a victim and a delinquent who seeks persecution; he forms gangs and uses the disguise of "an impassive and sinister clown whose purpose is to cause terror instead of laughter" (16).[3] Ultimately, the pachuco, in Paz's view, represents solitude.

In contrast, from the vantage point of Chicano cultural nationalism, Luis Valdez's influential musical *Zoot Suit* introduces the image of the pachuco as the social consciousness of his community, thus becoming a predecessor of the Chicano Movement. While some of the authors and filmmakers who create these characters are outsiders (much like Paz), others are very familiar with the world of Los Angeles's urban and suburban street gangs or were pachucos or gang members themselves, as is the case of Luis J. Rodríguez and Miguel Durán, author of the novel *Don't Spit on My Corner*. From this perspective, it is worth considering whether they manage to humanize pachucos and cholas by exposing and condemning the causes of their extreme alienation from mainstream culture or whether, on the contrary, they are just profiting from the readers' and viewers' curiosity or panic, and falling into stereotypes. As we will see, reaching varying degrees of commodification, some of these texts and films share both approaches.

Although the pachuco of the 1930s and 1940s, as Rosa-Linda Fregoso has noted, has become "a legendary figure of counterhegemonic masculinity for Chicano nationalists who see in him the embodiment of revolutionary identity" ("Re-Imaging" 72), today's Latino homeboy is often represented in a very different light. Maxson and Klein, who date the origin of the East Los Angeles urban street gang phenomenon to before World War II, present a demoralizing picture of the situation in Los Angeles County: in 1992, there were 1,400 listed gangs and 137,500 gang member residents, that is, over one-fourth of the gang members in the country (253). In their view, the limited scope of law enforcement exposure and the exaggerated interpretations carried out by the film industry, commercial television, and the news media have all contributed to a distorted stereotyping of street gangs that exceeds reality. According to their research, most street gang behavior (other than that of the relatively uncommon specialty gangs) consists "first and foremost, of noncriminal activity" (247), and when they do engage in criminal behavior, it is for the most part inconsequential. Yet, undoubtedly, gang crime since the 1980s has significantly tainted the image of Los Angeles and of Latinos in the United States.

The Spectacularization of Latino Gang Life

In the introduction to this book, it was established that writing can be a form of territorial reclamation or symbolic appropriation of space. In this subchapter, we will see how literature, the media, and film can also be conceived as strategic tools for cultural exclusion from the discourse of nation. Indeed, literary and cinematic practices can either encourage identification with national identities and projects or, on the contrary, leave readers and audiences on the margins. In this sense, the depiction of Latinos in film, the media, and commercial television has fomented new social and racial anxieties, particularly when a small section of this

community—pachucos and, years later, gang members—is dispropor-
tionately represented. Charles Ramírez Berg, from a different perspective, argues, "The case of Latino stereotyping in mass media involves
a discursive system that might be called 'Latinism' (a play on Edward
Said's Orientalism): the construction of Latin America and its inhabitants and of Latinos in this country to justify the United States' imperialistic goals" (4).

Within the context of the anti-Mexican hysteria that affected Euro-
American Los Angeles during World War II, Luis Valdez's musical play
Zoot Suit (written and first performed in 1979 but published for the first
time in 1992) portrays the worst side of the Los Angeles English-language
press.[4] The first Chicano play to be represented on Broadway, it opens
with racist headlines, such as "Zoot-Suiter Hordes Invade Los Angeles.
U.S. Navy and Marines Are Called In" (*Zoot Suit* 24), which unfairly
blame the flamboyant zoot-suiters for the so-called Zoot Suit Riots. As
Eduardo Obregón Pagán demonstrated in *Murder at the Sleepy Lagoon:
Zoot Suits, Race, and Riot in Wartime L.A.* (2003), this violent confrontation, which took place in May 1943, was actually caused by sailors and
soldiers stationed in the city. Other racist headlines describe the wave
of Mexican crime that is allegedly destroying Los Angeles. A mythical
character named El Pachuco who acts as a Greek chorus or, rather, as
the social conscience of his community, argues that "zoot-suiter" is, in
reality, a euphemism used by the press to attack Mexicans. According to
Charles M. Tatum, this is the role of El Pachuco: "to comment on and
undermine the motives of the Anglo characters (the newspaper reporter
who covers the Sleepy Lagoon incident and the trial, the liberal Anglo
lawyer who defends the four young Chicanos, the trial judge, and even
Alice Bloomfield, the woman who organizes a defense committee) as
well as to mock and goad Hank Reyna when he appears to weaken in
the face of the justice system" (76–77). He also tries to raise awareness
among other pachucos (or "streetwise Chicano youth" [List 1992, 190])
like Henry "Hank" Reyna, the leader of the so-called 38th Street gang,
inspired by real-life Henry Leyvas: "Because this ain't your country. Look
what's happening all around you. The Japs have sewed up the Pacific.
Rommel is kicking ass in Egypt but the Mayor of L.A. has declared all-out
war on Chicanos. On you! ¿Te curas?" (30). In fact, the play reveals a collective conspiracy led by the mayor and law enforcement, but especially
by the press, against the Mexican American community of Los Angeles. Alice, a young Jewish lawyer who is trying to help the youngsters,

informs the imprisoned Henry Reyna that according to the press, the alleged pachuco crime wave is being directed by fascists or by Japanese Americans from inside the relocation camps. In her own words, there are also ulterior motives for unfairly blaming these young Chicanos for the 1942 Sleepy Lagoon murder and the 1943 Zoot Suit Riots: "Are you aware you're in here just because some bigshot up in San Simeon wants to sell more papers?" (49).[5]

Christine List has noted how "El Teatro Campesino [founded by Luis Valdez in 1965] embraced the image of the pachuco (coded as gangster by Anglo media) and transformed him into a heroic symbol of Chicano identity" ("Self-directed" 192). In this tradition, Miguel Durán's semi-autobiographical novel *Don't Spit on My Corner* (1992) portrays a Los Angeles press that, spurred by World War II, foments racism and hate not only against Mexican American youth, but also against the Japanese. Although the autobiographical narrator, a pachuco of the 1940s named Mike, praises the *Daily News* for its sensitive reporting of the Zoot Suit Riots, he criticizes *Life* magazine and the rest of the Los Angeles mainstream print media: "All of this was reported in those two rags, the *Times* and the *Herald Express*. They wrote some inflammatory stories about how the Zoot Suit hoodlums were going to be cleaned out by servicemen and good riddance and all that shit!" (59). According to Mike, the press sensationalizes what it calls the "Zoot Suit Riots" and makes up sinister stories about saboteurs' intent to start a race war in the United States, while ignoring the fact that a Mexican American from Alaska has just received the first Congressional Medal of Honor for heroism in battle. As he explains, a year before the Zoot Suit Riots, in October 1942, the sensationalist print media took advantage of the Sleepy Lagoon murder case to demonize the young pachucos from the 38th Street gang and Mexican Americans in general:[6]

> What really hung on our heads was the bald-faced admission on the part of a judge that he didn't like Mexicans. During the trial those guys, besides not being allowed bail, were not allowed to shave or wash. They were also not allowed a change of clothes. The prejudiced newspapers had a ball with that. They were allowed to take all the pictures they wanted of these poor suckers. These pictures were fed to a public willing to believe any and all slanderous remarks. (126)

However, during certain periods, Los Angeles's English-language press showed interest for the concerns of Latino residents. In fact, during the

Figure 10 Scapegoating during the Great Depression: Deportation of Mexican Americans. Great Wall of L.A. (Photo by Tonya López-Craig)

1930s, the *Los Angeles Times* covered the mass repatriation of Mexicans and Mexican Americans, "criticized the Immigration Service's methods and called for an investigation of Walter Carr, director of the Immigration Service in Los Angeles, and his reprehensible raids" (Balderrama and Rodríguez 70). As can be seen in figure 10, one of the murals of the Great Wall of L.A. denounces this scapegoating scheme during the Great Depression. By the same token, one of the most important local journalists of Mexican origin during the 1960s was Rubén Salazar (1928–70), who worked as a staff writer and columnist for the *Los Angeles Times* and was also the news director for the local Spanish-language television station KMEX in Los Angeles. On August 29, 1970, while covering the third National Chicano Moratorium March against the Vietnam War (organized to protest against the disproportionate number of Chicanos recruited and killed) for KMEX, Salazar was killed in East Los Angeles. During a riot that broke out after the police tear-gassed the protesters, Salazar was shot in the head with a 10-inch tear gas canister and at short range while drinking a beer at the Silver Dollar Bar. Although a coroner's inquest ruled the shooting a homicide, the Los Angeles County sheriff's deputy who shot him, Tom Wilson, was never prosecuted. It is worth noting that, as a journalist, Salazar had been covering police brutality against Latinos as well as the numerous deaths of Latinos in Vietnam. It is also believed that he was under investigation by the LAPD and the FBI. After his death, Salazar became a martyr of the Chicano Movement and a symbol of the mistreatment of Chicanos by Los Angeles law enforcement and the U.S. legal system.

In contrast to the animosity and racial anxiety displayed by the Los Angeles English-language press, the Spanish-language print media has traditionally been a tool for unity and self-defense for the Mexican American community. For instance, *El Heraldo de México* and *La Opinión,* one of the nation's oldest surviving and continuously published Spanish-language newspapers (along with the New York–based *La Prensa*), criticized the racial overtones of the repatriation of one million Mexicans and Mexican Americans (approximately 400,000 of them from California) from the United States during the 1930s: "[*La Opinión*] gave the hearing and repatriation story an unprecedented four page coverage. In an article entitled 'Heridas que no cierran,' Injuries That Don't Heal, it discussed the background of the repatriation, its casues and the current ongoing situation" (Balderrama and Rodríguez 311). We find an example of this support in *Don't Spit on My Corner*, when Mike confesses his participation in the riots and then argues, "You read *La Opinión* and hear the news in Spanish. Mexicans are in the service, they are hard working, pay their taxes and try to be good Americans. Their reward is an ass-kicking and humiliation by the notorious Gladiators" (68). Like *La Opinión*, several other Spanish-language newspapers from Los Angeles have traditionally acted in defense of the Mexican American and Latino communities, often resorting to a transnational approach.

Moving on to cinematic practices, in spite of being in Los Angeles, Hollywood has generally ignored the existence of Mexicans, Chicanos, and Latinos. The misrepresentation of Latinos and Latino culture in American films has been evidenced in several studies.[7] In his subchapter "Chicanos on Television and in the News," Charles M. Tatum provides a recollection of data that coincide in their denunciation of the misrepresentation and underrepresentation of Chicanos on television and the media. With few early exceptions, whenever Hollywood wishes to add a touch of exotic ethnicity, it typically includes fair-skinned Caribbean or Spanish actors, such as Jennifer López, Antonio Banderas, Javier Bardem, and Penélope Cruz.[8] When Chicanos and Latinos from Los Angeles do appear in Hollywood films, they are usually given roles that cast them in an unfavorable light.[9] Nonetheless, a different take on this negative imaging of Latinos also exists. One of the first attempts to combat ethnic stereotyping through humor was carried out by the Chicano television character Francisco "Chico" Rodríguez, played by Freddie Prinze (born Frederick Karl Pruetzel; 1954–77) in the American sitcom *Chico and the Man*, which ran on NBC from September 13, 1974, to July 21, 1978. Later, self-stereotypification or counterstereotyping in comedy films, such as Richard "Cheech" Marín's *Born in East L.A.* (1987),[10] and those he co-directed with Thomas Chong (*Up in Smoke* [1978], *Cheech and Chong's Next Movie* [1980], *Nice Dreams* [1981], and *Still Smokin* [1983]) also produced a contestatory effect: "Cheech Marín's films show that an ethnic director can take a negative stereotype and, through humor, expose the stereotype as racist (among other things), thereby initiating the process of diffusing its significance for a general audience" (List 1992, 193).[11]

Among the many ways to approach the marginalization of Latino youth, one of the most dangerous is the spectacularization of gang life. In recent years, the Chicano homeboy from East Los Angeles has captured the imagination of writers and the film industry alike. The surprising success of television shows about street and prison gangs has added to the negative characterization of Latinos in motion pictures. Consider, for example, *Gangland,* a series on the History Channel dealing with prison and street gangs, including Nuestra Familia, 18th Street Gang, MS-13, Mexican Mafia, Black P. Stones, Hells Angels, skinheads, and Latin Kings.[12] Every episode was divided into different sections, each dedicated to a specific gang and introduced by the eerie music and special effects typical of contemporary horror movies such as *The Ring* (2002; a remake of the 1998 Japanese film *Ringu*). Along these lines, the narrator's tone is reminiscent of the voice-over used in action-movie trailers. Adding to the commodification of gang subculture, the first scene features the word *gangs* written in Gothic letters, supposedly tattooed on a young man's upper back.

To the program's credit, however, among the persons interviewed (most of them against a dramatically dark background) are not only police officers, but also experts from other fields (gang informants, U.S. attorneys, authors, academics). Yet, as is common in these types of programs, little interest is shown in investigating the social ills prevalent among the root causes of gang violence. Although one of the officers interviewed mentions overpopulation in the Chicago public projects and the flaws in the federally assisted system as part of the reason for the existence of gangs, most segments of *Gangland* are limited to sensation-alizing external signs (indicators of gang affiliation, codes of conduct, graffiti, "stacking" or "throwing up" a gang sign, hierarchical patterns, monikers, how they "mark their turf"). Tellingly, in a chapter that explores gang dress codes, a scene is included with four young Latino pedestrians dressed in what appears to be gang garb, thus implying that they are gang members. However, their outfits do not prove that they are gang members, because gang wear took hold in mainstream America long before. On the other hand, inclusion of Euro-American gangs (Hells Angels, Skinheads) on a par with urban minority gangs, while "politically correct," diverts viewers' attention from the fact that, outside of prison, gangs are, for the most part, made up of marginalized Latinos and African Americans.

In one of the interviews, Los Angeles mayor Antonio Villaraigosa admits that there are 40,000 gang members in the city and double that number in Los Angeles County.[13] Later, one of the informants claims that the Los Angeles riots of 1992 were "more or less" started by gangs. Other informants interviewed accuse gangs of being "heavily involved" in the five-day looting and murdering spree that caused one billion dollars in property damage. To underscore the gravity of the situation, the narrator postulates that "L.A., the city of angels, is also the gang capital of the world"; later, he introduces the concept of "race war" by adding that "the gang capital of the world is also America's most diverse city." Former gang members also point out that certain streets are no longer controlled by the police; instead, they are ruled by powerful gangs that are in the midst of a racial war to establish neighborhood boundaries. Although, according to *Gangland,* this war began a century ago when the first Mexican immigrants arrived in Los Angeles fleeing the violence of the Mexican Revolution, only in recent years has race become a key factor in gang violence. Murdering a perceived enemy from a rival ethnic group has become a sort of "badge of honor," one of the informants discloses; the more violent and bloodthirsty you are, the higher you rise in the gang's ranks. We learn that in these racially motivated turf wars, entire neighborhoods are taken hostage by the underground violence, and that innocent people, including children, are being killed just because of the color of their skin. As a result, notorious former enemies, the African American Crips and Bloods,[14] have had to join forces to defend themselves against attacks by Latino gang members, who outnumber them ten to one. As to the origin of this "interracial" hatred, another informant claims that it is fomented in prison. Inmates join prison gangs from their own race to survive; they fear lack of protection as well as retaliation from their own ethnic group. After their release from prison, these former inmates transfer this racial segregation and animosity to the mean streets of Los Angeles.

In a segment devoted to the 18th Street gang, considered the largest street gang in Los Angeles County (approximately 20,000 members),[15] the narrator condemns the fact that they are "harassing the citizenry." It is worth noting that the term "citizenry" is never used when dealing with gangs of other ethnic groups. This arguably implies that Latino gangbangers, even though most were born in Los Angeles, are not legitimate citizens and, therefore, "do not belong here." The suspicious terminology brings to mind the massive deportations, in the mid-1990s, of undocumented gang members of Central American origin, including those with American offspring. Therefore, the comment depicts the ideology of national exclusion that often informs the mainstream discourse of the media and certain politicians when they misrepresent pachucos as well as Latino homeboys and homegirls. Obviously, this type of nativism leaves these American-born Latinos outside the national project.

In direct contrast with this television show, when questioned about the random assassination of seventeen-year-old African American star athlete Jamiel Shaw, and of a six-year-old African American boy, by Latino gangs in March 2008, the LAPD and the City of Los Angeles denied that race was a factor in gang violence. Thus, in a press conference on March 5, 2008, that was aired by ABC, LAPD chief William Bratton gave this answer to KABC reporter Leo Stallworth when asked about racial tensions in South Los Angeles: "There are several, unfortunately, among you who every time we have one of these incidents want to make more out of it than it is. . . . We have to work with fact and speculation [. . .] You're a one-note band on this issue. . . . The rest of you [members of the press], seem to get it" (ABC7 n.p.). The obviously irritated LAPD chief denied, therefore, any racial motivation behind these crimes.

The spectacularization of gang life in television shows and films responds not to a secret conspiracy, but to market factors. No matter how irresponsible these portrayals may be, it is evident that the more sensational they are, the larger the audience. In this context, the police officer and former gang member Mona Ruiz recalls, in her autobiography or memoir *Two Badges,* how a student reporter who interviewed her ended up twisting her answers at will to sensationalize the story:

"Besides the inaccuracies, the whole tone of the article made me sound like some hardened gangbanger. Maybe the writer had seen too many movies or something, because he wrote my quotes up in street slang style and peppered them with expletives I knew I had never said. The story was dramatic, but it just wasn't true" (225). As a result, the Santa Ana Police Department where she worked was subsequently blamed by other local police departments of having low recruiting standards.

This same spectacularization of barrio gang violence is described in Alejandro Morales's short story "Pequeña nación" (Small Nation), included in an eponymous collection of three short stories. In it, a character named Micaela Clemencia and the Federation of Scissor Women criticize the mass media for reporting the violence caused by 4 to 7 percent of the Latino youth as the norm.[16] The image of the barrio as a space controlled by gangs is, according to them, a discursive fantasy. Paradoxically, whereas sometimes reporters are blamed for ignoring "brown on brown violence," in other instances they are accused of being parasites who profit from barrio violence. The news media are also criticized in Rudolfo Anaya's *Curse of the Chupacabra* (2006), a novel about the supernatural world of the Chupacabra (a popular figure in Puerto Rico, Mexico, and now in the United States), which is used as a metaphor to condemn drug abuse in Los Angeles's barrios: "Those not from the neighborhood often forgot the barrio wasn't just a place for gangs, drive-by shootings, and drugs. A solid working-class community was its real heart. . . . The news media never covers this part of the barrio, Rosa thought. It's always just the bad news they splash on TV" (58–59).

To return to the representation of Los Angeles Latinos in Hollywood, the release of the seminal film *Colors* marked the beginning of a series of sensationalized cinematic versions of Chicano gang life. Motion pictures about gang warfare, such as *American Me, Blood In Blood Out,* and *Mi vida loca* have carried the torch with varying degrees of stereotyping and glamorizing. A film that purposely avoids glamorizing Chicano gang life in Los Angeles is the bildungsroman *American Me* (1992), directed by Los Angeles–born Edward James Olmos (1947–). The action takes place both inside and outside a penitentiary, hence giving viewers the chance to observe mediated versions of street gangs as well as of prison gangs. It shows how the protagonist, a teenage thug named Montoya Santana (played by Panchito Gómez), turns into a powerful prison gang leader (played by Olmos). The first scenes, which include the rape of his nineteen-year-old mother by sailors during the so-called Zoot Suit Riots, expose a sociopolitical milieu that will later bring about the eventual tragic flaw of this son of old pachucos.

Later, while incarcerated in Folsom State Prison, Santana reminisces about his youth in East Los Angeles. In order to get "respect" (a sacrosanct word in gangbanger literature and film) in the barrio of 1959,[17] he created a *clika* (or gang branch) with two other friends, Mundo (Richard Coco and Pepe Serna) and a Euro-American named J. D. (Steve Wilcox and William Forsythe), who identifies with Mexican American culture: "Belonging felt good, but having respect, well, that feels even better," acknowledges J. D. In contrast, J. D.'s best friend, Santana, later criticizes the gang commandment of gaining and showing respect: "You know, a long time ago, two best homeboys were thrown into *juvie*. They were scared, so they thought they had to do something to prove themselves. And they did what they had to do. They thought they were doing it to gain respect for their people, to show the world that no one could take their class from them. No one had to take it from us, *ése*. Whatever we had, we gave it away."

Eventually, the three friends end up in Folsom State Prison, where they run the Mexican Mafia gang, also known as La Eme. After spending eighteen years in jail, fighting with an African American prison gang, the Aryan Brotherhood, and another Latino gang known as Nuestra Familia, Santana is released to a very different Boyle Heights from the one he knew as a teenager.[18] Soon, he joins J. D. in trying to take away drug peddling in East Los Angeles from the Italian Mafia. However, with the help of Julie (Evelina Fernández), a former gang member who has decided to change her ways and becomes his disgruntled new girlfriend, the former ruthless leader of the Mexican Mafia begins to see how drug addiction and gang violence are destroying his own community.

Rosa-Linda Fregoso has focused on the story that the film fails to portray. More specifically, she has criticized what she calls the "strategy of containment" of cholas and the erasure of female subjects in film. In her view, Julie's role as a character is reduced to a motherly shadow, and instead of witnessing her life as a gang member, the audience only knows of her gang tattoo when she is in the domestic and private sphere of her bedroom:

Who is this new subject, this Chicana whom Edward James Olmos claims is the heroine of *American Me,* the hope in our barrios? His story ends before hers can begin. In the final close-up shot of a cross tattooed on Julie's hand resides her untold story. It is the history of Chicana membership in gangs that unfolds not on the screen, but in my mind. The final weathered look in Julie's eyes sparks the painful silent memory of the female gang members I have known: Chicanas surviving and resisting la vida dura (the hard life). I often wonder why the story of Julie's oppression and resistance, why the pain of her rape is not up there, on the Hollywood screen, looking at me. (*Bronze Screen* 133–34)

Influenced by Julie, Santana tries to stop a murder after going back to prison, a sign of weakness that ultimately leads to his own death. His former best friend, J. D., sees no alternative but to have him killed. In all, if the scene where Santana is gang-raped after his imprisonment is an effective way to avoid glamorizing this lifestyle, the scene where he is stabbed to death by his followers represents the final condemnation. The film sends an unambiguous message that gang life leads to misery and early death. In this sense, Charles M. Tatum speculates that "Olmos's apparent intent is to shock young Chicanos and their communities rather than to attract a wide audience" (78).

A few months after the release of *American Me,* Taylor Hackford's *Blood In Blood Out* (also released as *Bound by Honor,* 1993), another film that tries to avoid the spectacularization of gang life, appeared in theaters. Interestingly, the film makes a perhaps unintentional incursion into the commodification of barrio gang life in a scene where Cruz, a former gang member who has become a locally well-known artist, is having a successful exhibit of his paintings. At the entrance of the art gallery we read the telling legend "Cruz Candelaria. The Soul of the Barrio." Inside, potential clients' superficial comments about the images of barrio pride in Cruz's paintings are implicitly ridiculed. Nonetheless, we also notice how Cruz's inability to behave properly in a sophisticated environment (he uses a homeboy handshake with one of the visitors), the antisocial behavior of his homeboys (who insist on entering the gallery without a pass), and his addiction to drugs may prevent his success as an artist. As an additional deterrent to pursuing the gang life, Montana, one of the characters, denounces the imprisonment of Los Angeles's inner-city youth as a lucrative business for the privately run California prisons: "Everyone who enters the joint thinks he's a man, but you know what he really is? A number worth thirty grand a year. They want us to come back and what's worse, they have us lining up to get in, *ése.* We gotta turn the system around. We gotta outthink 'em." Therefore, this scene warns Los Angeles's inner-city youth that the gangbanger lifestyle, no matter how glamorous it may seem to some, is tantamount to playing the game that powerful lobbies and corporations have scripted specifically for them.

Covering the years from 1972 to 1984, the film depicts the origins of the Vatos Locos street gang in the barrio of El Pico Aliso, in East Los Angeles. Two Chicano half-brothers, Cruz (Jesse Borrego) and Paco Candelaria (Benjamin Bratt), together with a cousin who has inherited his Euro-American father's light complexion, Miklo "Milkweed" Velka (Damian Chapa), decide to join forces. Later, we find out, their lives go in very different directions: Miklo is convicted of murder and sent to San Quentin State Prison; Paco joins the marines and, after his thirteen-year-old younger brother dies of a drug overdose, becomes an LAPD narcotics detective; and Cruz becomes addicted to heroin but manages to succeed as a visual artist. In spite of his white skin, Miklo gains acceptance into the San Quentin Latino gang "La Onda," by killing a Euro-American inmate (hence, the title of the film, which is also the motto of the prison gang Nuestra Familia).[19] After being released on parole in 1982, he is shot in the leg by his cousin Paco during an armed robbery. Miklo, whose downfall is the result of a combination of bad parenting, peer pressure, and an identity crisis, goes back to prison; this time he becomes one of the leaders of La Onda. To avoid the audience's identification with the antihero, several shots of the big East Los Angeles tree that symbolizes home and the essence of the barrio are often followed by prison and burial scenes. The film thus exposes the hardships of integrating back into society after joining a gang, becoming addicted to drugs, or being imprisoned.

Through a series of conspiracies and using his unsuspecting cousin Paco, Miklo's men kill seventeen of their rivals from the Aryan Vanguard and the Black Guerrilla Army gangs. Paco, who had been trying to arrange a truce between both gangs, is outraged at Miklo's behavior. Underscoring the idea that gang violence has nothing to do with Chicano cultural nationalism and ethnic pride, Paco cuts ties with him forever: "It's about our people out there, working, surviving with pride and dignity. That's raza; not lying and murdering. All you got is your white father's hate," he states after repeating that Miklo's activities have nothing to do with La Raza. Yet Paco manages to make peace with his brother Cruz, who, in the last scene, shows him an old mural of the three of them

Figure 11 Image of the Virgin of Guadalupe in a Mexican American market. (Photo by Tonya López-Craig)

by the Los Angeles River: "three *vatos locos* full of *carnalismo,*"[20] declares Cruz with pride; he also makes peace with himself after admitting his participation in Miklo's demise. Whereas the recreation of the environment in East Los Angeles begins with images of gang graffiti and warfare, Aztec murals and dances, and images of the Virgin of Guadalupe (similar to the one in fig. 11), the final scenes of the film show an aerial view of a never-ending city with thousands of streets, freeways and overpasses, and the ugly Los Angeles River. Perhaps this visual transition from the barrio to the rest of the city suggests the end of the ghettoization of the Chicano community.

In contrast with *American Me* and *Blood In Blood Out*, which consciously avoid the spectacularization of gang life, we have an example of a subgenre that Fregoso has termed "gangxploitation" in Chris T. McIntyre's *Gang Warz* (2004). The film, set in Los Angeles some time after the Rampart police scandals of 1998–99, was shot on location in East Los Angeles and Compton. Despite this realistic set, gang warfare takes shape in a glamorized confrontation between Compton's African American gangbangers and an East Los Angeles Latino gang, a struggle that is mostly ignored by a corrupt LAPD. In between both ethnic groups, we find rapper Chino XL (born Derek Barbosa), who is of Puerto Rican and African-American descent, playing a tough "biracial" (black and Latino, even though "Latino" is obviously not a "race") cop named Roe Connor, who is determined to single-handedly stop the violence. Connor's antagonist is Marco Cruz (Pablo Patlis), an unscrupulous and feared Latino gang leader, who has just been taken off death row and released from prison. The latter's evil nature is shown in a scene where he does not hesitate to strike his own mother. Eventually, his thirst for revenge against the cop who put him behind bars and the priest who testified against him brings about his own death. After numerous shoot-outs and car races, when the day is over, most of the gang members end up dead, which works as a moral lesson to the audience. However, not only is the market commodification of urban gang violence evident, but the overall representation of Latinos also falls into the usual clichés. In this sense, Justin Chang has pointed out that the film "can't disguise its essentially derivative nature, trafficking in standard-brand characters and dripping with self-conscious 'attitude.' At once simplistic and convoluted, full of macho posturing one second and embarrassingly melodramatic the next, 'Gang Warz' finally collapses under a series of 11th-hour revelations that make a mockery of the gritty, pseudo-documentary style" (n.p.).

Gang Warz is only one of the many films belonging to the "gangxploitation" subgenre that generate negative images of Latinos by focusing solely on the most abject margins of this community. These textual and cinematographic practices reinforce stereotypes by portraying young Latinos and Latinas as a threat to society, hence excluding them from the "national symbolic" and creating new social anxieties.

The Gang and the Barrio as Independent Counternations

In an episode of the History Channel's show *Gangland,* a member of New York's Latin Kings proudly declares: "My crown is my nation." The crown he is referring to is one of the main symbols of this Latino gang. As Monica Brown has pointed out, gang members often explain their violent actions in nationalistic or patriotic terms. Feeling excluded from the dominant discourse of nation and from the full rights of citizenship, they recreate, in their gangs and barrios, parallel structures modeled after the existing political organizations and rhetoric of U.S. nationalism. Consequently, they turn their backs on the "national symbolic" and devote their loyalty and "heroism" to their "counternation," which, in their view, empowers them: "gang membership for Latino youth is, in part, a means of restructuring their relationship with the American nation, a way—however illusory—of recuperating the subjectivity conferred by citizenship" (83). It is, she contends, the urban youth's reaction to the systemic denial of their right to American citizenship and to their exclusion from dominant notions of community and nation. As a result of this search for alternative "belonging," they "have forged their own counternational narratives through their gangs, which they represent as 'mini-nations,' using the rhetoric of patriotism and honor to frame their loyalties to the gang" (37).

As expected, this defiant attitude is reflected in the cultural production by and about Latino Los Angeles. We thus have one of the first examples of this defiant and nationalistic image of the barrio boy in Luis Valdez's *Zoot Suit*, where the playwright mythicizes the pachuco of the 1940s and turns him (and here I use the masculine pronoun intentionally since, as Fregoso has pointed out, the *pachuca* has a very limited role ["Re-Imaging" 83]) into a heroic figure. The pachuco, Henry Reyna's alter ego and social conscience (who, dressed in a zoot suit imitating African American youth's fashion, simultaneously mimics the inspiration for the zoot suit: Euro-American attire), raises awareness, among Mexican Americans, about a collective conspiracy led by the Los Angeles mayor, the local media, and the U.S. legal system. More importantly, he opens Henry's eyes to the fact that even if he joins the U.S. Army, he will continue to be excluded from the national project. As mentioned, the alienated pachucos, homeboys, and homegirls in gang narratives and films are the inheritors of the pachuco images created by Paz and Valdez.[21]

Likewise, in the first dialogue of the film *Blood In Blood Out*, a cab driver asks Miklo: "So, what's the difference between East L.A. and L.A.?" To which he responds, "It's a whole different country." Also, later in the film, his cousin Paco affirms his social dominion and the neighborhood's autonomy vis-à-vis the rest of the city by boasting that the police cannot arrest him in his own neighborhood: "Not in my barrio!" In another scene, while Paco's brother, Cruz, is painting the typical image of an Aztec warrior with a fainted or dead Aztec woman in his arms, he warns his younger brother: "Pay attention, *pelao*, I'm gonna teach you all about Aztlán 'cause this vato [Quetzalcoatl] is coming back someday to reclaim the Raza's kingdom." Therefore, we witness a double take on the ideas of nationhood and cultural difference: a lived or experienced reality goes hand in hand with a mythical one based on historical associations that prove the timeless nature and existence of such a nation.

Moving on to literature, the barrio of T-Flats, in Miguel Durán's *Don't Spit on My Corner* (1992), exerts a centripetal force that prevents young pachucos (the precursors of today's homeboys or cholos) from leaving its confines for a protracted time. The novel begins and ends in the same way, thus providing a sense of inescapable circularity. In fact, the first lines summarize its content succinctly:

> I hate my Barrio because I love her. I hate her because she can kill me. Yet, because I love her, I'll let her kill me. My Barrio is a jealous lover, she gave herself to me when I needed her. All I had to do was commit myself one hundred percent to her. My Barrio is vicious. If I don't embrace her, take care of her needs, protect her from her enemies, real or imaginary, right or wrong, she will put a jacket on me. I hate her, but I can't walk without her. I can't stand that jacket. It's a contract on my life. I don't want to die! (7)

Mike, the semiautobiographical protagonist, has to decide between two alternatives: a peaceful-but-boring life with the woman he loves, Penny, or the company of his best friend, David, along with a dangerous-but-exciting gang life in the barrio. Since he awkwardly refers to the barrio as a feminine entity (despite the word's masculine ending), it gives the impression that he must choose between two competing women. In the end, Penny abandons him, realizing that the street culture's grip is so strong that he will never be able to leave his gang days behind. In spite of the good advice and numerous warnings that he receives from several people, Mike's "jungle instincts" (133), that is, his addiction to gang life, is stronger than any other factor, including the fear of death. He often dreams of starting a new life far from the barrio corner where he is admittedly wasting his life, but those thoughts are ephemeral: he would always miss the thrill of the *vida loca*.

Like other pachucos and cholos in the texts and films studied here, the protagonist in *Don't Spit on My Corner* stays in his gang because his *vatos* provide the support that he cannot find at home, in school, or in mainstream society. Mike is reminiscent of Julián, a Mexican American character in Morales's *Barrio on the Edge*, but he distances himself from the other characters in that his main motivation is, avowedly, that he finds this type of life exciting and fun: "I sure didn't want my folks in on what I was up to, but I sure wasn't thinking about changing my life style either. It was too groovy" (53). Yet there is also a hint at a nationalistic spirit that connects this text to other gang narratives considered in this study. Trying to come to grips with his dilemma throughout this self-analytical novel, Mike ends up justifying his erratic behavior by comparing national patriotism and loyalty to that of his barrio. Thus, after he watches a war film with his best friend, he states, "Something like, 'Long live the United States!' or did they say '*Viva mi barrio*, Down with Japan!' We laughed. Countries at war are like Chicano gangs at war. Both are patriotic, they will fight, kill or be killed to protect their established rights!" (27). Mike later argues that his barrio is also his nation and therefore he has to defend it (hence, the title of the novel).

Along the same lines, after a probation officer convinces the young men to meet in order to plan a truce, the protagonist compares the gangs to Indian nations: "For my part, it all reminded me of a lot of Indian tribes sitting around a fire, first bringing up all the past trespasses against each other, then looking for honorable solutions and smoking the peace pipe" (51). Immediately afterward, he places his distrust of mainstream society in the context of U.S. national history: "I knew how the Indians felt when the Great White Father pulled his number on them" (52). The more excluded he feels from mainstream society and its national project, the more he is drawn toward his barrio and, more specifically, toward his gang's street corner: "They kept talking about how they only wanted patriotic Americans. I didn't feel I was one of those. I was a drag on society, being busted here instead of working in the industry or joining the service" (97). The barrio eventually wins the fight: the immature Mike is incapable of imagining a different lifestyle. The puzzling denouement of the novel seems to imply that his wife is not as important to him as is his gang and his barrio. Therefore, in contrast with Mona Ruiz and Geoff Boucher's *Two Badges,* and other texts and films, this novel does not carry a didactic or moralizing antigang message.

David R. Díaz, who describes the barrio as the foundation of Chicana/o urbanism, has summarized these two realities or forces (of attraction and repulsion) that are often described in Latino Los Angeles's cultural production:

In terms of spatial relations, it is historically a zone of segregation and repression. Uneven development, inflated rents, low wage labor, lack of housing, and the worst abuses of urban renewal best characterize barrios in the arena of urban policy. Conversely, within the context of everyday life, *el barrio* is the reaffirmation of culture, a defense of space, an ethnically bounded sanctuary, and the spiritual zone of Chicana/o and Mexicana/o identity. It is a powerful, intense space that has defined the independence and resistance of a culture that predates Euro-American influences on city life and urban form. (3)

Another text that portrays the homeboy's ambivalent feelings of attraction and repulsion toward his barrio is Alejandro Morales's first novel, *Barrio on the Edge* (*Caras viejas y vino nuevo,* 1975). Therein, he describes a nameless neighborhood that, as Francisco A. Lomelí argues in the introduction to the English version, could represent all barrios in Los Angeles: "What concerns Morales is an experiential, subjective barrio— a state of being rather than a place—that questions referents and the activity of referents" (6).[22] Genaro Padilla has also noted that, with this novel, Morales shunned his generation's tendency to romanticize the barrio experience by providing "a complex exposition of both the positive and the sordid elements" (1987, 164).[23] Indeed, as the English title foreshadows, it is a self-destructive space on the verge of implosion. As in the novels of nineteenth-century naturalism, all efforts made by well-intentioned outsiders (a schoolbus driver, a priest, and a young doctor who ends up killed by "those from the other side") are in vain.

The demoralized and angry Julián, one of two protagonists, is a suicidal boy troubled by a tumultuous relationship with his brutal father. Like other characters in the barrio, he has mixed feelings for his neighborhood. On the one hand, he is proud of his people for having taken over an area that used to belong to other social groups; he also feels protected there: "They respected him and his family in the barrio; no one looked at them with disdain. He felt very comfortable; but in the world of those others he felt like an intruder, knowing they were constantly screwing him. They used him, they looked at him like some kind of freak" (80). On the other hand, he realizes that it is an unbearably stagnant space flooded by hopelessness. In Lomelí's words,

> The barrio becomes a cruel distortion of what mainstream society produces and then rejects and abandons, much like a nonrecyclable pile of trash. . . . The barrio becomes ground zero, a sampling of urbanism lost in a no-man's-land that will later serve as on-ramps for freeways or parking lots for chain stores. More than an internal

colony with political and economic ties, it is the ruins of a land ravaged by stagnation and an insuperable hopelessness. (7)

To escape this dreary reality, his friends take refuge in music, alcohol,
and drugs. Julián's only escape from this vicious cycle is education, but
as seen later in this chapter, Los Angeles schools have not always been
welcoming to Latinos. Morales will retake this idea in his 2005 collection
of short stories *Pequeña nación,* in which, as the title suggests, the characters' gang, street, and barrio, and even East Los Angeles or the entire
city of Los Angeles, are often conceived as "small nations" or independent counternations that must be defended against outside invaders.

The visualization of the gang or the barrio as an independent counternation demanding loyalty and protection from its "nationals" resurfaces in the autobiography or memoir *Two Badges: The Lives of Mona
Ruiz* (1997), co-written by Mona Ruiz (1959–) and Geoff Boucher (1969–),
where the protagonist complains: "To grow up in the barrio is to grow up
seeing cops as an occupying army" (93). Another coincidence between
Don't Spit on My Corner and *Two Badges* is the portrayal of the hypnotic
effect that the barrio streets and corners exert on Latino youth. Ruiz
points out: "others want to relive those days when they felt they owned
the streets. If anything, the streets owned us" (10). In the case of Luis J.
Rodríguez's collection of short stories, *The Republic of East L.A.,* even the
title, which was inspired by the words of a barrio evangelist, suggests that
East L.A. is different from the rest of the metropolis, a world of its own
(to use the title of Matt García's book). Rather than simply noting the
"nationalistic" or "patriotic" feelings of gang members and barrio dwellers who create parallel structures modeled after U.S. political structures,
Rodríguez focuses on the root causes of these characters' disattachment
to the U.S. "national symbolic," and their creation of alternative loyalties.
Story by story, he explores these Latino communities' exclusion from
the dominant discourse and how they have been denied full citizenship
rights. Although Rodríguez depicts gang life as a dangerous and unwise
option that often leads to premature death, he considers gang activity a
by-product of unfair social conditions, hopelessness, and environmental injustice.[24] Similarly, in his autobiography, *Always Running/La Vida
Loca: Gang Days in L.A.,* Rodríguez humanizes the gang member first by
questioning the demonizing images of the cholo that appear in films and
the media, and then by defining gang life as a survival tactic to achieve
respect, protection, and a sense of belonging. Paradoxically, while his

arguments succeed in his objective of combating the stereotypes about gang members, he ends up demonizing the LAPD instead.

Latino Youth, Gangs, and the School System

As this cultural production shows, in many cases the marginalization of Latino urban youth and the creation of gangs begin in the schools, one of the key institutions within the barrio. Besides the cases of potential racial guilt on the part of Euro-American authors and filmmakers that I have suggested, there is a different type of racial guilt: the guilt for being a minority, for being of Mexican descent, shown by some of the characters in these works. This common feeling, as we will see in this subchapter, is inculcated by society in general, but mainly by one of the ideological state apparatuses (to use Althusser's term): the school system. Although the Marxist critic Louis Althusser conceives ideological state apparatuses in terms of social class, his notion could also be used to analyze racial relations in society. Along with "repressive state apparatuses" such as the police and the army, he claims, the state secures the reproduction of the "relations of production" by ensuring that people behave according to its rules through institutions (ideological state apparatuses such as schools, churches, and the family) that generate certain ideologies. Even when it is not in their best interest, this dominant ideology is later internalized by individuals and social groups, who, behaving according to its parameters, become subjects suited to perform their duties in the preestablished societal ways. According to this sort of conspiracy theory, our values, judgments, and decisions are not really ours: they are the consequences of social and ideological practices imposed by the state, which has made us in its own image. In this context, these texts and films depict ways in which, for generations, the Los Angeles school system has traumatized Latinos into thinking that they are ontologically and morally inferior to Euro-Americans.

Mike Davis has studied the deplorable situation of some Los Angeles schools: "Teenagers complain bitterly about overcrowded classrooms and demoralized teachers, about decaying campuses that have become little more than daytime detention centers for an abandoned generation" (*Ecology* 381). Stating that Latino high school graduation is only 53 percent, Davis highlights, among other factors, the effects of Proposition 13 (1978), which reduced tax-based funding of public schools: "A major study of the causes of Latino school-leaving, based on interviews with 700 dropouts in San Antonio, pointed to the 'lack of bilingual and

English as a Second Language programs, the concentration of Hispanics in high-poverty schools, lack of teacher preparation and low expectations for Hispanic students among teachers, administrators and society as a whole'" (*Magical* 113). Accordingly, young Latinos in these narratives and films often complain about their teachers' low expectations of them, about being taught subjects that are unrelated to their culture, and about not being allowed to speak Spanish on school grounds. Furthermore, some complain about how, on their way to school, they have to hide their books to avoid being "jumped" by other barrio boys.

In spite of these obstacles, most Chicano characters in Alejandro Morales's *Barrio on the Edge* acknowledge formal education as the only way out of the cruelty and hopelessness that afflicts their community. Several of them even berate Julián, one of the protagonists, for not accepting a scholarship. A gifted student and athlete, he hesitates between both worlds, "Goddam school, I'm not even sure if I'll finish, no, I will finish, because I do like it. I'd like to become one of those famous professors, or a famous writer, one who wins prizes, respected for what he knows. But I also like to fuck around, I like these people" (116). Eventually, he ignores his counselors and chooses drugs and violence over college. Later, however, the plot reveals the real reasons for this decision: Julián's seemingly unwise skepticism arises from a long history of discrimination in school.[25] He now is unable to overcome the distrust and resentment he harbored throughout the years.

In the same way, in *Always Running* Rodríguez describes Clemente and Garfield high schools as the epicenters of gang activity in their respective barrios. In these high school facilities covered with gang graffiti, students lack the most basic school materials, the dropout rate is as high as 50 percent, and fights and drug dealing are everyday occurrences. We also learn that, as a student, Rodríguez always felt unwelcome there and was routinely deprived of attention by his teachers—they would put him in the back of the room to build with blocks. His brother Rano, in turn, received a harsher treatment: they placed him in classes with mentally disabled children and held him back a year because of his limited English-language skills. Even worse, in Rodríguez's mind, the school system later succeeded in acculturating his brother: "he was in high school being the good kid, the Mexican exception, the barrio success story—my supposed model. Soon he stopped being Rano and even José. One day he became Joe. My brother and I were moving away from each other. Our tastes, our friends, our interests, were miles apart" (49).

When Rodríguez finally has a chance to attend better high schools such as Mark Keppel and Taft, he becomes the victim of a two-tiered educational system based on ethnicity and class: "They were mostly Mexican, in the 'C' track (what were called the 'stupid' classes), and who made up the rosters of the wood, print and auto shops" (83).[26] Eventually, we are told, Chicano students end up embracing the perception that their teachers have of them and become outlaws. In Rodríguez's view, high dropout and unemployment rates, together with police brutality and lack of social recreation, are the thresholds for gang activity and drug trafficking in the barrio; youngsters have too much leisure time on their hands. David R. Díaz has also linked the alienation of Chicano youth with the lack of socialization opportunities: "Youth demands for recreational and cultural programs and the facilities that meet these demands are a response to the negative influences of the gang and drug epidemics in U.S. society. Absent an adequate supply of parks and open space as an alternative to gangs and antisocial behavior, youth are vulnerable to negative social forces" (159). Yet *Always Running* also provides an example of empowering activism: after a few protests, students' demands are met and the school hires more Chicano teachers and introduces courses on Chicano studies.

Similarly, in Miguel Durán's *Don't Spit on My Corner*, the semiautobiographical protagonist considers Los Angeles schools the ultimate wake-up call about the marginalization of Mexican Americans. Although his father insists that school is not for Mexicans, and probation officers remind Mike that pachucos are not welcomed in schools because they never succeed, he earns a good reputation as a student and as an athlete. His tragic flaw, however, is revealed when his family moves from Inglewood to West Los Angeles, because he never feels accepted in the new high school: "I tried to fit in but couldn't. I ended up fighting because I refused to be Spanish and insisted on being Mexican and telling everybody I was. I was ignored by the kids, the teachers quit working with me, and in the gym the coaches were cold towards me. I wasn't used to this kind of treatment. It hurt me and affected my school work" (95–96). This sudden awareness about mainstream society's racism against Mexicans leads Mike to find an alternative refuge in his pachuco street gang. After this decision, all his problems begin, including a stay at juvenile camp for beating up some servicemen and their taxi driver during the Zoot Suit Riots.

The situation is even more dramatic in Yxta Maya Murray's novel *Locas,* where part of the plot takes place in and around Garfield Junior

High. One of the protagonists, Cecilia Silvas, describes the decrepit state of this center of operations for local gangs:

> Garfield's one of the schools they send us all to. What a low-down place that is, nothing but a concrete square all falling apart, the bricks rotted and a few windows smashed and patched up again with tape or thin wood board. . . . The rooms are stuffed full of kids and the teachers get so tired they're half crazy, the books have broken spines and there's fights in the halls. Garfield Junior High. I never learned a thing in there. (124)

The school's walls are the canvas where the spray-paint wars between rival gangs are fought. These gangs also sell cocaine and recruit children by force on its premises. Lucía, one of the gang leaders, ruthlessly argues that by turning children into drug addicts they are producing long-term business. After some gang training, these boys and girls become social psychopaths: "babies don't have hearts in them, they'll pull a trigger just to hear it go bang" (181), Lucía declares.

Attending school is an equally denigrating experience in *Two Badges,* where Mona Ruiz and her coauthor, Geoff Boucher, posit that nearly every public school in Santa Ana has a gang problem. In fact, they reveal that the F-Troop gang (to which Mona Ruiz belonged) originated in Smedley Intermediate School as well as in other junior highs in the area:

> It didn't take long to realize the wide intimidating corridors of Valley High School were like the rest of Santa Ana—carved up into distinct gang turf. . . . Some of the crosstown schools were ruled solely by one of the city's dominant gangs. F-Troop more or less "owned" Santa Ana High, and Saddleback High was known as a Del Hi Stronghold. But Valley was split uneasily among a handful of gangs when I arrived there in September 1974. (39)

Ruiz recounts her violent clashes with other students on school grounds as well as her frustration with counselors who refused to provide guidance and failed to warn her that she was missing three credits in physical education for her graduation. In *Two Badges,* we also find an interesting insight that does not usually appear in studies about gangs: "schoolies," that is, good students who are perceived as having an academic future, are left alone by gangs. Mona Ruiz's sister, Maryann, was immune to gang violence because of her strong commitment to studying.

Likewise, Danny Santiago's *Famous All Over Town* portrays Rudy, despite his obvious flaws, as a bright boy whose great potential has been stymied by spatial injustice and social inequalities. Although his school principal, his physician, and his family are aware of the protagonist's extraordinary intelligence, the determinism of the text makes it impossible for him to escape the social constrictions attached to his ethnicity. This novel joins the collective clamor against the discrimination against Chicanos in the Los Angeles school system, where several of Rudy's teachers turn against him. He first claims to have received bad grades in Spanish only because, from his perspective, his Mexican dialect was not good enough for his Euro-American teacher. Then, presumably blinded by racial prejudice, another teacher refuses to believe that Rudy can have an intelligence quotient of 135 and accuses the instructor who administered the test of inflating the outcome. In addition to these obstacles and to the lack of parental support, Rudy is aware that his police record and public bravado make him more popular among his peers than to earn good grades in school. This grim picture of the Los Angeles educational system notwithstanding, Danny Santiago coincides with the main message in Rodríguez's *The Republic of East L.A.*, Morales's *Barrio on the Edge,* and Patricia Cardoso's film *Real Women Have Curves,* when he proposes education as the best path for Chicano emancipation: "'Where did my father and mother go wrong?' I asked myself. Always fighting or snoring, they forgot the Best Things in Life. They wasted twenty-three hours and forty minutes out of every day. Possibly no education was the answer unless it was old age" (*Famous* 126).

In relation with his experiences in school, another important factor in Rudy's eventual failure is an inferiority complex (which is also noticeable in other Chicano characters in Antonio Villarreal's *Pocho* and Óscar Zeta Acosta's *The Revolt of the Cockroach People*) that plagues him with insecurities and identitarian uncertainties. Decades of Euro-American cultural indoctrination have led these characters to believe in their own ontological inferiority. For example, when one of the neighbors is trying to convince Rudy's family of the potential benefits of relocation, she suddenly corrects herself: "Why shouldn't we live like that? We're as good as them, or *almost* anyway" (128; emphasis added). Later, while Rudy is visiting this neighbor's new house, he is not persuaded that he could ever belong in that kind of luxury; in fact, the only moment in which he feels at home is when he finds a cockroach by the toilet. His fatalism and internalized racism are also apparent in his inner thoughts after Ernie, from the Boys' Club, begs him to stay in school: "Do your homework. Take an interest in sports. Be a credit to the Mexican race. So I could end up a well-paid barber if lucky? Or make big money in upholstery no doubt? . . . He thinks he can see right through a person and who is he anyway? Just a Mexican like everybody else" (281). After their conversation, when the well-intentioned Ernie offers him a ride home, Rudy reminds him that his home is no more; it has just been obliterated by the city authorities, hence eliminating any chance for his improvement as a person.

On a more positive note, and moving on to filmic representations of the Los Angeles school system, we come across Ramón Menéndez's 1988 film *Stand and Deliver*. This film was based on the real-life experience of Bolivian high school mathematics teacher Jaime A. Escalante (1930–2010). In it, we see the academic success of eighteen Latino students at Garfield Senior High School in East Los Angeles who pass the Advanced Placement Calculus Exam. The first scene shows the ugly Los Angeles River, supposedly working as a metaphor for the toughness of the inner city's social environment.[27] Against all odds, the determined Escalante (played by Edward James Olmos) is able to overcome the obstacles posed by his own health and by the reprehensible attitude toward education of his students' parents and friends. After painstakingly building up his students' self-esteem, he also has to fight society's racial stereotypes when, in a scene reminiscent of Danny Santiago's *Famous All Over Town*, both his colleagues and the Educational Testing Service (ETS) accuse the overachieving students of cheating on the exam. While Escalante's amazing success in Garfield Senior High School went from 1974 to 1991, the story portrayed in this film is an exception in the representation of the school system in Los Angeles's Latino cultural production.

The same optimistic tone continues in Patricia Cardoso's independent Spanish-language film *Real Women Have Curves* (2002), which tells the story of Ana García (América Ferrera), an eighteen-year-old Mexican American woman who dreams about leaving her uneventful life in East Los Angeles to go to college.[28] Although her teacher at Beverly Hills High School, Mr. Guzmán (George López), tries to convince Ana to accept a scholarship from Columbia University, her stubborn mother, doña Carmen (Lupe Ontiveros), refuses to grant her permission. Ana has lost hope but still rejects the destiny that has been drawn for her: getting married and working in a small garment factory run by Estela (Ingrid Oliú), her older sister. At her sister's factory, she daydreams about wearing the dresses they are sewing. She also encourages her coworkers to see the beauty in their own bodies and tries to raise awareness about the injustice of making dresses for eighteen dollars when Bloomingdale's stores sell them for six hundred dollars. Ana's boyfriend, Jimmy (Brian Sites), is a symbol of her desire to break loose from the confinement of her family life. He is a Euro-American classmate who has nothing to do with the image of the Euro-American oppressor and Other that usually roams the works under discussion. The last scene shows Ana, who, having accepted the scholarship, happily walks through the streets of New York, free from familial ties.

Real Women Have Curves counterbalances the degradation of Mexican Americans that prevails in so many Hollywood productions by portraying them in a positive light. While it denounces some of the hindrances that afflict the community (such as exploitation at work and lack of health insurance), the focus is not on its victimization; instead, Chicanas are true-to-life human beings whose determination helps them in their struggle against a double enemy: social marginalization and their parents' old-fashioned ways.[29] Again, the obvious solution to the community's problems is formal education. While she does not address the issue of education in her essay, María P. Figueroa has praised the stage play (first presented in 1990) by Josefina López (1969–) on which the film was based, for its resistance to mainstream society's hegemonic beauty: "In its denunciation of the hegemonic ideal of a thin curveless white body, López's play, *Real Women Have Curves,* discloses the 'outside' [body]: the 'fat,' Mexicana/Chicana/Latina, immigrant and working-class body, physically and historically existing on the margins of society as a viable body that matters" (272). She also points out the play's subversion of traditional and cultural gender roles outside the domestic realm: "these women leave the domestic space and assume an active subjectivity as seamstresses in the work place, constructing a newly redefined familial space in which they can exist and invest their minds, bodies, and souls" (275).

The last film to be considered in this chapter is *Walkout* (2006), directed by Edward James Olmos and produced by Moctesuma Esparza. It covers a foundational episode of the Chicano Movement: the historic 1968 East Los Angeles Walkouts (also known as Chicano Blowouts) by high school students in East Los Angeles (and later in Los Angeles County and the rest of the country).[30] These politicized students protested against poor academic quality for Chicano and Latino students as well as against the decreasing funding or nonexistence of courses in

Chicano studies in the Los Angeles Unified School District high schools.[31] Olmos was inspired by *Chicano! History of the Mexican American Civil Rights Movement,* a four-part PBS documentary series produced by Héctor Galán in 1996, which used real footage found in the vaults of some companies in Los Angeles. Part of this footage also appears in the closing scenes of *Walkout,* including a particularly gruesome one in which several police officers strike a young student while he is on the floor, and one of them aims at his neck. As Olmos explains, these 1968 images show blatant discrimination and prejudice against children from eleven to eighteen years old from several East Los Angeles schools: "You see on the documentary incredible acts of violence against these children. Men and women, boys and girls were beaten, bludgeoned, many were sent to the hospital. Many were injured but never went to the hospital. And nothing was ever said" ("Interview" n.p.).

The action of *Walkout* takes place in 1968, at the height of the national civil rights movement, when Paola Crisóstomo (Alexa Vega), a Chicana honor student at Lincoln High School, coordinates a school walkout to protest the mistreatment of Mexican American students in the school system. Tired of witnessing the indignities and humiliation to which her classmates are constantly subjected, she secures the help of her engaged Mexican American teacher and mentor, Sal Castro (Michael Peña), and her friend Bobby Verdugo (Efren Ramírez). The first minutes of the film, which is told from Paola's point of view, evoke the violent climate of that time with images of a weakening César Chávez and of police brutality against Chicano students. Subsequently, we see teacher Sal Castro complain to his students in East Los Angeles's Lincoln High School about the fact that, although Chicanos fought in the Battle of Gettysburg (on both sides) and in the Vietnam War, historians never wrote about it: "You're learning history from people who don't know your history," he states. The solution, he claims, is to have more Chicanos graduate from college so that, one day, they can recover their own legacy and history. The next scenes go on to show the lack of unity among Latino youth (they fight one another in the yard) as well as their Euro-American teachers' abusive demeanor: while they strike them for speaking Spanish in class, advisors recommend boys to become mechanics and girls, to prepare themselves to be secretaries. To raise his students' social consciousness, Mr. Castro takes them to a Chicano youth leadership conference and, on the way there, he shows them the beautiful homes where college-educated people live and the ocean, a new experience for some of the students.

He also recites Corky González's poem "I am Joaquín" and tells them about an article from *Time Magazine* entitled "Pocho's Progress," which is full of stereotypes about Chicanos.

Encouraged by Mr. Castro's enthusiasm, the students distribute a survey about Chicano attitudes toward school and education that, although it is at first dismissed by their teachers, will later prove to be instrumental in convincing the school board of the need for reforms. The presence of a Latino among the board members, Mr. Julián Nava (Edward James Olmos), also helps to have them take notice of the students' complaints. Eventually, following the example of the nonviolent struggles led by Dr. Martin Luther King and César Chávez, the minority students boycott the school system with their walkouts. The predictable result is police brutality and the manipulation of the events by a biased media, which accuses the organizers of having ties to the Communist Party and being infiltrated by outside agitators. Indeed, infiltration exists, but instead of "outside agitators," there is an undercover police officer among their ranks: in one of the demonstrations staged for the liberation of the East L.A. Thirteen (who have been charged with conspiracy to disrupt the public school system and face a possible life sentence in jail), Paola realizes that her boyfriend, Robert, has betrayed the cause and is actually one of the policemen guarding them. Yet the walkouts continue, this time with the presence of the families of students from five different schools. Now, Paola can even count on the support of her reluctant Filipino father.

Eventually, their voice is heard by the school board once they are allowed to present a list of their demands, which is based on the result of the survey they had conducted earlier: bilingual and bicultural education in all East Los Angeles high schools; the end of corporal and janitorial punishment; that teachers who show prejudice be transferred; that advisors and teachers cease to discourage Chicano students from pursuing a college education; that restrooms be open for all students at all times; and that students stop being punished for speaking Spanish on the school premises or for participating in demonstrations. As we learn at the end of this film based on real events, two years after the arrest of some of the walkout organizers, the East LA Thirteen (among them were several Brown Berets, including the producer of this film), their cases were thrown out of court on appeal.[32] The film's closing credits include interviews with some of the original organizers of these walkouts (including Sal Castro, Paula Crisóstomo, Victoria Castro, Carlos Montes,

Harry Gamboa Jr.,[33] "Milta" Cuarón, Bobby Verdugo, and Moctesuma Esparza), and with information about the results of their efforts: "By the Fall of 1969, Chicano student enrollment at UCLA increased from 40 to 1200 students. As the walkouts spread across the country over the next few years, Chicano college enrollment increased from 2 to 24 percent."

The LAPD as Just Another Gang

> We went after crime before it occurred. Our people
> went out every single night trying to stop crime before it
> happened, trying to take people off the street that they
> believed were involved in crime. And that made us a
> very aggressive, proactive police department.
> —LAPD Chief Daryl Gates (Boyer n.p.)

"The inner city," argues Philippe Bourgois, "represents the United States' greatest domestic failing, hanging like a Damocles sword over the larger society. Ironically, the only force preventing this suspended sword from falling is that drug dealers, addicts, and street criminals internalize their rage and desperation. They direct their brutality against themselves and their immediate community rather than against their structural oppressors" (326). In the Los Angeles context, this is as apparent as it is in any other large American city. And one may wonder, where do the local law enforcement agencies stand in this dilemma? "To protect and to serve" has been the official motto of the LAPD since 1963. Yet Latino Los Angeles's cultural production seems to answer this question with another rhetorical question: "And who, exactly, are you protecting and serving?" These works explicitly claim that instead of protecting Latino urban youth, law enforcement agencies have deepened their marginalization.

Eric Ávila has underscored the LAPD's thorny résumé regarding racial discrimination: "If the LAPD and its infamous Red Squad targeted union organizing in Los Angeles during the reign of the open shop, interracial mixing became the new scourge of law enforcement during the post–World War II period" (54). The increasing animosity between the LAPD and Los Angeles's minority groups was first exposed during the 1965 Watts riots that left thirty-four persons dead. When asked about the incidents, then–LAPD chief William H. Parker reportedly argued: "One person had thrown a rock, and then like monkeys in a zoo, others had started throwing rocks." More recently, the infamous Rodney

King beating and its ensuing riots (also known as the Los Angeles Uprising) in 1992 made this police department notorious worldwide.[34] Among several other scandals, the most controversial ones include detective Mark Fuhrman's role in the Nicole Simpson and Ron Goldman murder investigation in 1994, and the 2001 Rampart Scandal, involving the corruption of an antigang unit of the LAPD Rampart Division known as Community Resources Against Street Hoodlums (CRASH) in the late 1990s.[35] Perhaps the LAPD's chronic labor shortage has something to do with its long history of scandals, brutality, and corruption.

Although the LAPD has been featured in numerous films (*Lethal Weapon* [1987, 1989, 1992, 1998], *LA Confidential* [1990], *Crash* [2004], and *Changeling* [2008], among many others), as well as in radio and television shows such as *Dragnet* (radio: 1949–1957; television: 1951–59, 1967–1979, 1989, 2003), *The Shield* (2002–8), and *The Closer* (2005), the cinematic version of the gang-fighting LAPD has in Dennis Hopper's *Colors* (1988) one of its first examples. Set in the South Central Los Angeles of 1987, this film, which has been credited for creating a new subgenre, depicts the ruthless world of three street gangs as seen through the eyes of two Los Angeles cops in the CRASH program.[36] Surprisingly, it makes no distinction between Latino and African American gangs: all three gangs, the Crips, the Bloods, and the White Fences, are portrayed as ethnically mixed. Echoing Luis J. Rodríguez's criticism of the LAPD, the younger officer in the film behaves in a way that approximates him to a legal version of a gang member. Hence, in one of the scenes, after the hotheaded "bad cop," Danny "Pac-Man" McGavin (Sean Penn), sprays with paint the face of a Latino youth who has just crossed a tag (or gang moniker), the diplomatic "good cop," Bob Hodges (Robert Duvall), accuses him: "You're just like them, Pac-Man. Nothing but a gangster." The newcomer's explanation, that when a homeboy crosses a tag it means that he is planning to kill whoever sprayed it, fails to convince his veteran partner. To McGavin's chagrin, he also learns that the boy is his girlfriend's cousin.

Content with describing and condemning gang violence, the filmmakers make no attempt at exposing its root causes. Although in a scene an African-American man at a community meeting called by the police complains about unemployment, nowhere else in the film are historical racism and the discrimination that has marginalized Latino and African American communities stressed. In the last scenes, a sense of imminent Armageddon generated by gang warfare takes over the film, despite

Officer McGavin having learned the lessons taught by his now-deceased partner. Once again, the apocalyptic overtones, a staple in Los Angeles literature and film, seem to reflect racial anxieties that, perhaps subconsciously, inspire writers and filmmakers alike. Overall, the image of African Americans and Latinos, besides their token presence in positions of leadership within the LAPD, remains extremely negative and somewhat simplistic. Charles Ramírez Berg decries the stereotypical portrayal of Latino youth: "The Latino juvenile delinquent, a staple antagonist in Hollywood since the rise of the teen problems of the 1950s (*Blackboard Jungle* [1955]), and a denizen of either the slums of New York City (*The Young Savages* [1961]) or East L.A. (*Colors* [1988]), can be understood as not an altogether new stereotype but in many ways a continuation of an old one: a contemporary urban bandido" (41).

As to female characters, while most young women in the barrio are portrayed as the gangsters' sexual toys, Luisa Gómez, a waitress played by Cuban Venezuelan actress María Conchita Alonso, becomes Danny McGavin's lover and depicts the Hollywood stereotype of the Mexican spitfire.[37] As Rosa-Linda Fregoso elucidates, Luisa, who at first appears as a nice and subservient Chicana homegirl, acts as a cultural translator of the gang world for McGavin. It is precisely her passivity that, according to Fregoso, makes her attractive to the Euro-American officer. Later, however, McGavin feels disappointed upon finding her clad in sexy attire and cheating on him with a gang member at a party. Fregoso has interpreted this scene as a warning against the dangers of miscegenation: "The end of the film demonizes Luisa, reinscribing her as threat to the white race, an inscription serving to legitimize U.S. society's historic prohibition of mixed-race unions" ("Re-Imaging" 82).[38] Ramírez Berg comes to similar conclusions about this character:

> A contemporary incarnation of the dark lady is María Conchita Alonso's character in *Colors* (1988), another stereotype blend. She is the dark lady for the first half of the film (where she is the love interest of Sean Penn's Anglo cop), then suddenly reverts to the harlot (when she becomes the mistress of one of the gang leaders to spite the cop and to demonstrate how little he understands the realities of the barrio). According to Hollywood, then, beneath every Latino is a savage, a Latin lover, or both, and at heart every Latina is a Jezebel. (77)

Moving on to literary and testimonial representations of the LAPD, we find that, with few exceptions (*What It Takes to Get to Vegas, Don't*

Spit on My Corner, and *Two Badges*) a tendency abounds in Chicano and Latino cultural production to criticize law enforcement agencies in what may be called a discourse of defiance or resistance against police corruption and brutality. These works challenge the official story of social order in the city by proposing alternative images of the relation between Latino communities and the LAPD. For example, when LAPD helicopters,[39] squad cars, and motorcycles interrupt an unofficial lowrider parade in Rechy's *The Miraculous Day of Amalia Gómez,* a local resident describes it as "just the usual harassment" (44). Later, after Amalia witnesses how two squad cars ignore a fight between two Latino gangs in Sunset Boulevard, Rosario, a coworker at the sweatshop who acts as the voice of Amalia's conscience, provides an explanation for her: "They'll turn away as long as our own are killing each other, *corazón*" (132). In another scene, based on actual events, Amalia identifies the LAPD as just one more violent gang: "Only a short time ago cops had raided and smashed houses randomly in south central Los Angeles, and amid the wreckage they created in search of unfound drugs in the neighborhood suddenly under double siege, they had spray-painted their own *placa,* their own insignia: LOS ANGELES POLICE RULE" (114). Mike Davis has commented on this scandalous raid on a number of apartment buildings in the 3900 block of Dalton Avenue, where eighty-eight HAMMER troops destroyed walls with sledgehammers while yelling racial epithets and spray-painting "LAPD Rules" on other walls. After the incident, which took place in August 1988, no gang members were arrested, and no weapons were found; only two minor drug arrests were made (*City* 275–76). LAPD's Chief Daryl Gates, however, defended Operation Hammer:

> I finally said, "Enough is enough," and I put 1,000 police officers in what we called Operation Hammer in the South Central portion of Los Angeles. It was very, very effective, tremendously effective, but a lot of people criticized it. A lot of people criticized it and said, "It's a terrible thing. You're out there harassing all these people." We were harassing the gangs. What people don't know is that complaints were filed on 70 percent of those we arrested. (Boyer n.p.)

Along with the criticism directed at the LAPD, *The Miraculous Day of Amalia Gómez* includes scenes where agents of the Immigration and Naturalization Service (or *La Migra,* as is popularly known among Los Angeles Latinos) harass attractive Latinas in a sweatshop. There are even rumors that they rape workers at the sweatshops and kill undocumented immigrants at the border. Again, the protagonist's alter ego, Rosario, links her own suffering and the existence of gangs directly to the corruption of law enforcement agencies: "Don't you care about the women who work next to you?—arrested and sent back without even their wages! For God's sake, don't you see your own sons shoved around by cops only because they're Mexicans? Don't you wonder why they join the terrible *gangas,* and take *drogas*?" (54)

Luis J. Rodríguez further corroborates the comparison of the LAPD to a gang. In his autobiographical text *Always Running,* he singles out Los Angeles County's Sheriff's Department as a particularly brutal and unscrupulous agency. Thus, when talking about his son Ramiro, he states, "Not long ago, a few of his friends were picked up by police, who drove them around in a squad car. The police took them to a rival gang neighborhood. There they forced Ramiro's friends to spray paint over the graffiti with their own insignias—as rival gang members watched—and then left them there to find their way home. It's an old police practice" (9). Several other passages elaborate on how the LAPD instigates violence among rival gangs and even encourages drug dealing:

> In the barrio, the police are just another gang. We even give them names. There's Cowboy, Big Red, Boffo and Maddog. They like those names. Sometimes they come up to us while we linger on a street corner and tell us Sangra called us *chavalas,* a loose term for girls. Other times, they approach dudes from Sangra and say Lomas is a tougher gang and Sangra is nothing. Shootings, assaults and skirmishes between the barrios are direct results of police activity. Even drug dealing. (72)[40]

Moreover, the author accuses the LAPD of thwarting several cease-fires between rival gangs. Mike Davis corroborates this assessment when he argues that the "initial response of the LAPD and Sheriff's—especially the corrupt and tainted anti-gang unit, CRASH—was to do everything possible to sabotage and undermine the truce" (*City* xvi). The police in *Always Running* also use racial slurs against young Chicanos, arrest them without justification, place them with adults in prison, and kill them with impunity. Although in some passages the police become victims of gang members who "jump a cop" as part of their gang initiation, Rodríguez describes his work, in the preface and the epilogue, as an effort to prove how disproportionate and unsuccessful the LAPD's use of force has been throughout the years. In a meaningful scene, a Chicano deputy describes to the young Rodríguez one of their most despicable practices: they arrest every seventeen-year-old boy in the neighborhood to keep track of them over the years; "It ain't hard to figure out," the author elucidates, "that by the time some of the boys do something serious, they have a detention record a mile long and end up hard time—juvey or camp" (72). The LAPD's use of this illicit practice has been denounced by Mike Davis in *City of Quartz* (268) and by Miguel Durán in *Don't Spit on My Corner*. In this last novel, when young Mike asks a police officer about his unjustified arrest, he receives the following answer: "Oh, you're not being busted, but sooner or later you're going to fall. We might as well save time by having you on file now" (24). This way, police officers criminalize Latino urban youth and deny their right of citizenship at an early age. A few chapters later, Mike admits the success of their ploy: "Taking us in last year and mugging us had paid off for them, just like they said it would" (63).

We also have an allegorical and sardonic take on these fraudulent practices in Alejandro Morales's science fiction novel *The Rag Doll Plagues,* where we learn that, given the inevitable life-behind-bars sentences meted out to Chicano youth by the justice system, entire cities have to be built around prison facilities:

> Most of the population consisted of the Lumpen, the criminals and dregs of our society. The failure of our nation's penitentiaries to rehabilitate people had created a one hundred percent recidivism. No matter the sentence, it was understood to be life in a penal colony. The prisoners made the best out of a bad situation and encouraged their families to settle down outside the prison. Prison towns sprang up around the isolated penitentiaries. (137)

Using a more realistic approach, in his short story "Pequeña nación" Morales suggests solutions to prevent both gang warfare and police brutality in the barrio of Gerarghty. Under the leadership of a grade school teacher and amateur historian of East Los Angeles, Micaela Clemencia, the newly created Federation of Scissor Women takes control of their own community using only scissors as their weapons. Their tactic is to intimidate enemies by numerically overwhelming them, disrobing them, and then releasing them naked. Along with the encroaching local police (who are placed again on the same level as gangs), other people identified as obstacles to peace in the streets are city authorities, the news media, neglectful parents, and even some Chicano Hollywood celebrities.

Micaela accuses the police of "invading" the barrio, ignoring "brown on brown" violence, and showing interest in the community only when television cameras are around. She also concludes that the L.A. County sheriff's only objectives are to prevent upper mobility among Latinos and to justify their job by assuring the free circulation of alcohol and drugs in the barrio. With these objectives in mind, Micaela argues, they lobby the state of California and the federal government: "It was known that the union of policemen had hired the biggest agency of specialists in influencing politicians in order to protect its interests in the State and federal governments."[41] Indeed, Mike Davis has exposed the California Correctional Peace Officers' Association (CCPOA) as one of the most powerful and generous lobbies in Sacramento: "In 1990, for example, [CCPOA president Don] Novey contributed nearly $1 million to Pete Wilson's gubernatorial campaign, and CCPOA now operates the second most generous PAC in Sacramento" (*Ecology* 415). As a result, Davis continues, in "alliance with other law enforcement lobbies, Novey has been able to keep Sacramento in a permanent state of law-and-order hysteria. Legislators of both parties trample each other in the rush to put their names at the top of new, tougher anticrime measures" (*Ecology* 416).

After a group of gang members rape and strangle a sixteen-year-old girl as revenge against her boyfriend, the Federation of Scissor Women decides to take the law into its own hands: they burn a gang member's car, disrobe the owner, tie his shoes to his genitals, and then push him out on the street, where a truck runs him over. More interested in the gangbanger's death than in the strangling of the innocent girl, the county's sheriffs begin to interrogate people in the barrio. Yet no one gives them clear answers. When the women deem that the interrogations have gone far enough, they seize the weapons of the nine police officers, remove their uniforms, and release them naked to the streets, as they had done with the gang member. To increase the humiliation, they offer photographs of the naked sheriffs to the *Herald Examiner*. In revenge, police officers begin to harass young Latinos in Gerarghty and, after they label the Federation of Scissor Women a dangerous cult and accuse its members of selling drugs and accumulating firearms, they set the women's house on fire and all the women die.[42]

The LAPD is again to blame in Michael Nava's *The Burning Plain*, where Henry Ríos, the Chicano protagonist, believes that the corruption of some of its units is why lawlessness reigns in the city. Along with honest police officers (such as the gay officer who risks his job by collaborating with him), other rogue cops are accomplices in the gay bashing that takes place in West Hollywood. According to several characters, some members of the LAPD refuse to take hate-crime reports from gay victims so that they can continue to claim that the problem does not exist. Likewise, in the novel that follows in this Ríos series, *Rag and Bone,* an African American district attorney named Anthony Earl calls the LAPD "the Aryan Brotherhood" (153), and a few pages later, the Chicano lawyer makes this sarcastic remark: "This is the LAPD we're talking about, Kim. It would be shocking if they hadn't violated her rights" (225). At any rate, Ríos has not lost his faith in the judicial system and obstinately believes that law enforcement, despite its flaws, is the best way to achieve justice. In fact, in *Rag and Bone* he declares, "My years of legal training, my veneration for the law, made me want to argue the point" (262).[43]

Yxta Maya Murray provides an additional negative depiction of the LAPD in her novel *Locas.* At first, gangbangers seem to have the upper hand; they intimidate and challenge police officers when they "throw up that Lobos hand sign" (31) to show their gang affiliation. However, we later learn that the reason Manny lost his gang's respect was because of his failure to avenge the LAPD's brutal attack on a fellow gang member, which is described in graphic detail: "'How you like this, hey Mexican?' the heavyweight starts kicking Paco there in the side, in the ribs, his big black boot toe swinging up and digging into the bones, hard, so things start cracking. 'Fucking wetback.' Another cop hits him hard with those black batons, on his shoulders, his arms, his cheeks, making deep black and blue and red marks" (91). The novel also condemns the LAPD's tolerance of "brown on brown" violence and its double standard regarding drug trafficking: they are much more aggressive in enforcing the law when gangs sell drugs to college students than when gangs sell them in the barrio.

Whereas Latinos are usually portrayed as aliens to the body politic, young gang members become the ultimate outsiders. In this context of racial discrimination, class segregation, and economic marginalization, the street culture of resistance shaped by a number of rebellious practices (including gangbanging, substance abuse, and drug dealing) to which these characters adhere can be considered in terms of what Philippe Bourgois defines as "an alternative forum for autonomous personal dignity" (8). Marginalized minority youth try to appropriate and control public space as a sign of empowerment and emancipation. However, they often end up not only self-destructing, but also limiting the enjoyment of public life by inner-city residents; these live in constant fear of being attacked by them. This self-destruction is not only physical (through violence and drug abuse), but also civic. For mainstream society, their antisocial behavior is further proof that they do not belong in the national project, nor do they deserve the benefits of nationhood; they do not share the same values and commitments of the "citizenry." As Bourgois points out, "although street culture emerges out of a personal search for dignity and a rejection of racism and subjugation, it ultimately becomes an active agent in personal degradation and community ruin" (9).

As we see in some of these texts and films, the radical reaction by inner-city youth to structural oppression is in response to the provocations of law enforcement agencies. Expelled from the imagined cohesiveness of the national community through textual and filmic practices, the brutality of the LAPD and other exemptive strategies, minority youth create alternative types of "belonging" and "nationhood" that are equally exclusionary; these constructs develop along ethnic and class lines. To this effect, they use "national" symbolism and "flags," clothing, monikers, mottos, and hand signs. Incidentally, according to Benedict Anderson, the printing press and the printed material it produced became a tool for the rise of nationalism, since citizens identified with one another through sharing a common language. Street graffiti, such as that seen in figure 12, serves the same purpose: it produces a connection or common link among inner-city youth, who are often the only ones capable of deciphering it. As we have seen, their gangs and barrios resort to the same type of exclusionary practices and artificial borders that have marginalized them; they use them to reject the "nonbelonging" outsiders through equally imagined (and, therefore, constructed or false) notions of distinctiveness and cohesiveness. Paradoxically, the alienated Other establishes the right to reject admittance to anyone deemed alien to the group. At the same time, some of these narratives and films produce counternarratives, that is, textual and cinematographic images that disrupt the status quo by reintroducing Latinos to the discourse of the nation. They, consequently, expose and challenge the exclusionary agendas and representational strategies of "mainstream America."

In contrast with the texts and films examined, the image of the LAPD improves dramatically in Murray's next novel, *What It Takes to Get to Vegas,* where Dolores Zapata convinces city authorities to approve a 20 percent emergency increase in foot patrol officers in the barrio.[44]

Figure 12 Los Angeles graffiti artists. (Photo by Paige Craig)

Because they approve this request, the area experiences an immediate and drastic crime reduction. Coterminous images of this gentler side of the LAPD appear in Miguel Durán's *Don't Spit on My Corner,* through the character of Leo Pasterman, a member of the group guidance section of the probation department, whose job it is to help young pachucos leave gangs. The probation officer founds a club for recreational activities, organizes a talent show, and manages to arrange a truce between gangs, but, eventually, a brawl in a dance event that he had organized for the pachucos ends the short period of harmony. As in these two novels, the autobiography *Two Badges: The Lives of Mona Ruiz,* sharing several characteristics with testimonials, depicts both the good and the ugly sides of police departments by focusing on the Santa Ana Police Department (SAPD) in Orange County, thirty miles southeast of Los Angeles. In spite of the numerous cases of police corruption contained in this text, Ruiz considers the wrongdoings of a few officers in the SAPD an exception to the overall honest behavior of this police force. Thus, undoubtedly influenced by her new position as a police officer and her admiration of her two role models, Officer Billy Brown and Sergeant

Félix Osuna, she states in the introduction: "I want to be clear that the vast majority of my fellow officers in Santa Ana are clearly professional, dedicated and honorable men and women. For every negative encounter I have ever had, there have been, literally, hundreds of positive examples. The troubles and lapses in the department's history only show what a complicated, difficult mission it has taken on" (7).

Curiously, throughout the book and even in the didactic denouement of the story, which is somewhat apologetic of the SAPD and police departments in general, the coauthors emphasize the similarities between the structure and behavior of gangs and law enforcement agencies. In fact, analogies between both worlds are made eight different times:

> We always heard about cops who did the wrong thing, cops who did stuff as bad as any banger (94); to my young eyes, every offense was proof that the cops were just like the gang members (95); The same as in a gang, everyone seemed to be jockeying for position and sizing each other up (237); The nicknames reminded me of the gangs, like a lot of things in the PD culture (238); Rabbit would tell them that he never left the gangs, that he had just changed membership. "Now I'm in the Ross Street Locos, ése," he would rasp as he cuffed the junior homeboys. Ross Street was the site of the PD. "You never heard of us, man? Sheeeit, ése, we're the baddest. We go in any barrio we want, we got our colors and guns" (246); I always surprise people by telling them that, in some ways, my life isn't that different from when I was in a gang (278); Veteran cops and veteran vatos have the same look in their eye, and, sadly, more than a few share the same coldness in their heart (279); I know that many cops and gang members are more alike than either would like to admit, each sharing a thirst for action and an expectation that they deserve something more than the people who share the streets with them. (287)

According to *Two Badges,* women's subordination and fraternity-like masculinism are equally prevalent in both worlds. When Mona's friend, a boxer named Sal, insists that the police department purposely suppresses Latinos and that it has a negative influence on the barrio, she justifies their attitude by stating that gangs are worse: "I shrugged. 'I think you're wrong, Sal, but couldn't you say the same thing about the gangs? You're an old-timer: Don't the gangs bring more pain than they're worth?'" (215). Again, this reaction gives the impression that, according to Ruiz, the SAPD is a less-dangerous gang. Her association of police departments with streets gangs (be it explicit or implicit, conscious or unconscious) is undeniable. Even after Ruiz becomes a police officer, her "never-back-down" philosophy and her outrageous bravado are reminiscent of the tactics she learned as a gangbanger. To "claim" her territory, she drives around the neighborhood challenging delinquents and criminals by shouting, "Hey, hey, come out and play . . . Officer Ruiz is here to stay." (249).

Against her father's warnings, Mona joined the largest gang in Orange County, F-Troop, to look for excitement. During these years, she witnessed or experienced the parties, the cruising, and the drug dealing and consumption.[45] She also managed to survive the violence of gang "rumbles" and drive-by shootings. Paradoxically, this "education" on the streets ends up making her an ideal officer. For instance, she can now read war signs in the cholas' makeup, or recognize how gangbangers drive after they have stolen a car. She is also in a position to postulate her creed against authority abuse. Her harsh criticism of masculinism and of pockets of corruption inside the SAPD is often followed by didactic passages aimed at reducing antagonism between police officers and the community. Thus, she recommends her fellow officers not to always resort to arrests, to use "community policing," to treat people with respect, to offer nondemeaning solutions, and to act "like you expect good behavior out of them, and many will respond. And, at least once, they might even be heroes" (252).

Rather than fighting "the system," as most subversive characters in this chapter tried to do, the idealistic Mona Ruiz plans to transform it from within. "Her police badge," argues Monica Brown, "becomes a symbol of her status as full citizen, offering some degree of protection even against other racist, sexist cops" (123). Indeed, her joining the SAPD in 1989 could be seen as an additional attempt to attain the agency and power that gang affiliation and marriage had denied her. Once she becomes part of "the other side," she realizes that the relationship between the police department and the community should not be understood in Manichaean terms. Hence, her advice (which may be directed at fellow writers and filmmakers): "I learned that people can't be judged by where they are from, what they look like, or the uniform they wear—whether it is police blue or gangbanger baggy" (287; this reference to both "uniforms" is, of course, another comparison between gangs and police departments). At the end of *Two Badges* the reader is left doubting whether Mona Ruiz has fulfilled her own childhood dream or her father's—he had always dreamt of becoming a cop or seeing one of his children wear a badge. Furthermore, one wonders what parts of the story were left out or transformed, either by her co-writer's advice to make the story more "literary" or to avoid her having problems with superiors at the SAPD. Censorship and self-censorship are two plausible factors in this work.

Therefore, law enforcement agencies share an almost unanimous negative image in Latino Los Angeles's cultural production (perhaps the LAPD would have been included as one of the gangs in the History Channel's series *Gangland* if these authors and filmmakers had been consulted). They are deceptive in that they promise to be something that they are not. With few exceptions, most works fall into Manichaean views of this historically rocky relationship. At times, they offer a tedious and seemingly never-ending list of affronts and conspiracies perpetrated by the LAPD against the well-being of the city's Latino community. At other times, while it can open our eyes to American inner-city social injustice, reading some of these texts about homeboys' daily life and their thorny interaction with mainstream society and law enforcement agencies can produce a sense of involuntary voyeurism in the reader. As we saw in previous subchapters, there is a delicate balance in the politics of representation of marginalized social groups between (apparent) social protest and exploitation of their plight for the presenters' economic benefit.

In all, the study of the marginalized Latino urban youth in their traditional environment, the barrio, yields different realities and subjective experiences (perceptions, memories, desires, meanings), including the notion of an independent gang or barrio as a counternation modeled after U.S. political institutions. Their negative response to formal education functions as a microcosm of the neglect they feel within mainstream society, including the school system and law enforcement agencies. Their structures of consciousness and criminal activities represent a radical reaction to the negative feelings also experienced by many others in their community. From the more simplistic to the more sophisticated representations of their experience, a thin line exists between these cultural manifestations' attempt to expose the dangers of *la vida loca* and the "gangxploitation" subgenre in literature and film.

3

Gendered and Nationalistic Anxieties

> The inability of masculine cultural discourses thus far to portray
> Chicana urban identities, restricting them to the narrow private
> sphere of home, derives, in my view, from the threat to the
> Chicano "family romance" that her presence represents.
> —Rosa-Linda Fregoso, in *Cool Chuca Style*

In Latino Los Angeles's cultural production social anxieties are defined, for the most part, along "racial," ethnocultural, and class lines. Male-authored novels typically denounce mainstream society's strategies of exclusion of Chicanos and Latinos from the American national imaginary. Writings focusing on female subjects or authored by women, however, tend to expose social anxieties along gender lines and to denounce a double or triple oppression that is generated by poverty, racism, and gender inequalities. The same can be said of films focusing on women or directed by women. In this new approach, Chicano or Latino male characters, in general, sometimes become usurpers or oppressors, thus transitioning from victims of historical injustice to merciless victimizers. It is through the approach of women writers and filmmakers (or that of their female characters) to their own ethnic group that the creation of new invisible borders, the definition of gendered spaces, and the suppression of women's individuality and collective voice are more neatly revealed. Writing as a symbolic act of territorial and cultural appropriation takes on new meanings when we consider other parameters, such as gender and sexuality: Latina writing and filmmaking symbolically claim (public) space not only from hegemonic social groups but also from men in their own community. In the first subchapter, however, I argue that Kate Braverman's denunciation of machismo in the Latino community is an example of what James Kyung-Jin Lee has termed "multiculturalism as racial anxiety," which perhaps reflects her own uneasiness upon finding herself surrounded by people of Mexican descent in Los Angeles.

We also have texts and films wherein girls and women rid themselves of male oppression and reach positions of leadership within their own groups, barrios, or even street gangs, thus expanding their area of operations from the domestic space to the public space of the barrio or that of the entire city. Yet, as we will see in the second subchapter, some equate their liberation with emulating their male former oppressors. In this sense, Paulo Freire's *Pedagogy of the Oppressed* points out "sub-oppression" as a common tendency in the initial stages of the struggle for liberation: "Their ideal is to be men; but for them, to be men is to be oppressors. This is their model. This is their model of humanity" (30).[1] For these female characters, the suboppressor's model of "manhood," even when dealing with female characters, is that of the exploiter; they see their liberation as switching positions: from being oppressed to oppressing others, male and female. The third chapter closes this study with an exploration of what I have termed "de-barrioization," that is, a focal transition from the local (the barrio) to the national and global, in which authors and characters look for alliances with other emancipatory and decolonizing movements. This evolution affects nationalist views and opens the door to transnational and postnational alternatives. Just as the Chicano Movement was influenced by both internal forces (the Black Panther Party, Dr. Martin Luther King Jr., American counterculture) and external forces (the Vietnam War, revolutionary fervor in Cuba and the rest of Latin America, international decolonizing movements), in recent years Chicano communities and their cultural production have been changed by the arrival of new migratory waves (of Central Americans in particular) and the activities of other movements of men and women of color committed to equality and emancipation in different parts of the world.

Multiculturalism as Racial Anxiety

> Los Angeles, where anyone who isn't a moron can see
> that it's not an American city, it's a border town, the last
> great city of Mexico, its northern capital.
> —Kate Braverman (zulkey.com, 2006)

Raymund A. Paredes laid out in 1984 how Chicano barrios have been ignored by Euro-American authors writing about Los Angeles: "When one thinks of literary Los Angeles, one thinks of values and lifestyles associated with Hollywood, Beverly Hills, and the beach communities, but seldom with the sprawling barrio of East Los Angeles. As much as ever, Mexican-American culture seems curiously disconnected from general Anglo perceptions of the city, literary or otherwise" (240). However, two Euro-American authors gave their Latino characters a central position in their plots: while Danny Santiago had already published his novel *Famous All Over Town* in 1983, five years later, another Euro-American writer, Kate Braverman (1950–), filled this perceived lacuna with her second novel, *Palm Latitudes,* despite declarations, such as the one in the epigraph, which denote a barely veiled racial anxiety about the massive arrival of Latino immigrants.[2] This novel represents one of the first examples of literature "from the right side of the tracks" (T. Coraghessan Boyle's *The Tortilla Curtain* is a later example) set in Los Angeles to deal with main characters of Mexican descent. The plot unfolds in one second, in one single glance. It begins with Francisca Ramos looking at Marta Ortega and ends with Marta looking at Francisca; the rest are analepses and prolepses that tell the story of the last hours in the life of the seventy-four-year-old Marta and the path that led her to that moment in time and space. With poetic and hallucinatory prose, the author describes the barrios, the plaza of Olvera Street, and the growing re-Latinization of the metropolis, noticeable in murals, restaurants, stores, and businesses.

Palm Latitudes could be read against the background provided in Braverman's 2006 "accidental memoir," *Frantic Transmissions to and from Los Angeles.* The author describes herself here as "a guerrilla fighter, at war with the patrician demarcations between genres, which she [obviously referring to herself] called post-modern relics and vestiges of privilege that should be torched" (217). In the hostile urban territory demarcated in *Palm Latitudes,* Latinas find refuge in their solidarity. "Once a woman disappears," states Braverman in *Frantic Transmissions,* "she instinctively knows the names and histories of strangers. She recognizes kinship to all women standing on terraces or sitting alone on bus benches and porches" (35). Together with two other Latina protagonists (the prostitute Francisca Ramos and Gloria Hernández, a wife and mother who relieves her rage by killing her Anglo neighbor), the third protagonist is the seventy-four-year-old Marta Ortega, a Chicana matriarch who has raised two eccentric daughters. The solidarity and communion among these three protagonists are almost telepathic; they understand one another's plights with no need for verbal communication. The basis of their undeclared sisterhood is their deep resentment against men: they have spent their lives striving for survival in the patriarchal and unwelcoming worlds of Echo Park and greater Los Angeles. In this sense, David Fine has criticized the treatment of Latino male characters in *Palm Latitudes:* "its reductive view of Mexican-American males (all her Chicanos are ignorant, unfeeling *machos;* the only sympathetic males are the Anglo gay couple)" (*Imagining* 240).[3] While Fine is accurate in his description of Latino characters in *Palm Latitudes* (perhaps another sign of the author's racial anxiety), in Braverman's defense, although men are Euro-American in *Frantic Transmissions* and in her novel *Lithium for Medea* (1979), at one point or another most of them end up disappointing their female counterparts. The criticism is not directed exclusively at Latinos, therefore, but at patriarchy in general.

From a strategically essentialist perspective, Braverman also underscores the specificity of female social experience and emotional life. In her view, women share a collective intelligence that gives them access to an entire range of sensitivities (including magical perceptions) unknown to their male counterparts: "Women have waited millions of years, growing separate as another species, with visions and priorities no man-words, no man-measurements can comprehend" (*Palm* 37). Marta Ortega (along with another character named Josefina Jiménez) is, after all, a *curandera,* or folk healer. Latinas and, by extension, all women know one another; in fact, at one point in the novel, all women in Los Angeles turn on a lunar cycle and menstruate at the same time. Therefore, when Marta Ortega states that to be one woman is to be all women, it follows that by writing about abused Latinas, Braverman is writing about all abused women as well.

The author conceives of Los Angeles as "a city of subtle psychological apartheid, of them and us" (*Frantic* 15) and "of divisions based on accents, dialects, race, religious affiliations, and, of course, money" (*Frantic* 114). In this context, she attempts to write the novel from the perspective of the underclass (perhaps of women such as the ones in fig. 13). The narrative voice (and, again following James Kyung-Jin Lee's notion of multiculturalism as racial anxiety, one has to wonder whether there is some racial guilt here) openly identifies with the three main characters, not because they are women, but because they are socially underprivileged Latinas. Braverman expresses the same type of empathy in *Frantic Transmissions,* where the narrative voice disassociates herself from the stereotype of the wealthy Westside Jew to identify instead with

Figure 13 Newspaper stand on Broadway Street. (Photo by Paige Craig)

the multiethnic Angelenos whose families were uprooted by the construction of freeways: "We were already in the way. Our tract houses were razed for freeways. The city ordered this. They had a master plan. The new Los Angeles selected for another breed.... We were the offspring of disaster, personal, sociological, and climatic, the residue from failed families and farms, the legacy of sharecroppers, Mexican harvest workers, Asian refugees, and European ghettos" (117–18). She therefore feels entitled to speak for the (and as the) L.A. woman.

Braverman has declared her intent to tropicalize and femininize language in *Palm Latitudes*. Although language is indeed a key element in this text, the verb "tropicalize" brings to mind widespread stereotypes about Latin American literature in the United States (the pervasive association of the subcontinent's narrative just with magical realism, for example), which are congruent with Braverman's aforementioned tendency to adopt essentialist approaches. How she wrote the novel may explain the choice of vocabulary, the frenzied cascades of strong emotions and frustrations, and the abundance of evocative, lyrical passages, with some occasional overwriting: according to the author, while living in Echo Park, she began to write a long poem that became the plot of *Palm Latitudes*. This long narrative poem about the city of Los Angeles, however, had begun in her first novel, *Lithium for Medea*, as we may read in the first lines of the last chapter: "Los Angeles, brutal claustrophobic basin of delusion and ripoff, clutter, eerie, sticky, horrible. They came, they saw and went blind. O hallucination of urban gray slabs senseless and rotting behind me. Poor ruined sunsore and sadness for demented City of Angels, of white torment and hideous albino predator birds" (247–48). *Palm Latitudes,* therefore, is as much a novel about the trials of three Latinas surviving in a male chauvinistic world as it is a study of Los Angeles as a gigantic paradox. In consonance with *Lithium for Medea* and *Frantic Transmissions,* it reads as a love/hate relationship with a daunting cityscape whose elements can faithfully represent society's patriarchal views. In this sense, in *Frantic Transmissions* Braverman argues that there are two distinct and mutually exclusive configurations of Los Angeles: on one side, you have Hollywood's mythmaking machine and the city authorities with their global agendas and pharaonic projects; on the other, an underclass of local and multiethnic people who ride the buses every day and used to live in the neighborhoods that were bulldozed for public projects. Braverman conceives of *Palm Latitudes* as a novel about the latter: the invisible, economically deprived workers who are also an intrinsic part of the late capitalist machine, but who never had their own American dream. Freeways, sports stadiums, and other urban public projects were never designed for them; in reality, they were built around them or where their homes used to stand. In Raúl Homero Villa's words,

> As in the formal structure of literary allegory, the primary or "literal" narrative of Los Angeles' development is one of ceaseless modernization, of manifest improvements in the form and function of the city as an economic growth machine. At the secondary or allegorical level of conceptual significance, this master narrative of modernization has had radically contrary interpretations, depending on one's location in the metropolitan landscape of power. (2001, 235–36)

Palm Latitudes deals with a specific chronotope: the global city and its Latina denizens during the second half of the twentieth century.

As several critics have pointed out, the three Latina protagonists seem to be plays on female archetypes: the matriarch, the wife, and the prostitute. Among them, Marta Ortega rises as an epic figure that will challenge the reader's assumptions about Los Angeles, Latinas, marriage, interpersonal communication, and even magic. Although each of the four parts of the novel focuses on the daily life of one of these three women, it could be argued that the true protagonist is the oft-personified city of Los Angeles. As in John Rechy's novels about Los Angeles, prosopopoeia and pathetic fallacy are recurrent figures of speech in the plot of *Palm Latitudes*. Braverman's personifications, however, take the shape of metaphors, similes, or parallelisms between the female body and urban landscapes, a narrative strategy that works in two different directions. While in one passage the city of Los Angeles is portrayed as a "bloated diseased woman" (9) who keeps devouring more and more hills and natural spaces, in others Gloria Hernández compares herself to a city swallowed by the jungle that will one day be rediscovered, or describes "the slums" in her own body: "Once, May had spoken to me with delicacy and tenderness. That was before my interior regions became a slum, infested and abused" (182).[4]

The eradication of traditional neighborhoods and the destruction of natural habitat by urban sprawl mirror the personal suffering of the three Latina protagonists. Marta Ortega's own personal decline, for example, runs parallel to that of Flores Street in Echo Park. Another community mentioned in the novel is the Chávez Ravine barrio, which was uprooted by the Los Angeles Housing Authority to develop public housing under the National Housing Act of 1949. After the mostly Mexican American population was forcibly removed, the project for redevelopment was abandoned, and the construction of Dodger Stadium began (as Eric Ávila points out, the Dodgers' owner, Walter O'Malley, coveted this area "because of its proximity to Los Angeles' new freeways" [121]). In *Palm Latitudes,* however, the conflict is not exclusively between Euro-Americans and Mexican Americans. Mexican Americans are both victims and perpetrators of the disappearance of the emblematic barrio. Thus, Marta's brother, the developer Enrique Ortega, participates in the eradication of Chávez Ravine by speculating with land and buying old houses and orange groves to turn them into apartment buildings. This way, the guilt has to be shared by both groups.

At dusk, Braverman's downtown Los Angeles is almost deserted. Populated only by the lunatics and criminals who maraud the streets,

Figure 14 Los Angeles's Spanish and Mexican past: Ávila Adobe, the oldest building in Los Angeles. (Photo by Paige Craig)

it becomes a zombielike hallucination, a hellish underworld: "I considered hell, how brittle and hot it must be, parched, seasonless, incessantly whipped by winds pitted with the needles of cactus and the orbs of sharpened sand" (99). Although Francisca Ramos claims not to hate Los Angeles, overall the novel portrays the metropolis in a negative light. For instance, one of the city's purported flaws is its lack of a sense of history. Even though the omniscient narrator repeats the original Spanish name of the city and mentions several times that Los Angeles has Spanish and Mexican roots, she also claims that the city has no recognizable past in its architecture, a statement that figures 14, 15, and 16 refute. Yet Francisca enjoys this absence: "This incomplete city which seems to have no recognizable past, no ground that could be called unassailably sacred. This incomplete city that speaks of an impending terror. It occurs to her that what she most appreciates about this City of the Angels is that

Figure 15 Latino Los Angeles: Church of Nuestra Señora la Reina de los Ángeles in Plaza Olvera. (Photo by Paige Craig)

which is missing, the voids, the unstitched borders, the empty corridors, the not yet deciphered" (33). At one point in the novel, it seems that this lack of historical sense becomes a perception of the city having had no history. If we consider the previous passage, it is obvious that Francisca fails to acknowledge the existence of original stucco houses and other Mexican-style buildings around Plaza Olvera, or the Spanish missions in San Gabriel and surrounding areas.

Guy Sircello has eloquently interpreted the importance of nothingness and the sublime in *Palm Latitudes*:

Such language recognizes that tumultuous and accidental upheavals of the natural world, of history, of the human souls have nothing—a void—as their center and source, so to speak. It is experience of this nothing, then, with which Braverman's women, and especially the *bruja* Marta, are intimate. And it is also with respect to this nothingness that

Figure 16 Original house of the last Mexican governor of Alta California, Pío Pico, in Plaza Olvera. (Photo by Tonya López-Craig)

> Braverman constructs her biggest concrete symbol, as it were, in the novel—L.A. (548)

Yet Sircello fails to notice that the omniscient narrator's statement is preceded by two sentences (repeated later in the plot) that remind us of Los Angeles's Spanish and Mexican pasts: "This city which was once an outpost of Spain and once a region of Mexico. This city webbed with boulevards bearing the names of Spanish psychotics and saints" (33). Once again, the use of these derogative terms suggests the author's uneasiness about Los Angeles's Hispanic heritage and presence. Braverman's frequent use of part of the city's original name, Nuestra Señora la Reina de los Ángeles (she is missing the words "de Porciúncula"), from the onset of the narrative seemed to foretell her intention to underscore its Hispanic past. However, the possibility exists that the "lack of a sense of history" and "having no recognizable past" could respond to the implicit author's subconscious ethnocentrism. Some passages seem particularly puzzling: "She is grateful for the absence of history and its physical manifestations, the granite cathedrals of the imported God, the wide tiled plazas and the assault of church bells" (33). It is evident here that Francisca is happy to find no vestiges of Hispanic architecture because, as in the rest of the novel, Spanish, Latin American, and U.S. Latino cultures are inextricably linked to backwardness, patriarchy, and male chauvinism. If the novel is viewed from this perspective, Braverman's stance may well corroborate Raymund A. Paredes's claim that in "considering Los Angeles from a Mexican-American literary perspective, one begins with this fundamental fact: Los Angeles has been, since the mid-nineteenth century, a city uneasy about its Mexican-ness" (239).

This approach is especially problematic in a book whose title (appearing several times in its Spanish translation within the plot) reflects the negative impression that places like Los Angeles, Miami, Santa Clara, San Juan, Havana, Mexico City, or Caracas (note that all of them are populated mostly by Latinos) have made on the narrator, the characters, and, arguably, the implied author: "From her bus bench, she can see the orange-tiled roofs of Spanish-style houses planted in the sides of hills like a series of terra-cotta pots, almost ornamental. From a certain angle, this area could be Mexico City or Santa Clara, Caracas or San Juan. The pattern repeats itself *like an insane weaver or a cancer*, even in this southern city which seems only peripherally and accidentally American" (33; my emphasis), states the narrator. Therefore, the opening passage of the novel, so sympathetic to those brown people without a green card who are marginalized in the white realm of the City of the Angels, turns out to be deceiving. In spite of the apparent *intentio operis* of providing a feminist voice for subaltern Latina women striving to survive and surrounded by men whose only objective seems to be to subdue them through alcohol-induced violence, one can sense a condescending disregard for the Latino world in general. Here again, James Kyung-Jin Lee's notion of "multiculturalism as racial anxiety," discussed in the introduction, comes to mind.

The novel also points out the arbitrariness of national borders. Gloria Hernández comes to the conclusion that the international border is not in Juárez, Mexicali, or Tijuana: "I realized the border was merely a line a lunatic had arbitrarily etched across the surface of a map ...] The avocado trees and bougainvillea,[5] the slow blue coves and sea birds were identical with the lands we had left behind us in the country we called Mexico" (110). The real border, in her view, is language: it sits in her mouth, in the English/Spanish dichotomy. Yet, in spite of the similar topography on both sides of the border, Gloria conceived of the United States as a very distinct entity while living in Tijuana: "When winds blew from the north, I could smell America. It was an odor of clean tin, clean metal, clean sun and tamed rain. America smelled like time structured and welded into place" (107). North of the border, therefore, a clean, tamed, structured, and somewhat sensible chronotope determines emotional experiences and entices the character. By contrast, the air in Tijuana is "strange and bloody" (107), contaminated by prostitution and inebriated American soldiers. All things considered, the only positive images of Mexico (or any place populated by Latinos) are the references to the fetishized time of the Aztecs and the homeland dreamt by Marta Ortega's brothers, who mythicize it as an arcadia where men hunted eagles and jaguars in idyllic fields covered with tropical flora. That is, we find it in the land of the pre-Columbian Mexicans who present no threat to the Euro-American Angeleno citizens of today.

In *Palm Latitudes,* Latinos are unable to make sense of the city of Los Angeles. Only their barrio, which they see as a *pueblo* disconnected from the metropolis (its insularity deepened by its inaccessibility by bus), can provide a psychological shelter. Characters like Gloria Hernández and Octavio Herrera, while coming from drastically different environments, reject or even refuse to acknowledge the existence of a city that they deem peripheral to their lives. Time and again, they conceive of Los Angeles as the epitome of an urban dystopia: "A ruined city, Marta Ortega noted, with a center and not a heart. Once Los Angeles had been labeled the city of the future. But it had no core, it rotted at the edges and asserted a splendor which proved hollow, stillborn, its roots an illusion" (195).

As mentioned above, influenced by the scientific certainty that a powerful earthquake will strike the heart of this city sitting atop the San Andreas Fault, authors writing about Los Angeles are often tempted to resort to the apocalyptic imagery that lingers in the collective subconscious. *Palm Latitudes,* like so many other works set in Los Angeles,[6] forewarns of the inexorable arrival of Armageddon, and it does so through lyrical metaphors and allegories that include high tides and biblical plagues: "Night was resplendent with graveyards, saplings struck by lightning and the maniacal pools of neon which were the city, this illusion called Los Angeles that the ocean or desert would inevitably swallow" (100). The intertextualities with the Book of Revelation are obvious: when barrio dwellers interpret earthquakes, threatening Santa Ana winds, vicious wildfires on the hills, ashes that fall from the skies, and even what Braverman describes metaphorically as the "suicide" of an elm in Flores Street as omens of the impending destruction of the city, they flee to the churches to plead for God's forgiveness. In fact, the symbolic prediction and interpretation of events that characterizes this Jewish literary form permeates Braverman's novel. Just as most apocalyptic books were conceived as a source of hope in times of persecution, she provides a safety valve for her Latina protagonists in the advent of a new and better world that will erase this flawed one. In the end, the apocalyptic disappearance of the Chávez Ravine barrio against the symbolic background of the destruction of Tenochtitlán by Spanish conquistadores, together with the personal decline of the three protagonists, are interconnected to the point where they become one single event.

Besides the apocalyptic overtones that again Mike Davis considers a by-product of the authors' and film directors' racial anxiety, another coincidence between *Palm Latitudes* and *Bodies and Souls* is their ecocritical approach. Braverman underscores the catastrophic consequences of the never-ending urban sprawl and the dangerous contamination of "a sky littered beyond reconstruction" (10). She also criticizes the deplorable canalization of the Los Angeles River, a painful reminder of the long list of recent environmental fiascoes in Los Angeles.[7] As she did earlier with plants, clouds, and the city itself, the author now compares the "murdered" river to the suffering of Latina women: "I had small boulders for breasts, sand and cactus for flesh. A dead river, dammed with concrete, filled the juncture between my legs. I masqueraded as a woman" (109). But, above all the other personified natural elements in the cityscape, the novel's main symbol is the palms in its title: "with their tattooed legs, their inadequate skirts of straw and their guerrilleros. The palms, with their lashed bark flesh abandoned at the edges of ruined plazas, with the lost farmers at their feet, the legions of disappeared husbands and fathers and sons. The vats of oil, the plague of rum" (90). In yet another sign of social anxiety, palm trees, which remind the character (and presumably the implicit author as well) of places inhabited by Hispanics, bring about stereotypes about Latin America such as guerrilla fighters, poor peasants, run-down and sleepy plazas, machismo, and alcoholism. These majestic trees, which Hollywood films have turned into city icons, are reduced in the novel to pathetic phallic symbols whose green leaves resemble hands begging for absolution among piles of trash. Aside from the palms, however, the rest of the vegetation purifies an otherwise doomed city and provides an oasis of beauty inside an irreparably ugly world: Marta Ortega feels attuned with the universe because of her garden of hybrid orchids, Francisca Ramos finds refuge in her memories of the exuberant vegetation of Caracas, and women's perennial waiting for their men is eased by the company of flowers.

In this dejected urban landscape, the first of three Latina protagonists appearing is Francisca Ramos, a prosperous prostitute known locally as La Puta de la Luna (The Moon's Whore). Although disappointment with her Colombian lover has sent her life into a downward spiral, she enjoys a degree of agency and independence because of her solvency. At times, however, Francisca seems to be somewhat of a snob: she gets expensive manicures in Wilshire Boulevard and looks down on her clients, unsophisticated working men and Chicanos whose Spanish she finds atrocious. She is also intrigued by the empty eyes of a Latina worker, Gloria Hernández, whom she sees daily returning home from a downtown sweatshop. With no need for verbal communication, Francisca senses the reason for her sorrows and wishes she could "command her to step off the bus, to free herself from the configuration strangling her, to recognize there were no borders, no houses or men that could not be left, abandoned or run from" (30). Although Gloria knows that she is more intelligent than her family thinks, she still feels insignificant and flawed, partly because her husband and sons treat her as if she were a servant, and they also resent the fact that she never learned English and refused to assimilate to the new culture. Born in northern Mexico, the young and abnegated homemaker moved to the United States to help realize Miguel's (her husband) dream. Miguel, who always idealized this country, joined the U.S. Army and won several medals during the Vietnam War. He feels extremely proud of having become a U.S. citizen and tries to distance himself from recent, undocumented Central American immigrants. This attitude changes, however, after he falls in love with Barbara Branden, a liberal Euro-American neighbor. In an almost comical turn of events, Miguel no longer feels American and becomes re-ethnified, considering himself Mexican again. Suddenly, he starts to write poetry, grows a beard, wears a bandana, boycotts grapes (years after César Chávez's strike), idolizes Ernesto "Che" Guevara, and condemns the corruption of the U.S. government. In the end, poisoned by jealousy, Gloria goes insane, kills Barbara Branden and, in prison, refuses anyone's visit.

Francisca Ramos also empathizes with Marta Ortega, an elderly Chicana who sits by a polluted lake in Echo Park and becomes the protagonist of the novel's second part. Again, without having to resort to verbal communication, she senses that Marta's suffering must have a common denominator with hers. Indeed, when Marta was fourteen, her abusive father forced her to marry an alcoholic, ignorant, cruel, and unfaithful man, whom she later abandoned. Born in the heart of Los Angeles, near the Chávez Ravine area, she also witnessed the city authorities' relentless efforts to destroy her barrio through "whitening" projects: "The pueblo was considered backward, recalcitrant. The inhabitants were stupid as children. Or perhaps, by blood, congenitally moronic, incapable of grasping even the bold print of reality" (201).

Through the personal histories of these three Latina characters, the implicit author develops her views on Latino males; as mentioned, these become a synecdoche of all men. Most of these "Manuels or Josés" (13), as the narrator calls them disparagingly, ignore, beat, betray, and oppress their spouses through constant pregnancies.[8] Their aggressive nature, in Gloria Hernández's view, can be perceived from the moment they are born: "The boy baby, opening and closing his fists as if he were already angry and dreaming of spears, arrows, rocks which could be gathered, sharpened and thrown" (110). In turn, moved by convention, Latinas voluntarily enter the prison of marriage that stifles their uniqueness. They learn to become invisible and to spend their lives waiting for their primitive husbands, who they know will eventually disappear—cross the border, be imprisoned, suffer an accident while driving drunk, or abandon them for other women. In the novel, therefore, the institution of marriage and the ensuing dysfunctional family figure are the cornerstones of female disempowerment. In a similar vein, Marta tries to prevent her daughter Angelina from falling into this trap, by stating some outrageously reached conclusion: "Any woman waiting for a man is a whore" (264). To support the argument against eternally waiting for husbands to return home, the novel proves Marta right when one of her neighbors, Consuelo López, who had spent the entire length of the novel praying for her lover to come from Mexico as he had promised, feels disappointed by his laziness once he arrives.[9]

One of the biggest achievements of *Palm Latitudes* is its early portrayal of Latinas as educated citizens or as uneducated women who are nonetheless eloquent and intellectually sophisticated. In contrast, the novel describes the stereotypical pachucos in the barrio as potential felons who "dream of raping her [Francisca Ramos] beside the lake, or ripping her silk clothing from her flesh and taking her with force in the back seats of cars. They would like to grind her skin into concrete" (15). In turn, Francisca views them as unsophisticated crooks coming from insignificant Mexican villages who inevitably join gangs, abuse their wives, and end up in prison. To this cast of pathetic male characters, Francisca adds the assimilated Latinos who have erased their accents, wear suits, and use expensive colognes but are still troubled by a blatant inferiority complex: "Of course, they think they are Montezuma as he should have been. . . . Always, these men claim the uncorrupted blood of Mayan or Aztec royalty. Or they insist their grandfathers were born in Spain or France or Italy. She is mildly amused by how conventional and unimaginative their invented histories are. . . . She thinks they are ridiculous. Were they less ignorant, they would be pretentious" (12).

Women's Space and Female Gangs

The discourse of self-affirmation in many of the texts and films examined rests on images of bravery, manhood, and sexual prowess that relegate female characters to a subordinate position, as passive spectators or cheerleaders of the "true" male soldiers. For the most part, rather than being agents of their emancipation from structural oppression, Latinas embody the prize or status symbol that males receive for attaining money, power, and respect.[10] To cite only a few cases, women do not belong within the liberationist discourse of cultural nationalism narrated by Luis Valdez (note the limited role of the pachuca in his play Zoot Suit [Fregoso "Re-Imaging" 83]), Óscar Zeta Acosta,[11] Luis J. Rodríguez,[12] and other male authors under study. In their works, Latinas are described as a shadow of the barrio warrior, a trophy for his bravery, or a cheap commodity for homosocial relations. But, as will be seen in this subchapter, there are alternative ways of representing Latina life in the gang, the barrio, and the metropolis. These representations include female narrative perspectives and subjectivities, their conquest of public domain, and their positions of leadership (community activists, police officers, ruthless gang leaders). In some cases, however, their perceived emancipation and agency are reduced to an imitation of their male oppressors' abuses or to the fulfillment of someone else's dream.

"Within the Chicana feminist deconstruction of Chicano familial discourse," Rosa-Linda Fregoso has noted, "the figure of the Pachuca, chola, or homegirl is inadvertently overlooked as an agent of oppositional practices, despite her notable contribution to the politics of resistance"

("Re-Imaging" 78). From this perspective, in the following pages we will study the representation of the female gangbanger by male and female writers and filmmakers, from the abused figures that appear in Rodríguez's *Always Running* to their innocent games in del Fuego's *Maravilla* and their subjugation in Ruiz and Boucher's *Two Badges,* all the way to their progressive emancipation in Anders's film *Mi vida loca* and the positions of leadership that they attain in Murray's *Locas.*

Rodríguez's text provides a brief introduction to female gangbanging that is later developed in Yxta Maya Murray's first novel, *Locas.* Most homegirls in *Always Running* are subservient, passive victims of their male counterparts' chauvinism, as illustrated in the scene where a girl's "initiation" consists of having sex with a gang member. This preamble to her street-gang life prefigures her plausible lack of agency and her reification as a sexual toy for male peers. In other passages, however, homegirls become more aggressive: "Some of them called themselves cholas. They had long, teased hair, often peroxided black or red. They had heavy makeup, skirts which hugged their behinds, and they were all the time fighting, including with guys. The cholas laughed a lot and knew how to open up to every situation. They talked back, talked loud and talked tough" (44). The most prominent is Payasa, Rodríguez's girlfriend for some time, whose strange behavior—she is unable to be intimate unless she is under the influence of drugs—is partly explained by her brothers' cutting her tongue if she lost a fight at school. *Always Running* is, therefore, one of these works where the self-proclaimed new urban Aztec warriors who affirm their cultural identity and sometimes protest their marginalization ultimately turn into also merciless suboppressors of young Chicanas. Cholos use the female body as a site where they inscribe their virility, or as an object through which they take vengeance on rival gang members by damaging their "legitimate property," that is, by humiliating, striking, or raping their women.

One of the tactics that fictional homegirls in these works use to rid themselves of subservience to their male counterparts is the creation of their own, independent female gangs, modeled after male gangs. Maxson and Klein, having studied gender as a factor in gangbanging, acknowledge the existence of female street gangs: "Gangs are primarily male but clearly not exclusively so. Ten males to one female or less are common, but four-to-one, two-to-one, and even one-to-one ratios have been reported. Independent, fully autonomous female gangs have been and remain fairly rare, but otherwise the form of female involvement, from auxiliary groups to full integration, has shown considerable variety" (248). From this perspective, Consuelo Concepción "Cece" Contreres, the protagonist of Laura del Fuego's first novel, *Maravilla* (1989), refers to her 1960s group of East Los Angeles friends as a "gang." By today's standards, however, Las Belltones seems closer to a girl club than to a female street gang.[13] Several activities that the autobiographical protagonist describes separate this group of pachucas from today's concept of a street gang. First, their initiation seems quite harmless: "The initiation rites: no make-up for a month; no talking to guys for a week; wearing blouses and sweaters backwards for one week; doing chores and running errands at the club meetings and social events until someone new had been initiated. Our club jackets were mint green, with a black bell and a musical note emblazoned on the back under *Belltones E.L.A.*" (11). Later, in contrast with the often life-threatening consequences of leaving a gang today, Cece's punishment for not attending gang meetings and, subsequently, for leaving the Belltones is that members stopped talking to her. Despite description of violent fights against racist Euro-American girls, the killing of a male friend by the LAPD, and Cece's drug addiction, coupled with that of her best friend's boyfriends (most males in the barrio are described as junkies and irredeemable "losers"), the pachucas' daily activities (including trying on wedding dresses) seem innocent and innocuous compared to those of pachuco characters in works such as Luis Valdez's *Zoot Suit* and Miguel Durán's *Don't Spit on My Corner*. In any case, Rosa-Linda Fregoso has praised Laura del Fuego's early depiction of pachucas' sexual exploration and their liberating image outside the domestic domain:

> Though *Maravilla* stops before consummating homosexual desires, these scenes of Cece's homoerotic pleasures and her homosexual bonds with other girls nonetheless disclose the novel's homosexual subtext. [. . .] By hanging out with girlfriends, cruising the streets, or fighting rival gangs, Cece and her cohort of pachucas refused to be contained in the home or limited by the prevailing views of female comportment. ("Re-Imaging Chicana" 81)

In contrast with the mostly legal and nonaggressive activities of the pachucas in *Maravilla*, a novel published eight years later, *Locas*, by Chicana author and lawyer Yxta Maya Murray (1970–), describes in detail the violent reality of today's female gangs.[14] The same pachucas or cholas that rarely had a voice or a visible role in male works now take center stage.

Although, as we will see, the paths for resistance they choose seem highly questionable, they nevertheless articulate, in their own way, an oppositional discourse against patriarchal rules. The novel explores, in more depth than *Always Running* and from a female narrative perspective, the daily lives of female gangbangers, focusing first on their submissive involvement in drug gangs, and then on their creation of an independent gang. Cecilia Silvas, sister of a pioneer gang leader named Manny, narrates the first chapter. Most of the action takes place in the East Los Angeles neighborhood of Echo Park, an area that, like Las Lomas in *Always Running,* is concealed by invisible borders: "See, if you live in Echo Park, you don't see *California.* You don't see sharp-dressed people who work in offices and shop in stores. Instead all you see are power lines and broken sidewalks, clika tags scrawling up and down the walls and cholos hanging on the corner with their hairnets and cigarettes and thick black shoes" (187), complains Cecilia. On a rare occasion where the characters venture outside the barrio (other than to sell guns or drugs), Cecilia and her friend from a rival gang, Chucha, notice in the looks that people give them that they do not belong in the economically privileged space of Beverly Hills. They have crossed the invisible boundary marker within the city, only to realize that, whether they like or not, they carry this visible border (the color of their skin) with them.

Like the semiautobiographical character in Acosta's memoir *The Autobiography of a Brown Buffalo,* Cecilia constantly describes herself in derogatory racial terms.[15] Interestingly, the way that characters perceive skin color and indigenous phenotypes differs depending on the judged person's gender: "I got these square hips and shoulders, like a little fat box, and I'm Aztec looking with a flat brown face, too dark to be any real good. Thick hands. You can be that way if you're a man, but a girl has to be light and thin and small all over" (55). The protagonists' low self-esteem, which becomes an inferiority complex (even self-hatred when both Cecilia and Lucía use racist, sexist, and homophobic epithets to describe their own ethnic group, gender, or sexual tendencies), is informed by the double standards of the mass media and the LAPD: "Some C-4s opened up on them and killed a rubia. Made it all over the TV. And even though we've got a hundred dead brown babies in these parts and there ain't nobody crying about them, after the gabacha girl got hit there was black-and-whites driving down my streets thick as locusts" (243).[16]

Unlike most gang and "gangxploitation" films and texts, Murray speculates about the circumstances that give rise to violent street gangs.

Whereas Rodríguez, in the epilogue to *Always Running,* argues that no one wants to hurt his own people,[17] Murray suggests that there is, in fact, a predisposition to evildoing in some of her characters. Cecilia, for instance, has to fight her instinct to participate in illegal gang activities, because, as she admits, it is in her blood. Likewise, *Locas* coincides with *Always Running* in its underscoring of the barrio's sheer poverty as a reason for gangs but adds greed as another factor, when Cecilia testifies: "People thought we started the Lobos or any other gangbang because we loved seeing blood. They called us animals, made their little speeches. But it was money just like anything else. My brother's a businessman, a leader" (11).[18] On *Gangland,* Detective Christopher Brandon, a member of the Los Angeles County's Sheriff's gang unit, seems to concur by stating that gangbanging is "all about making money. That's just the bottom line."

The type of gang first described by Murray in *Locas* belongs to what gang scholars label as "specialty gangs," that is, "groups whose general goal is to reap the profits of specific forms of crime" (Maxson and Klein 246). More specifically, once Manny Silvas's Echo Park Lobos move from gun selling to drug dealing, their "clika" becomes a "drug gang." In spite of the Echo Park Lobos' boastful display of pride, however, Lucía describes their gang activities as a mere delivery service: they take illegal merchandise from Echo Park to different parts of their territory, which extends to Long Beach. Societal power struggles find their replica within inner gang circles when Chico, Manny's right-hand man, creates a rival gang in Echo Park's Eastside. Consequently, numerous innocent neighbors are killed. Besides being bloodthirsty and greedy, all characters claim to be looking for empowerment. They believe that the time has come to regain lost respect and demand their piece of the American Dream, after years of seeing their parents selling fruit and flowers on freeway exits, cleaning houses, or busing tables in restaurants.

Isela Alexandra García cheers how Murray links Lucía's awareness of her people's marginalization to her gang attraction but criticizes the characters' questionable motivations for becoming members or leaders of gangs:

Both author and protagonist fail to see the scope of desires in these women that gang membership promises to fulfill. Among these desires: group solidarity, economic independence, and escape from the restrictions of conventional female behavior—each in the context of protection from exploitative relationships—and further, the desire to resist the pressure to assimilate exerted by social institutions, especially by the schools Latinas attend. (67)

Yet Murray provides a range of factors other than those García points out: in addition to poverty, greed, and a natural predisposition to wrongdoing, young characters in the novel equally express a need for love, empowerment, protection, and respect. In Lucía's case, her determination to emulate her boyfriend Manny and become a *jefa* (boss) stems from the resentment she feels for all the mistreatment that her mother had to endure at the hands of her husband and other male partners. By the same token, although Monica Brown underscores the absence of nationalistic ideology in this fictional female gangbanging, Lucía's attainment of money, power, and respect within the tenets of the street economy may be understood to be in consonance with the "upward mobility" philosophy of "mainstream America." In this sense, Philippe Bourgois argues:

> Like most other people in the United States, drug dealers and street criminals are scrambling to obtain their piece of the pie as fast as possible. In fact, in their pursuit of success they are even following the minute details of the classical Yankee model for upward mobility. They are aggressively pursuing careers as private entrepreneurs; they take risks, work hard, and pray for good luck. They are the ultimate rugged individualists. (326)

Locas, therefore, fictionalizes gang life from the perspective of young Latinas who are trying to rebel against a male hegemony that is repeatedly criticized through the use of the word *macho* (seven times in the plot). While Latino adolescents in the novel disrespect and abuse their female friends, men beat their daughters if they become pregnant before marriage or beat their wives while inebriated or because they are frustrated for being unemployed: "you can tell when a woman gets beat by her man because she walks away. Keeps far from her own people. A woman that gets beat doesn't want a soul to find out. She thinks they'll judge her wrong. That they'll say it's her fault" (81). The plot also portrays male chauvinism through the homosocial relationships that permeate gang politics. Cecilia recalls how, despite not being considered a pretty girl, many young men wanted to date her only because she was Manny's younger sister. Against this disturbing background, the story depicts interactions within and among drug gangs in Echo Park as a male-dominated environment where servile girls and young women are abused and called "sheep." They stand at the lowest levels in a well-defined hierarchy that ranges from the gang leader, to his "right hands," the younger "taggers" who spray graffiti, and to the dishonored third-raters, those taggers not good enough to become right hands. This struggle against a dominant patriarchy limits, according to Monica Brown, their inclination to conceive of their gangs in nationalistic terms: "The nationalist sentiments and explicit critique of dominant national culture present in male gang narratives seem to be absent for the female protagonists, who offer more local critique, especially of oppressive gender hierarchies" (91).

In alternative chapters, two teenage girls, Lucía and Cecilia (Manny Silvas's girlfriend and sister respectively) narrate their experience during a violent period that is divided into three intervals (1980–85, 1985–90, 1997). Manny has created a powerful gang that runs a profitable business selling guns and drugs, but Lucía and Cecilia slowly undermine his power through their personal quest to emancipate themselves from male oppression. In the end, the aggressive Lucía, having learned to manage a gang by helping Manny with the finances, takes over as the new *jefa*. Nonetheless, she has to use her new boyfriend, Beto, as a figurehead, as she cannot avoid her male dependency. In this context, Philippe Bourgois has blamed society for minority women's tendency to fall into this type of situation:

> Poor women should not be forced to seek desperate alliances with men in order to stay sheltered, fed, clothed, and healthy. Current welfare policy explicitly encourages mothers to seek men with unreported illegal income. In this vein, the lack of safe, affordable child care in the United States contradictorily encourages mothers to stay at home and have more babies rather than seek careers in the legal economy, because anything they might earn goes to pay for private baby-sitters. (324–25)

Lucía develops a set of strategies to approach gangs and then to attain power. At first, she resorts to her sex appeal, and once Manny is no longer useful, she makes sure to show that she can be more violent and unscrupulous than her male peers. Having learned valuable lessons on gang life from Manny, when Lucía groups girls for her new clika, the Fire Girls, she replicates the "jumping in," whereby the initiate must fight all gang members at once. However, she knows when to deviate from the male norm. When it comes to female psychology, she observes that "a woman gang's different than a man's cause women need more love" (212). Therefore, these feminine needs and values show that rather than mere emulation, there is, along with characteristics associated with male gangs, some creativity in independent female gangbanging. Besides guaranteeing respect to her initiates, Lucía becomes a sort of mother figure for lonely girls who escape from dysfunctional families. She becomes progressively heartless and bloodthirsty, recruiting children from the local junior high and selling them narcotics. However, in the denouement of the novel, she feels guilty about her recruits' young ages.[19]

A more cerebral Cecilia also looks for empowerment, first in a frustrated motherhood, and then in a romantic relationship with Chucha, a young woman from the rival gang. At first, she has internalized traditional male chauvinistic indoctrination and believes that a woman can feel fulfilled as "a real person" (62) only through motherhood. After a miscarriage, she wonders whether it happened because her husband beat her every night or because it was God's punishment for obeying her brother's order to sell drugs at a junior high school. In the novel's last pages, Cecilia, now making an honest living cleaning homes, is proud of having avoided *la vida loca* (gang life) and quenches her thirst for revenge by mocking her bedridden brother. Although overwhelmed by guilt for past actions and homosexuality, she no longer feels the need to get pregnant to be accepted by others. However, Cecilia's new life (she has become religious and attends Mass with her mother) still bears the marks of self-alienation and cannot be considered a success story. In Monica Brown's words, "having conformed to the role expected of her by her mother and society in general, she has a 'stable' home of sorts. Cecilia does nothing but work as a cleaning lady, sleep, eat, watch telenovelas, and pray, but inside she secretly rejects the fire and brimstone God who tells her to pray and not complain" (103). By becoming a churchgoing domestic worker and her brother's caretaker, Cecilia has renounced the public sphere of the streets. Instead, she has returned to the invisibility of domestic life (the private space of the family's home and the limited public sphere of the church) as expected in a male-dominated society. Paradoxically, through devotion to their priest, elderly women replicate the homegirls' dependence on men: "Around here the viejas fall crazy in love with padres like they're don juans" (197), notices Cecilia. Therefore, Cecilia no longer benefits from the liberating achievements attained by pachucas, whose bodies, according to Fregoso, "refused to be contained by domesticity or limited by the prevailing orthodoxy of appropriate female behavior" ("Re-Imaging" 78).

Because of their newfound self-sufficiency, Lucía and Cecilia no longer have to keep quiet, serve food to their male counterparts at meetings, or satisfy them sexually at will. Since Lucía is now recognized as the de facto boss in the barrio, she has earned her longed-for agency. She is proud to "own" a certain number of streets and dares to drive a car, scream at men, and dress like a chola rather than wearing sexy clothing. Other homegirls have also gained independence from cholos, at the price of imitating their antisocial behavior. Nevertheless, the novel leaves an aftertaste of hopelessness and futility that offsets the sense of victory: not only is Lucía haunted by guilt, but she also has limited her chances at happiness by shutting out her feelings from the world. Undoubtedly, the two female protagonists have internalized the overpowering male chauvinism that has always ruled their lives. Lucía's lifelong struggle is a sort of claim to manhood: "I was made to be a man, strong and tall and looking out for number one. Got stuck with pussy, and ain't nothing you can do about it" (109), she complains. Rather than creating a path of liberation for women in the barrio, Lucía only wishes to be allowed to operate in the world of men so that she too can collect "a piece of the pie." Lucía thus confuses her liberation by replacing her former oppressors with taking advantage of helpless girls and women in the barrio. As Monica Brown puts it,

> for many girls and women, gang membership is less about a revolutionary break from oppressive patriarchal structures than it is about belonging, community, and a sense of personal agency. Female gangs seem more likely to mimic or mirror abusive practices by men than to surmount them. . . . Unfortunately, female gang members' roles are less revolutionary than reflective of dominant patriarchal ideology that sees violence, intimidation, and coercion as a means to power. (90)

Murray, therefore, draws social anxieties among Latinas in Los Angeles's barrios along gender rather than racial lines. If readers are interested in constructive female alternatives to male gangbanging, they are found in the activities carried out by Dolores, a character in her next novel, *What It Takes to Get to Vegas*. Although Murray brings to light a virtually unknown world to Chicano literature, she has been accused of resorting to worn-out stereotypes. David Hernández, for example, has criticized her exoticization and eroticization of this fictional Los Angeles barrio controlled by drug gangs (153). Likewise, Monica Brown has argued, "Unfortunately, by choosing to organize her narrative around men, Murray falls into some of the same stereotypical patterns of representation of gang girls—as hypersexualized femmes fatales or as desexualized 'masculine' lesbians" (93). And later, she adds, "Murray has fallen into the trap of linking aggression and lesbianism, and, even more reductively, of linking lesbianism with the desire to be a man" (106).

Moving on to a different medium, we find that well-intentioned films such as *Mi vida loca* (1993), written and directed by the Euro-American Allison Anders and portraying the lives of female gang members in Echo Park, have the downside of focusing exclusively on the most negative aspects of Chicana life, thereby reinforcing existing stereotypes, including dependency on welfare.[20] Yet, as Rosa-Linda Fregoso posits, this film differs from the stereotypes that abound in the "gangxploitation" subgenre: "To Anders's credit, she refuses the cinematic strategy of glamorizing violence, depicting instead gang violence off-screen. She does, however, show its tragic human consequences" ("Hanging Out" n.p.). In the film, a sisterhood of independent, young, single mothers has to overcome all sorts of difficulties in part because their boyfriends and husbands are either dead or imprisoned. When Sad Girl (Angel Avilés) becomes pregnant by her best friend's boyfriend, a drug dealer named Ernesto (Jacob Vargas), the two young women begin a feud that is interrupted only when Ernesto is shot by one of his customers. Subsequently, Angélica/Giggles (Marlo Marron), an older *veterana* who has just finished a four-year prison term for a crime committed by her boyfriend, convinces Sad Girl and Mousie (Seidy López) to reconcile, become independent, and stop fighting over men. In a scene, she shows her new stance by refusing to exchange gang hand signs with her friends. She later defends a homegirl by pointing out to the LAPD that they are photographing her illegally, given that she is a minor. Taking advantage of the homegirls' admiration for her having been in prison, she takes on a leadership role and organizes them so that their voice can be heard in the barrio. Together, they plan to convince homeboys that the proceeds from Ernesto's lowrider truck should go to Mousie and Sad Girl. The film also shows a consequence of gang life: with a criminal record and no formal education, Angélica will find it difficult to get the job she needs to become independent from men.[21]

Unfortunately, as Fregoso points out, while the film shows detailed attention to mannerisms and speech, it does not depict accurately the specificities of the daily experiences of inner-city youths. She is thereby criticizing teenage Chicanas' lack of interaction with female adults as well as the film's trivialization of gang warfare: "The battle between Chicano gangs is over the control of turf and scarce economic resources, not lowrider trucks" ("Hanging Out" n.p.). Indeed, gang warfare may be understood in terms of a capitalist economy that strives to eliminate competition and control profitable markets. For this reason, Murray's novel *Locas* and Anders's film *Mi vida loca* have been equally criticized for their limited scope in the representation of the girls' motivations to join or create gangs. Perhaps such criticism detracts from these works' importance of being, respectively, among the first novels and the first commercial film to deal with the underworld of female gangs.

The subjugation and the social anxieties of female gang members are even stronger in the previously discussed autobiography *Two Badges*, by Mona Ruiz and Geoff Boucher. In a scene reminiscent of the rape of a drugged teenager by Luis J. Rodríguez's friends in *Always Running*, Mona Ruiz recalls how gang members raped a girl drugged on heroin: "Later, I heard, some of the gang members ran a train on her that night, taking turns raping her while she was too groggy to fight back or even care. The girl was humiliated, and because the gangs are driven by a male code, the disgrace of that night's events was pushed on her alone" (58). As Ruiz explains, the girl was blamed for the attack because the boys' actions were "expected." Since girls, she continues, were the only ones blamed for out-of-wedlock pregnancies, they became outcasts in the barrio or disappeared. Ruiz also devotes numerous pages to describing the constant mental and physical abuse that she suffered at the hands of her boyfriend and, later, husband Frank Ruiz. Not only did he forbid her to attend college or find a job, but he also beat her when she was pregnant, often threatening to kill her. When she desperately sought help, male police officers and priests closed all doors for her. In all, Ruiz's autobiographical narrative has testimonial overtones in that she denounces the physical and psychological abuse constantly inflicted on young urban Latinas by fathers, husbands, gang members, and police officers.

Like *Locas*, Murray's second novel, *What It Takes to Get to Vegas* (1999), includes two female characters who choose different paths in life. The Zapata sisters, each in her own capacity, refuse to follow in their abused mother's footsteps and strive to recover the family's lost pride. On the one hand, we have Rita Zapata, who sees no way out of her precarious life in the barrio other than to marry a wealthy man.

Although her many affairs with aspiring boxers in the barrio ruined her reputation, Rita regains her hope once she meets Billy Navarro, a successful young boxer who is supposed to offer her the respect she has been longing for. However, her happiness will be short-lived. At first, the enigmatic title of the novel seems to suggest that if an East L.A. woman wants to enjoy the wealth of a prosperous man, she must also be willing to tolerate his infidelities and mistreatment. This anagnorisis takes its toll on Rita's mental health: her emotional distress is such that she ends up hating all men, and in an act of temporary madness, she tries to drown her baby nephew, while thinking about all the suffering that men have inflicted for three generations on the women of her family. In the end, she shoots Billy Navarro, after he had temporarily restored the long-awaited dignity to her life.

Her sister Dolores (like Cecilia in *Locas*) finds a more rational way to free herself from her social anxieties and a dependence on men. She rejects Rita's subservient demeanor and opts, instead, for political commitment at a local level. In spite of the novel's title, this alternative is obviously the one that Murray finds more appealing. After a thirteen-year-old boy dies of a drug overdose, Dolores gains awareness of the gravity of the situation in the barrio. Her fruitful activities are contrasted, in a seriocomic way, to those led by Pedro, a local activist obsessed with Anglo conspiracies: "After the Rodney King riots died down in '92, he just started getting more and more Malcolm X every day. He didn't just kick around Rabbit Street talking about grapes and telling folks to vote now. He'd become Mr. Back to Aztlán. He hated the Man, la migra, brown-baiters, race-traitors, English-Only, school busing" (65). Pedro creates the Xicano Warriors and tries to convince men in the barrio to join him in a march in Washington, D.C., to protest against the National Immigration Services. As expected, his efforts are unrewarded and he ends up being ridiculed by several characters. When Pedro argues that double consciousness is the reason for the widespread violence in the barrio (young Chicanos conform their identity to the way they are perceived by others), Dolores views his explanation as mere male chauvinism: "You call a man the devil long enough and he'll start living up to that name, girl!" . . . "Hoosh! That's a bunch of macho baloney, Pedro" (66).

Instead of identifying enemies like Pedro, Dolores focuses on problems within the Chicano community, including gang warfare. Consequently, she secures an increase in police activity in East Los Angeles. Her commitment, it must be noted, may be considered unique in this literary and filmic cycle. Determined to combat brown-on-brown violence, Dolores confronts her husband (an action that will cause his death) by placing "Wanted" signs with his brother's picture on it, after the latter kills two neighbors. She also creates the Latina League and develops a neighborhood watch, an antigang hotline, daycare pools, project jobs, and a rape crisis center at her immigrant clinic. Eventually, she gets the attention of the city council and the local press, and when a reporter asks her whether she is interested in running for office, she considers that possibility. Therefore, whereas her sister Rita thinks about suicide and telephones Billy obsessively, Dolores is heading a full-fledged campaign for Chicana emancipation:

> She hated the gangs more than ever and in the last couple weeks had been saying she didn't just blame them for violence and drugs but also for all the lost jobs. She said they were bad for the Chicano reputation in the national media, or something like that, and it was because of gangs that brown men couldn't get good work these days. She also said that Latinas should get ourselves self-reliance because we'd all been taught from day one to depend on a man for everything but those days were over and we needed to get in touch with our feminisms and our brown female power. (260–61)

As we have seen, the narratives and films about pachucas and Latina gang members problematize, from a feminist perspective, the masculinism of their male counterparts, and the image of the male suboppressor who envisions Latino liberation at the expense of women.[22] Some also depict female characters as agents of oppositional practices and propose a new consciousness that leaves room for the self-affirmation and agency of Latinas beyond the traditional domestic space and the omnipresent focus on the girls' sexual promiscuity. Within the more general counterdiscourse of resistance against patriarchy, female gangbanging often represents a flawed version of this new subjectivity, which confuses the desire for emancipation from male hegemony with reproducing the same parameters of oppression. These texts also highlight the victimizing role of gang rape, domestic violence, and even motherhood for disenfranchised Latina gang members. From a different perspective, literature and films about gangs present the economic function of this sad occurrence as a by-product of capitalist dynamics in the control of drug markets. In a sui generis version of mainstream society's "pursuit of happiness," male and female gang members try to escape their marginal position in economic and sociopolitical terms. In spite of all the flaws pointed out by critics, films such as *Mi vida loca* and texts such as *Always Running, Two Badges, Maravilla,* and *Locas* echo the reality of Latina gangbanging, which had hitherto been overlooked in gang literature and films. Latina gang involvement, as we have seen, may reach many different levels of complexity, from complete subjugation to positions of leadership. Because of this cultural production, it is no longer "present but invisible" or simply reduced to stereotypical images that reflect the media's fascination for the hyperviolent girl of minority groups (Chesney-Lind and Hagedorn 3). As Meda Chesney-Lind and John M. Hagedorn propose, "It is vital that we stop constructing images of girls' participation in gangs that endlessly compare them to boys and their gangs, or worse, get caught up in notions that girls, and their groups, are simply appendages or mirror images of boys' gangs" (3).

"De-Barrioization" through Transnational Activism

> "Post-nationalism" may have acquired its current
> purchase among border literati precisely because of the
> massive reassertion, over the last generation, of the physical
> and cultural continuity of Mexico in the U.S. Southwest.
> —Mike Davis, *Magical Urbanism*

Postnationalism is a process of human exchange that supersedes the traditional centrality of the nation-state, its borders, and its national identities. In this subchapter, however, I use the term *postnationalist* not in reference to the nation-state (the United States), but rather to the nationalism of the Chicano Movement of the 1960s. The type of postnationalism to which I am referring does not pose a significant threat to the nation-state.[23] In turn, transnationalism refers to the new patterns of migration that are transforming the culture of diasporas. Workers would emigrate to other countries to settle. Because of new advances in global transportation, however, they are now able to return to their native countries more often, and as a result, settlements have ceased to be entirely permanent (in the case of the Chinese diaspora, this type of migration began as early as the nineteenth century).[24] In other words, movements of people have become more fluid, and old emigrants have now turned into migrants. Where once there were points of departure and arrival, today's workers are able to migrate to several places or to move back and forth between countries, thus creating strong transnational ties (at times to various "home" countries). In economic, cultural, and ideological terms, the transnational relations along the international border between the United States and Mexico have been studied in depth in Gloria Anzaldúa's seminal study *Borderlands/La Frontera* (1999), a cornerstone of border studies. However, for many decades these exchanges have gone well beyond the border area. The Mexican community, because of its country's proximity to the United States, has been exercising this back-and-forth migration for decades. Today, exchanges between people of Mexican descent at both sides of the border are further nuanced by global trade as well as by other Latino and non-Latino migrations that are accelerating the creation of additional postnationalist predispositions and identities. Regarding the topics pertinent to this chapter, transnational activities and postnationalist attitudes have transformed the regional approach that first characterized the Chicano Movement.[25]

Transnational activism in Los Angeles began with the *crónicas* (short narratives written in Spanish-language newspapers).[26] From Los Angeles, Francisco P. Ramírez and Ricardo Flores Magón verbally fought for the emancipation of Mexican people on both sides of the border. According to Richard Griswold del Castillo, *Regeneración,* the Los Angeles newspaper in which many of Ricardo Flores Magón's crónicas were published, "downplayed Mexican nationalism and emphasized multi-national, multi-ethnic working class solidarity in a struggle against liberalism and capitalism [and] advocated violent revolt, anarchy and the total destruction of the existing order" ("Mexican" 42). Their efforts are testimony to the close political ties between Mexicans and Mexican Americans since early in the twentieth century. As shown in the next subchapter, looking beyond nationalism and national borders to resolve U.S. Latino/Latina problems has endured.

The New Mestiza's Activism Looks beyond National Boundaries

In her writing, Graciela Limón abandons nationalist discourses while embracing transnational activism and postnationalist dispositions. Her novel *Erased Faces* (2001) establishes connections between Chicanismo and Zapatismo to envision an ideal Chicano community in Los Angeles.[27] The plot's theoretical premises can be found in the writings of several

Chicana theorists. Chela Sandoval, for example, proposes to establish an alliance with decolonizing movements of men and women committed to emancipation and equality: "It is a location wherein the praxis of U.S. third world feminism links with the aims of white feminism, studies of race, ethnicity, and marginality, and with postmodern theories of culture as they crosscut and join together in new relationships through a shared comprehension of an emerging theory and method of oppositional consciousness" (17). Flexibility and mobility are two key words in this new tactical subjectivity that denies ideology as the final answer. More specifically, U.S. Third World feminists identify the benefits of establishing alliances with women of color, that is, the "new mestizas, 'Woman Warriors' who live and are gendered 'between and among' the lines, 'Sister Outsiders' who inhabit a new psychic terrain which Anzaldúa calls 'the Borderlands,' 'la nueva Frontera'" (Sandoval 5). In this subchapter, I shall study how Limón establishes a dialogue between Chicanismo and Zapatismo to offer Zapatista women fighters as behavioral models to Chicanas in Los Angeles and, by extension, to all U.S. Latinas. This text exemplifies the lasting influence that Zapatismo had on Chicana leadership and on Chicana cultural production. Among the many potential aspects of this impact, Limón's novel mainly exposes two: the evolution from a male-modeled to a feminist and egalitarian form of leadership, and the transition from nationalistic to transnational, postnational, and pluralist views.

Coinciding with the signing of the North American Free Trade Agreement (NAFTA) on January 1, 1994, the Zapatista National Liberation Army (Ejército Zapatista de Liberación Nacional; EZLN) began an uprising in the southern Mexican state of Chiapas that would change the image of revolution and revolutionaries in Latin America:

> Subcomandante Marcos and his ski-masked indigenous followers took over San Cristóbal de las Casas and issued their "Declaration of the Lacandón Jungle," a manifesto declaring opposition to the Mexican state, its land policies, and NAFTA. The rebel action was timed to coincide with the enactment of NAFTA and attract the attention of the international press to the plight of the Maya peoples of Chiapas, a place where cattle ranchers and coffee producers have traditionally pushed Indian peasants off their lands. (Raat 201)[28]

Soon this local movement had repercussions and became the prototype for other groups seeking social justice and autonomy. North of the border, this historic event would have lasting influence, as seen in its cultural production and in its activists' strategies.[29]

In recent years, Chicana activists and artists from the Los Angeles area have taken part in several meetings with Zapatista rebels.[30] Although Zapatistas have expressed their enthusiasm for sharing and learning from Chicano cultural workers, when these offered their "support," they received, as Flores explains, an unexpected answer:

> When people from different parts of the world visit with the Zapatista, they (from a very Western perspective) frequently ask (at worst from a point of view of pity and superiority), what can we do to help you? How can we support you? The Zapatista answer is commonly, you can help by helping yourself, by struggling from your own foxhole: "We hear there are serious problems with your youth, gang warfare, drugs, with discrimination of minorities, particularly Indians and blacks, is that true? Is that true?" They are saying that we're going to walk together on this one. (McLaren 9)

In many ways, the publication of Limón's *Erased Faces* can be considered a landmark in the literary representation of the increasing impact of Zapatismo on the Chicano Movement. The romance between two fictional characters, Adriana Mora, a Chicana from East Los Angeles, and Juana Galván, a Tzeltzal woman, in the Lacandón jungle one year before the 1994 Zapatista uprising, symbolizes the implicit author's goal of internationalizing the predicament of the Chicano community.[31] Her use of English, Spanish, and indigenous languages in the novel is part of the same strategy. Although Juana's subsequent assassination eliminates the possibility of a long-term relationship between the two women, the foundation for a fruitful dialogue between the Zapatista movement and the Chicano community has been symbolically laid through feminist dialogues. Therefore, by expanding her outlook from the traditional nationalist position to an internationalist and pluralist view of the conflict, Limón puts Chicanismo in perspective with other social justice movements.[32] In this sense, she seems to agree with Néstor García Canclini's position:

> to overestimate one's own culture—as nationalistic, ethnic, and class movements involved in liberation struggles do—does not always constitute prejudice or a mistake to be regretted; it is in several cases a necessary stage of rejection of the dominant culture and an affirmation

of their own. The irrational elements that are part of these processes, the chauvinistic temptation, can be controlled in two ways: through self-criticism from within their own culture and through solidaristic interaction with other subordinate groups or nations. (9)

Through mirroring narrative strategies, Limón establishes parallels between racist attitudes in Los Angeles (Adriana is not fully accepted in the barrio because of her father's African descent) and the ancestral ethnic antagonism between indigenous people and mestizos or *criollos* in Chiapas. Transnational solidarity, consequently, is presented as a way to leave this interethnic fighting behind. Along with issues of racialization, justice, and sociopolitical struggle, several chapters of *Erased Faces* focus on the sphere of gender and sexuality. Domestic violence, as suffered by Juana Galván, is central to the plot. At first, indigenous men shift their aggression toward their employers to their wives, suppressing them through constant pregnancies and battery. As a result, in contrast to other texts by or about the Maya like *I, Rigoberta Menchú* (*Me llamo Rigoberta Menchú y así me nació la conciencia,* 1983), where marriage is not criticized, here the institution is depicted as a tool for the subjugation of women.[33] As discussed, Limón develops the topics of gender oppression and homophobia through the description of a lesbian love affair between the protagonist and Juana Galván, which obviously challenges normative heterosexuality. The novel claims pluralism for the Chicano Movement, not only through the recognition of feminist discourse and diverse ethnocultural identities, but also through the literary representation of alternative sexual identities. The author resorts to a contrapuntal technique to intertwine the account of this "forbidden relationship" with the narration of the struggle for freedom and survival of Orlando Flores, the Lacandón indigenous character whose real name is Quintín Osuna. Ultimately, Orlando's affliction is a synecdoche of the suffering of all indigenous people in the Americas. Therefore, the Zapatista uprising draws three decolonial voices—Adriana, the mulatto Chicana from Los Angeles, and two indigenous characters, Juana and Orlando.

Set against the historical background of the Spanish conquest of the Americas, these fictional characters interact with real-life Zapatistas (Subcomandante Insurgente Marcos, Comandanta Insurgente Ramona) along with earlier historical characters (Hernán Cortés, the Spanish conquistador; Bartolomé de las Casas, the Spanish Dominican

Figure 17 Sculpture of Aztec emperor Cuauhtémoc by Lincoln Park. (Photo by Paige Craig)

priest who defended indigenous peoples in the Americas; Cuauhtémoc, Aztec ruler from 1520 to 1521 [see fig. 17]; and Motolinía, a Franciscan missionary who wrote two historical accounts about the Aztecs).[34] From the first page of the novel, where we read about Adriana's nightmare, the Mexican army and the Spanish conquistadores are allegorically blurred into one group. Through this narrative device, the novel "others" both colonizers: sixteenth-century colonial power and contemporary Mexican mestizos. Chan K'in, the mystical Lacandón character, also provides an indirect explanation for this narrative technique: "The people of this forest know that each one of us has lived not only once, but in other times. What is happening to us now is a repetition of what happened to us then" (21). Hence, perhaps in keeping with the Chicano Movement's fetishization of Aztec heritage, Adriana Mora learns that she is the reincarnation of the heroic Mexica woman Hutizitzilín.[35] Through these magical reincarnations and the repetition of colonial structures, these episodes emphasize the cyclical nature of history: the current situation of the Maya of Chiapas is very similar to their circumstances five centuries before; the Mexican army is the reincarnation of the Spanish conquistadores. Today's situation for the natives, therefore, is a continuation of the abuses that Fray Bartolomé de las Casas denounced before the Spanish crown.

Likewise, although it opposes violence, the Catholic Church depicted in the novel, represented by the bishop, shows a sympathetic stance toward the indigenous people and to the EZLN.[36] Like the actual church in Chiapas, it seems to adhere closely to the tenets of liberation theology. In the end, the faces that had been hidden through oppression are now hidden by the owners' choice with ski masks identical to the one that Mayor Insurgente Maribel wears on the cover of the Arte Público Press edition. Orlando Flores unravels the mysterious title of the novel, "masking our faces in order to give a face to our people" (94). Limón also explains that the masks that Zapatistas wear symbolize the renouncement of their individual identity "in the desire to bring identity to one people" ("Zapatistas" n.p.).[37]

A well-intentioned Adriana has arrived in Chiapas with the subconsciously patronizing goal of supporting the indigenous uprising by recording the daily lives of Lacandón women, thus providing them with a voice. In spite of her initial charity-oriented mentality, in the end, the young freelance photojournalist ends up benefiting the most from the intercultural exchange. She is pleasantly surprised to find that Chiapaneco women are not only active participants in the *guerra contra el olvido* (war against oblivion), but that they have also taken leadership roles. The political scientist Kathleen Bruhn contends, however, that a leading role for women was not in the original EZLN plans, but "it got there through the back door" n.p.). When recruiters went to the villages, men were away working as day laborers; therefore, the only ones that could be addressed were their wives. Once recruited, these women began to demand the right to speak and be respected, the right to study, to be drivers, etc. (see the Zapatista Women's Revolutionary Law in note 169). Women's position in the EZLN evolved from necessity and became revolutionary in the indigenous community (Bruhn n.p.). The decision to join the Zapatistas becomes an empowering experience for Juana and the other women who followed in her footsteps, and who make up half of the insurgent force: "She frequently thought of the many village women she had met during the past months, of their reticence and passivity, and she wondered how it was that women of the force had transformed themselves" (218). With Adriana's return to Los Angeles in 1998 after her four-year stay in Chiapas, the reader is implicitly invited to envision how she will import and implement, in her own community, the Zapatistas' utopian dreams, participatory democratic structures, and leadership organization, just as Roberto Flores (Limón's friend and colleague) is trying to do in real life.

The novel introduces ethnic and class conflict with the trials of the third protagonist, Orlando Flores. Along with a brief appearance by Subcomandante Marcos, he is the refreshing exception among numerous depraved male characters, including El Brujo, Cruz Ochoa, Palomón Cisneros, Absolón, and Rufino Mayorga. Some indigenous men become tarnished in the novel by becoming suboppressors once they join the army. Likewise, some passages denote a deliberately soft criticism of certain Zapatistas' motivations. In one, for example, the omniscient narrator reveals that Orlando Flores is moved by personal revenge: "Memories of Don Absolón, of his son Rufino, of El Brujo, and even of his friend Aquiles, filled him with an insatiable desire for vengeance, making him forget his commitment to justice, to freedom—all the ideals that had led him to join the insurgents" (183–84). Orlando eventually experiences moral growth and regrets having killed his former friend Rufino Mayorga, by burying him in the mud, as revenge for the assassination of his parents.[38] Orlando realizes that his parents' death has not been vindicated, and his vengeance has lowered him to the level of his former master. Therefore, the involvement of Adriana, Juana, and Orlando (Quintín Osuna) in the political struggle is guided by inner conflicts and identity crises, rather than by a conscious political commitment. Kathleen Bruhn points to this driving force as one of the novel's successes: while Marcos, as the Zapatista spokesman, presents their struggle to the world as one against neoliberalism and NAFTA, Limón brings these relations of dependence and exploitation to a regional level and allows her characters to express their internal motivations ("Zapatistas" n.p.).

As to the feminist perspective prevalent in *Erased Faces*, the title of chapter 11, "Why Don't You Come and See?" is an invitation to learn from the EZLN's organizational strategies. Limón confessed to me that the Chicano Movement, during its first years, was deeply male chauvinistic. Most Chicanas, she recalls, rejected feminism as a "gabacha thing" and opted for "supporting their men." After visiting Chiapas, Limón had to overcome her own prejudice, realizing how much more egalitarian was the

relationship between male and female Zapatistas. Thanks to the eman-
cipating impulse of the Zapatista uprising, she mentioned, indigenous
women had become very organized and even aggressive when needed. In
this chapter, Adriana Mora arrives at the Zapatista camp in the mountains and immediately notices that women are active participants in the
insurgents' meetings. Equally surprising to her is the dialogical interaction between the *comandancia* and rebel soldiers: decisions are made
through broad consultation and consensus, without stifling discussion.
Thus, when Orlando announces the next step in the struggle, various
men openly express their contrasting views: "These words unleashed a
torrent of remarks and questions that pelted Orlando from different
directions. Juana had never witnessed such outspoken men. Her experience had taught her that silence was usually her people's response. She
saw, however, that Orlando answered every inquiry and comment looking each speaker in the eye" (90). As in the scene where a Zapatista rebel
confronts Orlando's decision to recruit women, the revolutionary is not
always portrayed as a flawless and angelical being. Showing the results
of the consciousness raising initiated in the Lacandón jungle, when the
male-chauvinist insurgent vehemently opposes the idea, the Zapatista
women, who literally embody Chela Sandoval's "Woman Warriors,"
become enraged.

In light of these passages, it is clear that the ideas of unity-in-diversity
and feminism-in-nationalism are crucial to Limón's novel. It implicitly
encourages adoption of Zapatista third-space feminism by the Chicano
community in Los Angeles as well as in the rest of the nation. Limón's
"decolonial imaginary" challenges fixed boundaries by including gender
and sexual orientation as important critical categories and sources of signification, along with class, race, and culture. Within this context, in the
last chapter, a completely transformed Adriana lends her voice, though
an interior monologue, to the women of Chiapas and, in particular, to
her deceased lover, Juana, the victim of a hate crime: "She was erased
because she had been strong, because she had been a leader, because she
was *una india*, but most of all because she had committed the forbidden
act: She had been in love with another woman" (253–54).[39]

In *Erased Faces*, Zapatista indigenous women, the same "othered"
women who always were invisible to traditional historiography, challenge
their inferior status by using the revolution to their advantage and by
exposing chauvinism in male revolutionaries. They put the Zapatista revolution to the test by addressing gender issues and introducing women's

sexuality in their discourse, thus creating a third space of separation that Emma Pérez has called "sameness-in-difference." With its testimonial traits and its neo-indigenist approach, the novel subtly presents the feminism-in-nationalism construction followed by the fictional Zapatistas as a "social struggle" prototype that should be copied by Chicanas and Chicanos. In the Zapatista movement appearing in this text, most men and women advocate women's rights and gender equality. Contrary to the assumption that lesbianism is rejected among Mesoamerican indigenous societies, the novel's male characters are either indifferent to or tolerant of lesbian relationships such as Juana's. This recognition of sexual-preference diversity in a racialized group like the indigenous Zapatistas of southern Mexico is celebrated in *Erased Faces* as a prototype for another racialized group in the United States, the Chicano community, despite obvious differences in their circumstances.

Social changes resulting from armed struggle have facilitated indigenous women's access to an agency that they lacked for centuries. In the novel, they have the capacity to initiate action and resistance freely and autonomously. Their oppositional consciousness disrupts the traditional association of their identity with passivity and abnegation. They challenge power relations and protect women's rights by positioning themselves at the center of the uprising and questioning their male peers' discourse when needed. Limón is aware that the social construction of "race" in the southern states of Mexico has important connections with that of Los Angeles: with southern Mexico's Mayas as well as with Los Angeles's Chicanos, ethnicity (and often indigeneity) has been a reason, if not the basis, for their disenfranchisement. The author expands the border imaginary by proposing the resistance of these "othered" and ethnicized women from Chiapas as a model for Chicanas, another Mexican-origin group. Anna Sampaio likewise has studied the connections between both ethnic groups:

> Both populations have comparable socioeconomic and political positions relative to their national populations. That is, on key indicators . . . both have consistently been ranked in the lowest percentile. [Both] are linked to forms of colonialism . . . [Both] have been effectively pushed outside the realm of traditional government institutions and public policy making and positioned largely as second-class citizens. . . . While hundreds of Chicana/os and Latina/os from the United States have gone to Chiapas to witness the rebellion, a

better indicator of this affinity has been the adoption of cultural symbols, the creation of "sister communities" and support organizations
in the United States. (49)

By dedicating the novel to the memory of those who perished in the
massacre of Acteal in 1997, Limón speaks from a situated perspective.
In the epilogue, she presents her book as an expression of support for
Zapatismo and an earnest denunciation of the oppression of indigenous
people in southern Mexico. Echoing Gloria Anzaldúa's groundbreaking
premises in *Borderlands/La Frontera*, *Erased Faces* reclaims gender and
sexuality (in addition to class and race/ethnicity/culture) as an additional
organizing principle in Chicana/o literary and cultural studies. Moreover, Limón's novel mirrors Chela Sandoval's endorsement of a new
epistemology based on the multiple identities and worlds represented
in mestiza consciousness. The gynocentric perspective of *Erased Faces*
therefore moves to a transnational context by dialogically interweaving
the worlds of Chicanismo and Zapatismo.

Questioning the Limits of the Mexican and Chicano Imagined Communities

Together with this transnational perspective, it is important to note that,
as mentioned, Adriana Mora, the Chicana protagonist in *Erased Faces,* is
a mulatta. As Limón admitted to me, she has been criticized for considering this character a Chicana, although she has African blood. Yet, considering herself a Chicana, Limón is of African (she has cousins in Jalisco
with African phenotype) and Sephardic descent (from her family line
in Sonora).[40] This narrative strategy, coinciding with Gloria Anzaldúa's
description of a new mestiza consciousness characterized by its flexibility, plurality, and hybridity, exposes the traditional representations of
both Mexican and Chicana/o cultures as homogeneous (or only Spanish
and indigenous) as mere nationalist fabrications or "imagined communities." In these times of globalization, Limón chooses a postnationalist, comparative, and interethnic perspective for her contribution to the
collective agenda of denouncing patriarchal exclusionary practices and
restoring agency for (and by) today's Chicanas. Her novel emblematizes
the new impetus to move beyond the nationalistic approach to the Chicano community. Along the way, she creates, by mixing chapters set in
Los Angeles with others in Chiapas, a literary version of the Los Angeles

Chicana community that she would like to see. Rather than describing reality, *Erased Faces* explores and maps a space of potentiality.

This widening of perspectives in Limón's narrative is also reflected in her recreation of the arrival of Central Americans, the new Latinos, to Los Angeles.[41] As does Héctor Tobar in *The Tattooed Soldier* (1998), Limón, in *In Search of Bernabé* (1993), conceives of Los Angeles as a key component in a set of global circumstances and places. The author confessed to me that her worldview has radically evolved throughout the years. While in the 1970s she was almost a zealot of the Chicano Movement, which went so far as to exclude people who considered themselves Mexican Americans rather than Chicanos, the movement's accepted term, she now sees her extremism as parochial. Admittedly, her volunteer work with Central American refugees in 1980s Los Angeles, along with a trip to El Salvador in 1990, when she was part of a delegation assigned to investigate the assassination of several Jesuit priests, opened her eyes to a different reality. In her view, the relatively new presence of Central Americans in the metropolis has widened the initial objectives and changed the concept of Chicanismo by including global circumstances.

As the title, *In Search of Bernabé,* shows, the protagonist, Luz Delcano, spends many years looking for her son, after his disappearance from San Salvador in the midst of the chaos that followed the burial of Archbishop Óscar Arnulfo Romero in 1980. The transnational nature of the plot is self-evident in the character's travels from El Salvador, through Guatemala and Mexico City, to Los Angeles, and back to El Salvador. The novel, inspired by the author's trip to El Salvador, describes the metropolis through the eyes of frightened and powerless immigrants who are trying to escape punishment or death, while looking for missing family members in the north:

> Like children, Luz and Arturo looked around, craning their necks, curiously peering through the windows and seeing that people waited for their turn to step onto the street. Luz thought it was silly the way those people moved in groups. No one ran out onto the street, leaping, jumping, dodging cars as happened in Mexico City and back home. Right away, she missed the vendors peddling wares, and the stands with food and drink. (77)

In contrast with other works, Los Angeles is here represented differently because of the civility of certain citizens, who are modeled after real people. The protagonist spends time in a Hollywood church that serves as sanctuary for undocumented immigrants. She moves to a small apartment in 1989, only to see her friend Arturo killed by a Salvadoran death squad that breaks into their house. After the crime is officially labeled "gang-related," Luz is deported to El Salvador, leaving only this statement for the city: "I'll never return to this place of death" (87). Therefore, always within the context of a global scenario, Los Angeles becomes a refuge for displaced and fleeing people as well as a stage for political assassination. By including Salvadoran characters, Limón again extends the world of migration and resistance beyond the limits of the Chicano and Mexican experiences. And, coinciding with the story in *The Tattooed Soldier,* not only oppressed immigrants, but the suboppressors belonging to death squads also move to Los Angeles in *In Search of Bernabé.*

On the same note, Limón's *The Day of the Moon* (1999) includes other types of Mexicans living in Los Angeles, not so much the descendants of pre-Columbian groups who are now fleeing exploitation, but oppressors who moved north with their pockets full of money. Characters like don Flavio Betancourt, who typifies racism and classism among Mexicans, represent the other side of the coin, that of wealthy Mexican immigrants. As is common in postcolonial societies, he is proud of sharing the phenotype of the colonizers. Having inherited his father's fair complexion, he chooses to forget the "embarrassment" of his mother's indigenous roots. His daughter Isidora, on the other hand, does not share his racist views and falls in love with an indigenous man. Although don Flavio loves her, he is unable to overcome his racial prejudice and never consents to their relationship. The novel also includes characters of Mexican descent who were born in the American Southwest before or after the Mexican-American War and who do not consider themselves *indios.* On the contrary, they view themselves as the Native Americans' "Other"; they are, in fact, their masters and exploiters, or the descendants of the latter.

This plot challenges the Chicano Movement's strategic identification with an often-mythicized Aztec past. Rafael Pérez-Torres has questioned the romanticization of the Indian by the nationalist discourses of the 1960s through the 1980s. Feminist Chicana critic Gloria Anzaldúa also observes: "Many of the *mestizos* who, beginning in the seventeenth century, move north into what would become New Mexico, California, Texas, and other states were actively involved in genocidal campaigns against Native populations. The unproblematic claim by Chicanos to indigenous ancestry thus helps erase a troubling part of the Chicano past in relation to Native peoples" (14). In the end, however, racism vanishes in the novel when one of the last members of the Betancourt family, a mestiza youngster named Alondra who mixes the Spanish and English languages to her family's dismay, returns to the land of her ancestors and decides to find her roots among the Tarahumara (Rarámuri) Indians in the state of Chihuahua.

We find a different type of postnationalist deconstruction of the imagined Chicano community in Danny Santiago's *Famous All Over Town*, where the protagonist and several members of his family equate indigeneity with backwardness and ignorance, and call each other "Indian" when they perceive an action as unintelligent or violent. Chicano characters' awareness of how they are perceived by mainstream society in the United States changes their perception of Mexican ethnicity south of the border. Although early in the novel Rudy's father, Rodolfo, calls his wife *india* as a term of endearment, during the family's trip to Mexico, this term acquires a different connotation: Rudy, his sister Lena, and their father deride the indigenous origins of the mother's side of the family and those of most Mexicans. The professed ethnic and nationalistic pride that they exhibit in Los Angeles turns into internalized racial anxiety and self-loathing once they visit Mexico. Rodolfo Medina, in particular, drops his mask when he points out his in-laws' dark skin as an indelible sign of moral inferiority. Similarly, he and Rudy find a source of pride in commodity fetishism: they feel superior to their destitute Mexican relatives, who own no appliances, telephones, or automobiles. Therefore, an achievement of *Famous All Over Town* is the paradoxical contrast between their deceptive pride of being Mexican in Shamrock Street and the mental dislocation made apparent by their trip to Mexico. As Laura Browder points out, Danny Santiago approaches the characters' serious identity crises from a humoristic perspective: "much of the comedy of this very funny novel is predicated on the trouble people get themselves into when they invest too many of their assumptions on what it means for others, or for themselves, to belong to a particular racial or ethnic group" (*Slippery* 238).

Rudy's poor impression of Mexican nationals stems from his contacts with undocumented workers and with men who took part in the Bracero Program.[42] He resents, above all, that they make passes at Mexican American women although they have wives back in Mexico. In one scene, after certain migrant workers react submissively to Rudy's provocation, he states condescendingly: "The TJ's [men from Tijuana] looked at each other, then decided to laugh too. Not having papers does

wonders for people's disposition" (94). The derogatory remarks continue as he mocks their clothing: "they were exactly what some wetback
would buy in hopes to look native-born American" (99). In all, although
Rudy's principal, Mr. Pilger, had hoped that knowing his family's roots
in Mexico would be a source of empowerment for the boy, the latter
cannot identify with a place that he deems unattractive and so backward
that a girl his age, one of his distant cousins, had her body sold by her
destitute parents to the "President" of the town and his friends. In this
context, when Rudy, having internalized stereotypical images of Mexico,
sees a big cactus in the Mexican desert, he grumbles: "All it needed for a
picture was a burro and some clown with a big hat over his eyes. If this
was my father's famous Mexico, you could give me the U.S. any time"
(214). At this point in the novel, before his neighborhood is obliterated,
Rudy's true source of pride is the city of Los Angeles and its "American
Way of Life."

Likewise, Rudy's father's disenchantment with his beloved (and idealized) Mexico increases gradually during the trip. Back in Shamrock,
Rodolfo Medina was a member of the Aztecs' Club and had always taken
pride in distancing himself from mainstream American culture. While
Rodolfo daydreams about inheriting his mother-in-law's lands and
moving back to Mexico, he tells his son Rudy that it is the country of his
ancestors and, therefore, his real *patria* (fatherland). He also dismisses
his wife's concerns about the corruption of Mexican customs officers
and tries to appease her by reminding her that they are "brothers." Soon
thereafter, however, he is appalled to see that while customs officers treat
blond Euro-American tourists in a friendly manner, they falsely accuse
him of planning to sell the clothes found in their trunk. Furthermore,
right after he imagines that the boy washing his car must have led a
heroic life of work and sacrifice, the latter steals the gun he had hidden
inside the car. As his wife must bribe the inspector with her gold ear-
rings, Rodolfo sees his long-standing patriotism fade away: "And after
that, on our long road south, my father never saluted the Mexican flag
again, and he talked more English than I ever heard him speak in L.A.,
and louder too" (215). It is suggested that, following the trip, Rodolfo
becomes progressively de-ethnified.

The novel's last pages stress the author's skepticism regarding the
Chicano Movement's traditional tactics. Once all has been lost and
Shamrock Street has been razed as a result of an "urban renewal" proj-
ect promoted by the Southern Pacific Railroad and the city authorities,

Rudy realizes that he needs to still believe in something. Moments later, he addresses his "Chicano Power" bumper sticker by telling it to shut up; slogans have been proven useless. He also conveys the story's message by indirectly asking for the reader's empathy: "How would you feel, man, if they came onto your street and tore it down. What would you do?" (276). It is implied that, despite his disappointment and occasional suicidal thoughts throughout the text, he has not given up his determination to keep the street's memory alive, because it is the only means he has to prevent history from repeating itself. Finally, according to Browder, the fact that Danny Santiago happened to be a Euro-American writer "passing" as a Chicano also poses questions about issues of cultural nationalism: "*Famous All Over Town* is a novel that critiques the notion of ethnic essentialism and violates audience expectations of ethnic autobiography. It presents the ability to cross ethnic boundaries not only as possible but as necessary to successful survival in America" (*Slippery* 236).

These postnationalist views continue in *The Burning Plain* (1997), the sixth novel in the Henry Ríos series by the Mexican American author Michael Nava (1954–).[43] The protagonist of this novel, Henry Ríos, is an openly gay Chicano detective, criminal-defense lawyer, and gay activist who is trying to survive in Hollywood, a cradle of homophobia, as embodied in the sadistic killer whose murders are investigated by Ríos and who turns out to be a Hollywood filmmaker.[44] Tellingly, the same old barrio of East Los Angeles that is at the heart of so many narratives by Chicana and Latino authors is entirely dismissed by some of Nava's characters. Instead, West Hollywood (the equivalent of San Francisco's Castro neighborhood or Manhattan's Greenwich Village) takes a prominent presence and becomes a synecdoche for the entire metropolis.[45] This choice suggests that the text is not as concerned with the marginalization of Chicanos as an ethnic minority as it is with discrimination on account of sexual orientation. In this sense, Ralph E. Rodríguez, in his study of the Henry Ríos series, maintains that throughout these novels the protagonist challenges the heteronormativity and other controlling structures that have dominated the Chicana/o imaginary: "Henry must construct his identities through the discourses of family, race, sexuality, and home. Each of these shaping forces poses substantial challenges to this gay, post-nationalist, Chicano subject" (34).

Like John Rechy's novels, Nava's noir fiction has been studied mainly from the perspective of gay and lesbian studies.[46] Yet whereas Rechy concentrates for the most part on the marginal underworld of male hustlers, Nava provides a wider array of gay characters. Among other successful Latinos in the novel, we have Alyssia Morán, a Latina publisher; John Fuentes, a Latino judge; and Inez Montoya, a Chicana lawyer and politician who runs for mayor (in *Rag and Bone*, she has bigger political ambitions: she has become the first Latina to hold statewide office, and she will run for the U.S. Senate).[47] This inclusion of Chicano characters who are professionals again contributes to the de-barrioization process of Chicano literature. Likewise, the promiscuity of many of Rechy's characters (which some critics have associated with a feeling of guilt about their sexual tendencies) contrasts with Ríos's behavior—he usually seeks love relations rather than casual sex. Ultimately, the inquiries of this tragic figure plagued by loneliness, an alcoholic past, a "workaholic" present, and the memories of a lover lost to AIDS are an offshoot of his soul-searching. In George Klawitter's words, "What undoubtedly endears Ríos to many readers is his believable human frailty" (295).[48]

Rather than exposing the victimization of Chicanos and gays (or their intersection, which Ríos represents), Nava is more interested in recreating how they overcome the restraints posed by a heterosexual and Euro-American mainstream society. Furthermore, most of his Chicano and/or gay characters, despite the persistent discrimination and aggression they suffer, cannot be considered marginal or subaltern, since their professions provide them with agency or social power within U.S. society. In spite of his talent, Ríos has never attained the influence, prestige, and economic rewards that his friend the Chicana politician Inez Montoya thinks he deserves, not because of racism or homophobia, but because of his own personal choices and sense of ethics. As we see in the seventh and last novel of the Henry Ríos series, *Rag and Bone* (2001), thanks to affirmative action and Montoya's support, Ríos becomes a judge. Therefore, in contrast with many other "invisible" Chicano characters in the works examined here, Ríos "belongs" within the American national project and nation space. His is one of the many ways of "being Chicano" in Los Angeles, thus expanding the meaning of *Latinidad* in Latino Los Angeles's writing, and portraying it as an open category rather than as a monolithic and homogeneous identity. The "Chicano space" of assimilated second-generation Mexican Americans in his novels consequently is no longer the barrio, but the entire metropolis and country. As in Rechy's *Bodies and Souls*, in *The Burning Plain* no internal borders exist for Chicanas and Latinos: they freely go beyond the traditional barrio areas whereby they take the entire city for their own. David Foster has underscored how this development distances Nava's Chicano characters from subalternity: "the ranging by the protagonist over the space of the city is also a form of legitimization for the subaltern, in that it provides him access to spaces that counter the principle of ghettoization, which is integral to the marginalization of groups excluded from power: the denial of spatial access is an effective and integral part of the deprivation of power as is any other strategy of discrimination" (73).

Although social anxieties about spatial mobility have virtually disappeared among Chicano characters in Nava's narrative, other types of social tension are so intense that Angelenos, we are told, have become used to (perhaps addicted to) violence. One of the lawyers describes this seething cauldron of racial hatred: "I've got swastikas at synagogues in Fairfax, arson threats at black churches in South Central, and some asshole going around Union-Pico, pretending to be the INS and extorting illegals" (248). Through unfavorable descriptions and scattered observations, Ríos's subjectivity and that of other characters (his friend, Richie Florentino) depict a nearly uninhabitable place where intolerance (mostly, ethnic and sexual prejudice) thrives below a gigantic cloud of smog that, as previously mentioned, is ubiquitous in Los Angeles literature. Although this smog is the reason for the beautiful colors of the sunset, it also reflects, through a pathetic fallacy, the characters' pessimistic views on the city: "a dirty veil that curtained the city and left its inhabitants to stew in their own filth" (65). Besides the thick smog, an even more sinister and dangerous type of pollution threatens the city: bigotry. In particular, homophobia is, in David Foster's view, "the core issue of Nava's work" (74). In effect, Angelenos in *The Burning Plain* are segregated much as was done under the late South African apartheid system, hence the characters' use of the word *ghetto* to describe Boystown, the gay meeting place within West Hollywood. According to Ríos, although gay men moved to that side of town in search of safety, by grouping in a certain place they became easy targets of increasingly violent hate crimes, another reflection of Angelenos' social anxieties.

Pervasive hatred (and, in particular, hatred against homosexuals) is the inspiration for the metaphoric title of the novel. While there are several literary intertextualities, those with Dante's *Inferno* are the most recurrent.[49] In one of these passages, when a young poet compares Los Angeles to the seventh circle in the *Inferno* (where Dante placed homosexuals and violent men), the protagonist's friend, Richie Florentino, scornfully protests: "'Please,' he said, lighting a Marlboro. 'Hell is where you go when you want a vacation from LA'" (30). This symbolic scene takes place in a laundry room where the uppity Poets' Liberation Front has decided to hold a poetry reading. A synecdoche of the city of Los Angeles, the sweltering laundry room is suddenly divided by an invisible and uneasy line between the humble Latino families who are there to do their laundry, and the young, presumptuous Euro-Americans who want to read or hear poetry. In this awkward situation, Ríos describes himself as "the only dark-skinned person to cross the invisible line separating the two groups" (30).[50] Nava, therefore, conceives of Los Angeles as a schizophrenic dual city characterized by sharp economic and sociopolitical polarizations, a peculiarity that constitutes a recipe for social chaos: "I followed Richie's directions to a bad stretch of Sunset in Silver Lake, a neighborhood that increasingly defined what Los Angeles was becoming. In the hills above the reservoir that gave Silver Lake its name, the terra-cotta, white-walled houses of the affluent sprawled like a Mediterranean village, while down in the flats stood the graffiti-covered tenements of the poor" (29–30).[51]

David Foster has compared this novel's apocalyptic references to those included in Rechy's *Bodies and Souls*: "*The Burning Plain* is as much a paradigmatic Los Angeles novel as Raymond Chandler's were, and it has much of the same intensity of apocalyptic description as John Rechy's *Bodies and Souls* (1983)" (89–90). Indeed, as in Rechy's *Bodies and Souls,* in this city where dilapidated bungalows exist along with million-dollar châteaux, where opulent shopping areas stand in contrast to humble *taquerías,* one can hear the whisper of death everywhere. The stars of the "Walk of Fame" thus remind the narrative voice of gravestones; tour buses take tourists to the sites of celebrity suicides and murders; and yearly violent deaths are so numerous that a few unsolved murders are acceptable. These apocalyptic overtones that, in Mike Davis's opinion, are usually "rooted in racial anxiety" (*Ecology* 281) connect the novel with much of the literature and film set in Los Angeles. Prefigured by the customary references to mudslides, earthquakes, wildfires set by madmen, and Santa Ana winds that tear down palm branches and break traffic lights, the civil war–like situation into which the metropolis has been plunged for decades will inevitably end in Armageddon: "In war, the bottom line was who was winning. The cops knew it wasn't them. Violence was escalating in the city, rising like the temperature in a kettle on a low flame, so gradually and inexorably that before we knew what was happening we'd all be boiled alive" (107).

Referring to the writings of John Rechy and Michael Nava, Ricardo L. Ortiz has noticed "the way they negotiate the ambivalence they feel toward the past, toward their origins in both their cultural and sexual dimensions" ("Sexuality" 118). Indeed, although the setting in *The Burning Plain* is unquestionably urban, there is a nuanced nostalgia for the bucolic and agrarian culture of olden days, long ago replaced with urban sprawl. Yet, according to Ríos, at least something positive may come out of the unstoppable suburbanization in the state: the bigotry that drove him out of his hometown will be moderated by the urban lifestyle. References to the never-ending orange groves of old are followed by memories of the city's glamorous past as expressed by some characters while driving through MacArthur Park, a neighborhood populated by "brightly dressed throngs of Mexican and Central American immigrants" (239). Sixty years earlier, we learn, this area was the equivalent of today's Beverly Hills. Although it may seem odd that a Mexican American protagonist (and his implicit author) would be lamenting, perhaps condemning, the transformation of formerly opulent neighborhoods through Latinos, the temptation to speculate about a possible case of false consciousness is tempered when the idealistic narrator rushes to balance his remarks by explaining that, paradoxically, happiness reigns amongst the poor: "One Sunday we stumbled into this district of sad, decaying wealth and cheerful, teeming poverty. We looked at five-hundred-dollar sweaters at Bullock's, then ate fish tacos at a storefront taquería down the street. Later, I thought, the city's schizophrenic nature had never been clearer to me than in that afternoon of cashmere and salsa" (240). In the end, Ríos neutralizes this passage with a few remarks about the coexistence of disparate social realities within one neighborhood.

Curiously, we find a similar reading of the new look of MacArthur Park in Rechy's novel *The Miraculous Day of Amalia Gómez:*

They had looked at the glistening lake at night. Romantic couples huddled in rowboats floating on the water crowded with water lilies.

Now the park looked like a ravaged battlefield.

The most destitute—the wasted bodies of men and women, flesh on bones—congregated in one corner of the park, separated by tangles of rusted wire. The grass had died. (142)

Rechy also feels compelled to show a more positive side: "So many pretty young women in the area! Amalia noticed with pleasure; they were so new in Los Angeles that they wore little makeup, if any, dark shiny hair loose or braided, and they were still so shy" (*Miraculous* 142). There-fore, in both novels (as in Nava's *Rag and Bone*),[52] we see how the recent arrival of destitute Central American immigrants has turned a roman-tic getaway into a dangerous garbage dump filled with homeless people and drug dealers. Could these scenes suggest possible racial anxiety on the part of Rechy and Nava about the massive arrival to Los Angeles of people from their own ethnic group (even if they are Central American immigrants)?

Returning to *The Burning Plain*, we surmise that Ríos's ostensible false consciousness originates from a latent resentment against his own people. He knows, for example, that many hate crimes that victimize gays in West Hollywood are committed by gang members from the Latino neighborhood of Boyle Heights. In addition, the protagonist's description of his father as a brutal macho who used violence to pre-vent him from being homosexual is one of the ways in which Mexican-ness is introduced in the text.[53] This dysfunctional relationship with his Mexican father, which made Ríos sever ties with the rest of his family, also spurred him into a relentless search for justice, particularly for the gay community. Now, his dealings with gay victims and victimizers as well as with macho, homophobic Latinos remind him of the pain of his repressed childhood memories.[54] Besides his father, other characters of Mexican descent in the novel exacerbate his de-ethnification and his resentment against his own ethnic group. One is Montezuma Gaitán (whose first name, incidentally, epitomizes Mexicanness), a Chicano police officer, gay basher, and murderous vigilante who cannot conceive of a Mexican homosexual.

Embittered by his own social group's rejection, Ríos unapologetically declares, in a sort of self-imposed alienation, that he no longer wants to belong to *La raza*. As a result, his cultural translations are glossed in a way that distances him from his people's language and culture. When Gaitán addresses him with the insult "desgraciado," Ríos clarifies: "'There's no English equivalent.'... 'It's a kind of Mexican tribal curse'" (81). The use of the term *tribal* in this context sounds demeaning and uninformed, since the epithet *desgraciado* is not Chicano argot, but a word commonly used in all Spanish dialects.[55] Yet no matter how much he tries to disassociate himself from his ethnic background, he continues to be identified with Mexicans by Euro-American characters. As part of Nava's representational strategy, in this novel being Chicano becomes a choice for the protagonist. *Latinidad* becomes a flexible notion: Ríos can enter or leave it at will, depending on his mood, memories, and needs of the moment. In fact, his sharing of certain ethical values (including respect for people's sexual inclinations) overshadows the allurement of other types of affiliations along ethnic or national lines. As Ralph E. Rodríguez has noted, with Ríos's character Nava "offers alternatives to the prescribed understanding of what it means to be a man in the Chicana/o community—new understandings that do not stigmatize homosexuality" (54). Concomitantly, these passages reflect the veiled tension and animosity between assimilated Mexican American Angelenos and first-generation immigrants.

Henry Ríos also shows a certain degree of double consciousness in *Rag and Bones,* where he again uses questionable vocabulary in his description of a Latina: "I dreamed I was in a pawn shop on Spring Street, a neighborhood that seemed like it belonged in Mexico City rather than L.A. A greasy old woman stood behind the counter, arms crossed, an unlit cigarette clamped between her lips" (60–61). Here, the epithet "greasy" is reminiscent of "greaser," the old racial slur used against Mexicans. Likewise, Nava goes against the grain of recent Mexican American literature and film by implying that Mexicans are better off, both socially and professionally, living in the United States than in their native country. Thus, Inez Montoya compliments her friend Ríos by telling him:

> "In the little Mexican village where you and I would have lived a hundred years ago, you would have been the priest."
> "And what would you have been?"
> "Someone's wife," she said. "The mother of his thirteen children. Instead, I'm raising millions of dollars to get myself elected to the senate. I'm going to make it, too." (285–86).

As we have seen in this last chapter, current feminist and gay writing puts nationalist discourses and ideologies to the test. Helena María Viramontes, Graciela Limón, Danny Santiago, Michael Nava, and other authors question the Mexican and Chicano imagined communities, problematizing the position of women and homosexuals, the classist and ethnic divisions within Mexican communities, and the Chicano Movement's unproblematic identification with indigeneity. In some cases, they propose a pluralist and postnationalist widening of perspectives from the local to the global, which will allow Chicanas and Chicanos to learn from other decolonizing movements and racialized ethnic groups (including the experience of women in these communities) within and outside national borders. Some authors also incorporate in their texts the experiences of another important diasporic Latino community: the Central American immigrants in Los Angeles. This metropolis, despite its geographical location, not only demands to be part of border studies but also shares a border mentality within its city limits.

Conclusion

> The Anglo conquest of California in the late 1840s has
> proven to be a very transient fact indeed.
> —Mike Davis, *Magical Urbanism*

As Natter and Jones postulate, any discussion of identity has to include
the question of boundaries: "hegemony not only perpetuates processes
and identifications to which 'identity' may then become attached, it does
so spatially, by disciplining the meanings and practices associated with
any social space. This structuring, historically and geographically, has
served the aim of stamping both identity and space with a resolute cor-
respondence: every identity has its place" (153). Accepting this premise,
we must wonder, What is the place of Latino identity in Los Angeles?
This study reveals that such a place extends far beyond the traditional
barrios. The traditionally local identity of the Chicano has given way
to a broader, more encompassing national, transnational, and postnationalist Latina/o identity, one that is no longer territorially defined.
The foundational vantage point of the mythical Aztlán has now been
complicated by more-fragmented narratives and less-stable and politically eroded positionalities. Therefore, whereas some authors claim the
Greater Los Angeles area as the space that Latinos share with other ethnicities, others, such as Graciela Limón, evince a transnational and postnationalist identity. This identity replaces essentialism and exclusionary
politics with a focus on situations and concerns shared with other struggling minority groups.

Many cultural artifacts examined in this book are antihegemonic,
because they undermine a perceived stability and the traditional boundaries of Latino identity. In the face of an expanding process of worldwide
transculturation and, more importantly, of the globalization resulting
from the commercialism of multinational corporations, they propose
an identity that is (like all cultural identities) in continuous formation

and motion, just as the spaces where this identity is unfolding. As both physical spaces and cognitive mappings are expanded and transformed with disregard for the limitations of such concepts as national economy and nation-state, so are these identitarian processes and cultural identities. In the eyes of many of these authors and filmmakers, the celebration of flexibility, difference, contingency, and in-betweenness (to use Homi Bhabha's term) has become more useful than the search for sameness and identity. In a sense, this cultural production realizes a type of "disidentification" similar to that proposed by Natter and Jones.

> The form of resistance more antithetical to hegemony is one that refuses the emplacement of categorically designated identifications, while offering a potentially effective strategy for reconfiguring nodal points of both identity and space. In this regard, disidentification—even while generally thought of as being outside the economy of production—becomes a tactic that enables a refusal of concepts—e.g., the "private" and the "public"—that ground such economies. (158)

By the same token, these works show that in the imaginary of Chicano and Latino cultural production, the quintessential border, the international line (or, rather, the international wall) that separates the United States from Mexico, has always been complemented by invisible miniborders within the confines of the city itself, which can be drawn along "racial," ethnocultural, linguistic, class, gender, sexual, institutional, and even mental lines. These miniborders are the reflection of the social anxieties mentioned in the introduction: every social group seems to feel that someone else is "taking over." From this perspective, we may ask, Why do a study about the imaging of Los Angeles in Latino cultural production and about the fictional and cinematic representation of Latino Angelenos? Like Héctor Tobar, Mike Davis, David Rieff, and others, I believe that, in the twenty-first century, Los Angeles is exporting its evolving identity (perhaps a composite of reality and the virtual reality that Hollywood and other media have always exported) to the rest of the country. Subject to different historical and hegemonic forces (and to the largest border of all: the global border between North and South, between wealthy nations and poor-nation immigrants), this hybrid cultural identity is (and will be) the result of a long process of transculturation among Euro-American, Latino, African American, and Asian communities, which developed throughout the last century. Among these four groups, Latinos are becoming an increasingly determinant factor.

In *Translation Nation* (2005), Héctor Tobar formulates a sort of Zeitgeist for Latinos in Los Angeles that he counters to a presumed WASP worldview, ruled by "Protestant work ethic, individualism, and an obsession with orderliness in all matters, public and private" (5). In his view, the Latino contribution to this new U.S. identity is an embrace of "informality, excess in emotion, the dissembling force of rebellion, and the idea of strength in collectivity" (7). The Euro-American response to the Latinization of the country, argues Tobar, has followed a consistent pattern: "denial, anger, acceptance" (18). Whether or not readers agree with Tobar, his assertions lay bare the Latinization of Anglo North America. This process is increasingly debated not only in the media and the arts, but also in academic circles. Scholarly studies like José David Saldívar's *Border Matters: Remapping American Cultural Studies* (1997), *Latino/as in the World-System: Decolonization Struggles in the 21st Century U.S. Empire* (2005), edited by Ramón Grosfoguel, Nelson Maldonado-Torres and José David Saldívar, and *Latinos in a Changing Society* (2007) by Martha Montero-Sieburth and Edwin Meléndez, together with numerous publications for the popular market, show the unfading interest in the Latinization of the United States.[1]

The previous chapters explored, from different, and sometimes contrasting, perspectives, the racial and social anxieties emerging as a result of this amalgamation. In my view, they are a crucial factor in the process of image making of a city that has often been conceived as the avantgarde of a new North America. As we have seen, the glamorous world of Hollywood stars, life in the affluent western districts, hardboiled crime fiction, and the disaster novel set in Los Angeles represent only a minimal aspect of the daily life of a metropolis that has become a locus of interaction among working-class minority groups. In all, this contestatory cultural production represents a valid alternative to the erasure of the Latino presence from anthologies of Los Angeles literature as well as to the self-image that Hollywood films disseminate worldwide. Perhaps these two mutually exclusive self-representations, the Latino and the Euro-American, mix reality with the individual and collective fantasies of their respective communities.

Inevitably, the sheer vastness of the area (a sixty-mile circle, according to Edward Soja) makes its imaging fragmented and, at times, even contradictory. Each of these fragments, however, reflects a palimpsest of individual and collective struggles, a trajectory that goes from the initial lack of access to spatial and social mobility to the representation of Latina professionals who no longer see the barrios as metaphorically independent nations with their own invisible borders. As shown, among these characters we can find different levels of identification with the collective project of the nation-state or with the city itself, ranging from a feeling of full citizenship or integration with the city to the subaltern's resentment over their exclusion from the spatial and imaginary space of the city and the nation. This cultural production, therefore, depicts a long history of struggle to build a spatial infrastructure where Mexican American and Latina subjectivities can emerge. This process of subject formation goes hand in hand with the emergence of an oppositional discourse that evolves from the projects of national liberation of the 1960s, through the reaction against the nativist California propositions of the 1990s (aimed, for the most part, at limiting Latino agency), to today's significant increase in political visibility and the national debates about undocumented immigration. Although the economic recession that began in the last months of 2008 seemed to have reduced mainstream social anxiety about undocumented immigration, the 2010 signing into law, by Governor Jan Brewer of Arizona, of the nation's toughest bill on undocumented immigration has reignited the debate.

While this book has concentrated on the overarching topic of the literary and cultural representations of mainstream Los Angeles's social anxieties about the Latino presence and the massive arrival of Latin American immigrants (and on the related social anxieties that Hispanics—Chicanos, Latinos, and Latin American immigrants—feel as well), a similar study is yet to be carried out about the correlative effects of the new waves of Asian migration and capital investment. As Aihwa Ong explains, "For many middle-class Americans, unease over being displaced in their neighborhoods and in their native social order, and anxiety over the American city as being 'too open' to foreign capital and influence, are linked to a wider undercurrent of panic over 'losing out'—in jobs, wages, home ownership, and wealth—to the economic dynamism of the Asia Pacific countries, as embodied in the Asian newcomers" (108–9). A comparative study of the social anxieties produced by Asian and Hispanic presence and migration waves would undoubtedly produce additional questions and answers to the ones provided here.

Appendix 1
Chronological List of Literary and
Testimonial Works

Daniel Venegas, *The Adventures of Don Chipote, or, When Parrots Breast-Feed* (1929)
Octavio Paz, *The Labyrinth of Solitude* (1950)
John Rechy, *City of Night* (1963)
John Rechy, *Numbers* (1967)
Óscar Zeta Acosta, *Autobiography of a Brown Buffalo* (1972)
Óscar Zeta Acosta, *The Revolt of the Cockroach People* (1973)
Alejandro Morales, *Barrio on the Edge* (1975)
Luis Valdez, *Zoot Suit* (1979)
John Rechy, *Bodies and Souls* (1983)
Danny Santiago, *Famous All Over Town* (1983)
Kate Braverman, *Palm Latitudes* (1988)
Laura del Fuego, *Maravilla* (1989)
John Rechy, *The Miraculous Day of Amalia Gómez* (1991)
Alejandro Morales, *The Rag Doll Plagues* (1992)
Miguel Durán, *Don't Spit on My Corner* (1992)
Graciela Limón, *In Search of Bernabé* (1993)
Luis J. Rodríguez, *Always Running* (1993)
T. Coraghessan Boyle, *Tortilla Curtain* (1995)
Helena María Viramontes, "Neighbors" (1995)
Helena María Viramontes, "The Cariboo Café" (1995)
Yxta Maya Murray, *Locas* (1997)
Mona Ruiz and Geoff Boucher, *Two Badges* (1997)
Michael Nava, *The Burning Plain* (1997)
Héctor Tobar, *The Tattooed Soldier* (1998)
Graciela Limón, *The Day of the Moon* (1999)
Yxta Maya Murray, *What It Takes to Get to Vegas* (1999)
Carlos Fuentes, *Los años con Laura Díaz* (1999)
Graciela Limón, *Erased Faces* (2001)
Michael Nava, *Rag and Bone* (2001)
Luis J. Rodríguez, *The Republic of East L.A.* (2002)
Alberto Fuguet, *The Movies of My Life* (2003)

Alejandro Morales, "Pequeña nación" (2005)
Rudolfo Anaya, *Curse of the Chupacabra* (2006)
Kate Braverman, *Frantic Transmissions to and from Los Angeles* (2006)
Mario Acevedo, *X-Rated Bloodsuckers* (2007)
Helena María Viramontes, *Their Dogs Came with Them* (2007)

Appendix 2
Chronological List of Films and Documentaries

Gregory Nava, *El Norte* (1983)
Ramón Menéndez, *Stand and Deliver* (1988)
Dennis Hopper, *Colors* (1988)
Edward James Olmos, *American Me* (1992)
Taylor Hackford, *Blood In Blood Out* (also known as *Bound by Honor,* 1993)
Allison Anders, *Mi Vida Loca* (1993)
Héctor Galán, *Chicano! History of the Mexican American Civil Rights Movement* (1996)
Patricia Cardoso, *Real Women Have Curves* (2002)
Chris Fisher, *Nightstalker* (2002)
Chris T. McIntyre, *Gang Warz* (2004)
David Ayer, *Harsh Times* (2005)
Edward James Olmos, *Walkout* (2006)

Notes

Foreword

1. One of the first decisive critiques of the 1970s model of Chicano literary history is Ramón A. Gutiérrez's "Nationalism and Literary Production: The Hispanic and Chicano Experience."

2. The global has different transnational ranges, from the radically different and distant to near but remote in time, stemming from colonial relations with Spain. See Ahrens, *Violence and Transgression in World Minority Literatures* (2005); Poot-Herrera, Lomelí, and Herrera-Sobek, eds., *Cien años de lealtad en honor a Luis Leal* (2007); Francisco Lomelí and Clark A. Colahan, eds. and trans., *Defying the Inquisition in Colonial New Mexico: Miguel de Quintana's Life and Writings* (2006).

3. See Leal, "The First American Epic" (1989); in addition, Padilla, "Discontinuous Continuities" (1993). Also, Lomelí et al., eds., *Nuevomexicano Cultural Legacy* (2002).

4. See Díaz del Castillo, *The Conquest of New Spain* (1963), 82.

5. Frémont (2001, 532). For the earlier falling of the pole and flag on top of Gavilán Peak, see p. 460.

6. In his memoir, Frémont rewrites the meaning of "telling a story," particularly when the audience is an alien people on the path of Manifest Destiny. Telling a story teaches others to retell the same anecdote with a similar or greater pathos. This is how the lesson in storytelling is taught by Frémont to the Tlamath nation: "When the Tlamaths tell the story of the night attack where they were killed, there will be no boasting. They will have to tell also of the death of their chief and of our swift retaliation; and how the people at the fishery had to mourn for the loss of their men and the destruction of their village. It will be a story for them to hand down while there are any Tlamaths on their lake" (496). The storytelling lesson does not end with the Tlamath: on their trek through forests and mountains, Frémont and his men come across a member of another native nation. After a brief exchange of gunpowder and arrows, "the Indian was killed and his scalp put up in the trail *to tell the story*." Frémont continues: "We were getting roughened into Indian customs" (496; my emphasis). Frémont's manner of telling a story would eventually become the core curriculum in U.S. public schools: Mexican Americans in Texas, for instance, knew by heart the (one-sided) story

of the Alamo. Chicano historians have since examined and challenged Frémont's storytelling legacy and institutionalization in U.S. public schools.

7. Frémont, 565.

8. See my review of *Rewriting North American Borders in Chicano and Chicana Narrative*, by Monika Kaup (Peter Lang, 2001), in *Modern Language Quarterly* 64.4 (Dec. 2003): 508–13. Kaup's historical analysis suggests different ways to conceive *origins* or foundational dates: 1848 for Chicano cultural nationalism, 1910 for Mexican immigrants, and 1519 for Chicana feminists. "Far from being trivial acts," Kaup argues, "conceptual starting points represent significant delimitations for any intellectual project. A beginning—1848 or 1519—is never simply given; it is a significant choice"(222).

Introduction

1. Of course, when eight years later I decided to move to Texas, my teary-eyed Angeleno friends felt sorry for my daughter, who would have to grow up in a cultural desert run by the Ku Klux Klan . . .

2. To avoid the repetition of the spelling "Chicana/o" and "Latina/o," I shall alternate between the masculine and feminine genders. As is well known, several terms have been used throughout the years to refer to people of Mexican or Latin American descent living in the southwestern United States. All these terms, like most words, are loaded with metaphoric meanings that provide a wealth of information about the perception of Chicanos and Latinos by Euro-Americans as well as the self-perception of Chicanas and Latinas. In the context of identity construction and representation, terms that indicate origin or location such as *Mexican, Mejicana, Californio, Mexican American, Chicana, Hispanic, Latino,* and *La raza* (along with neologisms and racial epithets like *greaser, messcan, pepper belly, zoot suiter, beaner, wetback, pachuco, vato, cholo,* and *loco*) have all described this population at one time or another. In a sense, the changing vocabulary reflects the evolution of this population as well as the mainstream's perceptions of it. By the same token, despite the fact that New Mexican Latinos and Latin American immigrants tend to identify more with the term *Hispanic,* I have chosen to use the term *Latino* instead, because of the history of racism that the term *Hispanic* has had in the United States since it was adopted by the Nixon administration in the 1970s. I agree with Mike Davis, however, when he points out that "both labels fail to acknowledge the decisive quotient of indigenous genetic and cultural heritage in the populations they describe. Both meta-categories, in fact, were originally nineteenth-century ideological impositions from Europe: 'Hispanicity' from Liberal Spain and 'Latinity' from the France of Napoleon III" (*Magical* 12–13).

3. Reyner Banham, in his *Los Angeles: The Architecture of Four Ecologies* (1971), coined the term *surfurbia* to suggest the influence of beach environments

(represented by the three S's: sun, sand, and surf) on the construction and sub-urbanization of the contemporary metropolis.

4. Richard Rodríguez was born to Mexican immigrant parents in San Francisco, California, and grew up in Sacramento, California. Before settling in Las Lomas, Rodríguez's family had lived in Watts, a primarily black community with a Mexican section known as La Colonia. The area housed workers of the large industrial con-centration that Los Angeles had in those days (before factories such as Goodyear, Firestone, General Motors, Bethlehem Steel, and American Bridge closed down), when deed restrictions or restrictive covenants prevented them from moving to other neighborhoods. The U.S. Supreme Court outlawed restrictive covenants in 1948. He now lives in San Francisco. He is also the author of *Hunger of Memory: The Education of Richard Rodríguez* (1982), *Mexico's Children* (1990), and *Brown: The Last Discovery of America* (1992), and works as an editor at San Francisco's Pacific News Services as well as for *Harper's* and the *Los Angeles Times*.

5. The Tongva are also known as Gabrieleños. They belong to the Shoshon-ean linguistic group.

6. The study of the Bonaventure Hotel as a postmodern building by Fredric Jameson would be a good example of this type of perception.

7. The term *ethnoburb* was first coined in 1997 by geographer Wei Li, of the University of Connecticut.

8. The concept of "chronotope" was developed between the years 1937 and 1938 by Mikhail Bakhtin in "Forms of Time and the Chronotope in the Novel: From the Greek Novel to Modern Fiction" (1973).

The five counties of the Los Angeles region are the following: Los Angeles, Orange, Riverside, San Bernardino, and Ventura.

9. In *Decade of Betrayal: Mexican Repatriation in the 1930s* (2006), Francisco E. Balderrama and Raymond Rodríguez study the traumatic consequences of the unconstitutional deportations and coerced repatriations by which Los Angeles lost one-third of its population of Mexican origin in the first half of the 1930s.

10. "In 1990, working-class Latinos accounted for more than half of Los Angeles County's manufacturing workforce, although they constituted little more than a third of its population. . . . Inside the city limits, the Latino pres-ence in the manufacturing sector has increased to more than 72 percent" (Valle and Torres 16).

11. "The established barrios in the Los Angeles area in the 1950s," Raymond A. Rocco explains, "included communities like East Los Angeles, whose neigh-borhoods included Lincoln Park, Belvedere, and Maravilla. Other important Mexican communities were located in San Gabriel, San Fernando, Wilmington/ San Pedro, and a small barrio in the Venice area" (367).

12. Although Richard Rodríguez popularized the term "browning of Amer-ica," it had been used before the publication of his 2001 *Brown: The Last Discov-ery of America*.

13. There are six million Latinos (Chicanos and new Latin American arrivals) in Los Angeles and Orange counties, and the city of Los Angeles has as many Spanish speakers as Anglophones. At a national level, the Census Bureau has recently estimated that approximately forty-five million Latinos live in the United States (more than half of them are Mexican Americans). The number, therefore, equals Spain's population and surpasses all Spanish-speaking countries except for Mexico. Latinos are not only the largest but also the fastest-growing minority in the United States.

14. This same horizontality prevents a young Richard Rodríguez from considering Los Angeles a great city: "Great cities were tall cities. New York promised most glamour for being the tallest, the coolest, the farthest from these even rows of green; this hot, flat Valley floor. . . . Billy Rockers sent me a postcard from L.A. once—white, horizontal, vast—a vast Sacramento" (*Days of Obligation* 150).

15. The story is obviously very different in Spanish-language channels. As David E. Hayes-Bautista argues, Spanish-language commercial advertising presents "the public with more positive imagery of Latinos. In contrast to contemporary English-language news portrayals—gang members, welfare mothers, illegal immigrants—these new images treated Latinos as human beings with dreams and ambitions" (145).

16. Óscar Acosta began to call himself Óscar Zeta Acosta in July 1970 during his campaign for sheriff (Calderón 93). In *The Autobiography of a Brown Buffalo*, he confesses that he moved to Los Angeles in search of literary material for his book: "I took Doc Jennings' [his literature professor's] advice and hit the road to Los Angeles in search of experience in June of 1957" (148).

17. Daniel Venegas was the chief editor of the Los Angeles weekly newspaper *El Malcriado*. While Venegas's is plausibly the first novel about Mexican immigrant workers in the United States, the first example of a novel about Hispanic immigration, explains Kanellos, is Alirio Díaz Guerra's *Lucas Guevara*, published in New York in 1914 (2000, 9).

18. In this context, in *The Republic of East L.A.* Luis J. Rodríguez coincides with much of this cultural production (including Gregory Nava's 1983 motion picture *El Norte*) when he suggests that Latinos would have been better off had they stayed in their own countries rather than to end up in this "mad city, fuck-it-all-and-blow-you-away city," as one of the characters describes Los Angeles in the short story "Chain-Link Lover" (161). Rudy, a homeless alcoholic in "Shadows," embodies this idea: "He was the specter of their deepest aches, a reminder of what happens when you leave so much of the old for the new. How once compact communities and families could turn up on the other side and completely fractured—about what it was they sacrificed to find 'the good life' in America" (26–27). The same warning against moving to the United States closes the collection with "Sometimes you dance with a watermelon," where Rosalba

"danced for her people, wherever they were scattered, and for this country she would never quite comprehend. She danced, her hair matted with sweat, while remembering a simpler life on an even simpler rancho in Nayarit" (239). In contrast, when, in Richard Vásquez's novel *Chicano* (1970), Neftalí finds out that his two sisters work as prostitutes and states "it would have been better had we stayed in Mexico," his sister reminds him about their life before arriving in the United States in the 1930s: "Don't you remember, brother, the hunger, the nothing we had, no clothes, beans and corn every day, a big occasion when we had a chicken? Well, now I eat chicken whenever I want. Hortensia and I have a room all our own, on the edge of the barrio, where we buy things we like, that we never dreamed we could own in Mexico" (55). Alex M. Saragoza has criticized the tendency to oversimplify this issue in Mexican films such as *Las braceras* (1981): "most of the recent films on immigration made in Mexico convey a simplistic message: crossing the border to the United States spells eventual doom. . . . This message, however, contradicts the presence of an enormous population of *mexicanos* with many years of residence in the United States" (118–19).

19. As its Web site indicates, the MOLAA is the only museum in the western United States that exclusively features contemporary Latin American art.

20. As stated on its Web site, the Bilingual Foundation of the Arts also provides educational resources and training opportunities for theater artists, translates and presents Hispanic theater works, and produces bilingual theater for the general public.

Chapter 1

1. Banham's notion of "autopia" refers to highways and the experience of driving as iconic ways of life in Los Angeles.

2. The image of this district remains uninviting in Mario Acevedo's *X-Rated Bloodsuckers:* "Of course. The San Fernando Valley was to porn what Maine was to lobster fishing" (4).

3. The MS-13, or "Mara Salvatrucha," for example, has a presence in numerous suburbs.

4. Alberto Fuguet lives in his native Santiago de Chile and is one of the leaders of the McOndo literary "movement" (although he does not consider it a movement). He has published the volume of chronicles *La azarosa y sobreexpuesta vida de Enrique Alekán* (1990) and the collections of short stories *Sobredosis* (1990) and *Cortos* (2004), as well as the novels *Mala Onda* (1991), *Por favor rebobinar* (1994), and *Tinta Roja* (1996). He has also published scripts such as *En un lugar de la noche*, included in his book *Dos hermanos* (2000), and edited, along with Sergio Gómez, the anthologies of short stories *Cuentos con walkman* (1993), *McOndo* (1996), and *Se habla español* (2001), and in cooperation with the Bolivian Edmundo Paz Soldán, *Voces latinas en USA* (2000). In an interview

with Ernesto Escobar Ulloa, Fuguet disaffirms the autobiographical nature of *The Movies of My Life* but admits that it is a personal book and that it echoes key episodes in his life.

Other works by T. Coraghessan Boyle are the following: *Water Music* (1981), *Budding Prospects* (1984), *World's End* (1987), *East Is East* (1990), *The Road to Wellville* (1993), *Riven Rock* (1998), *T. C. Boyle Stories* (1998), *A Friend of the Earth* (2000), *After the Plague* (2001), *Drop City* (2003), and *The Inner Circle* (2004). Boyle grew up in Manhattan and has taught creative writing at the University of Southern California since 1978. He lives in Santa Barbara, California. He has won numerous awards, including the PEN/Faulkner Award for Fiction in 1988 for *World's End*.

Although the term "tortilla curtain" refers to the U.S.–Mexico border, it is more frequently used in southern Arizona's talk radio, rather than in California.

Echoing the popularity of *The Tortilla Curtain*, a film based on this plot, featuring Kevin Costner and Meg Ryan, is now in development. The American musical group Eddie from Ohio also has a song titled "Cándido and América," which is based on Boyle's characters.

5. It is worth noting here that some ecologist groups are changing their position toward a new anti-immigration stand, as one can read in the article "A 'Hostile' Takeover Bid at the Sierra Club" (Knickerbocker).

6. Stereotypes also affect Latino characters in this novel. Thus, Cándido ponders his people's fatalism: "Cándido was listening to the woman cry softly beside him and thinking about that fatalism, that acquiescence, the inability of his people to act in the face of authority, right or wrong" (172). Prejudice and bigotry affect these characters as well; not only does Cándido have preconceptions about Euro-Americans, but he also disparages América because of her indigenous blood.

7. Other commonplaces resurface in the pages of *The Tortilla Curtain*, including the inevitable natural disasters (earthquakes and wildfires) and the apocalyptic views of destruction, which appear in the movies for which the racist Jack Cherrystone is doing trailers.

8. This animalization of street gangs is evident, for example, in Kate Braverman's *Palm Latitudes:* "These Dreamers and Chicos and Charmers recognized we were content in our insignificance. We offered neither resistance nor interest in their rituals of cars and knives, in the territories they patrolled and guarded like dogs, moving in packs, marking the edges of their squalid domain" (117).

In the fifth chapter of his *Ecology of Fear*, Mike Davis has studied the adaptation of coyotes to "the pet-and-garbage ecology of the suburbs" (246) as well as the reaction of Los Angeles suburbanites to these types of attacks.

9. Don Chipote warns Mexican readers who may be planning to move to the United States against dishonest Mexican Americans who will inevitably try to take advantage of them. Likewise, the two negative Chicano characters in *El*

Norte are Don Mocte, who makes a living by manipulating recent immigrants, and Enrique's Chicano coworker, who turns him in to the Immigration and Naturalization Service after the latter receives a promotion in his job.

10. The etymological origin of the name of these winds is uncertain. However, it is believed to be an English translation from the Spanish *vientos de Satanás* (Satan winds).

11. "El problema es que a mí me cuesta odiar a Estados Unidos, algo que acá en América Latina es un *dirty little secret*" (135). Later in the same interview, Fuguet explains how José Donoso told him that nothing literary could come out of Encino.

12. "McOndo para mí es lo que se siente cuando estás en Downtown, Los Angeles" (n.p.).

13. The image of Los Angeles's inner city, South Los Angeles this time, as the epitome of barbarism is succinctly presented in the first scenes of a recent film, David Ayer's *Harsh Times* (2005). While the protagonist, a Euro-American soldier who returns from the Gulf War suffering from post-traumatic stress disorder, and his Chicano friend are buying beer in a Korean convenience store, they hear two Latinos running and shooting at each other in the inner city's mean streets. Subsequently, the Korean owner comes out with a gun in his hand, and ready to shoot. Moments later, the protagonist's car is stopped by a corrupt LAPD officer who ends up recommending a place to them where they can sell their gun. David Ayer recently returned to the portrayal of corruption in the LAPD in his crime drama *Street Kings* (2008), starring Keanu Reeves and Forest Whitaker.

14. Whereas in the system of economic production formulated by Henry Ford, workers had specialized tasks in a production line, post-Fordism, the dominant system in most industrialized countries since the late twentieth century, is related to a service economy, new information technologies, consumption, and white-collar or specialized jobs.

15. As Wolch explains, "In 1990–1991, an estimated 12,600 to 204,000 people were homeless in Los Angeles County at some point during the year, and between 38,420 and 68,670 people were homeless on any given night" (390).

16. In 2007 there were 1,815 homeless people in Antelope Valley; 6,411 in San Fernando Valley; 9,942 in San Gabriel Valley; 22,030 in Metro Los Angeles; 6,703 in West Los Angeles; 11,670 in South Los Angeles; 5,580 in East Los Angeles; and 4,457 in South Bay/Harbor. Fifty percent of homeless people in greater Los Angeles are African American, 24 percent are Latino, and 19 percent are Caucasian. Incidentally, in August 2008, the FBI accused three Southern California hospitals, City of Angels Medical Center, Los Angeles Metropolitan Center, and Tustin Hospital and Medical Center, of a scheme to enlist homeless persons for unnecessary health care. Apparently, they recruited hundreds, perhaps thousands, of vagrants, including drug addicts and people with mental illness, in order to charge the government for the stays. Allegedly, millions of dollars have been

billed to MediCal and Medicare. According to a report by Shaya Tayee Mohajer, "The investigation began in 2006 as Los Angeles police looked into reports that hospitals were dumping homeless patients on Skid Row streets" (2).

17. Héctor Tobar was born and raised in Los Angeles. He is the son of Guatemalan immigrants (his father was a leftist military police officer in the Guatemalan Army) who moved to Los Angeles in 1962. He is the author of *Translation Nation: Defining a New American Identity in the Spanish-Speaking United States*. He is currently the Mexico City bureau chief of the *Los Angeles Times* and has published hundreds of newspaper articles. In 1992, he won a Pulitzer Prize for his coverage for the *Los Angeles Times*, as part of a team, of the so-called Rodney King riots. As a reporter for the *Los Angeles Times* during the 1980s, Tobar was exploring urban violence and Central American homelessness when he came up with the idea for the novel: "a social worker at the agency El Rescate told me a story about a client of hers who had spotted a death-squad member in MacArthur Park" (Tobar's home page). *The Tattooed Soldier*, a finalist for the PEN USA West Award for Fiction, is currently in its fifth edition in paperback.

18. For example, in Rodríguez's *Always Running* one of the characters claims that most Angelenos did not even imagine that such places existed around them until the first suburbs where created: "We were invisible people in a city which thrived on glitter, big screens and big names, but this glamour contained none of our names, none of our faces" (20).

19. Since, according to Jennifer Wolch, this type of action is common in Los Angeles, Tobar's scene was probably inspired by real-life events: "the City of Los Angeles shut down 'Justiceville,' a 60-person, organized encampment located on a former playground in Skid Row, removed a group of homeless living on the steps of City Hall, and bulldozed a camp of 125 people living behind the Union Rescue Mission" (Wolch 415).

20. In the first chapter of *Translation Nation*, Tobar describes the real-life political rally at MacArthur Park, as well as the trials of Fidel Chicas, the inspiration for José Juan's complaints about El Armenio, an employer who refused to pay him for six days of hard work.

21. The image of Los Angeles's downtown is equally negative in Acosta's *The Revolt of the Cockroach People*. Perhaps as a continuation of his apparent self-hate, his autobiographical protagonist translates his anger into dystopian images of an inner city populated mostly by people from his own ethnic group: "I find myself alone in my tiny legal office on the tenth floor, high above the Cockroaches on the streets of spit and sin and foul air in downtown LA" (21). Later, Acosta (who was born in El Paso, Texas, but grew up near Modesto, in California's San Joaquin Valley) extends this perception to the entire city:

But already my bones have told me that I have come to the most detestable city on earth. They have carried me through the filthy air of a broken city filled with battered losers. Winos in tennies, skinny fags in tight pants and whores in purple skirts all ignore the world beyond the local bar, care about nothing except where the booze comes cheapest or the latest score on the radio. Where I am, the buildings are crumbling into pieces. The paint is cracked and falling to the streets covered with green and brown phlegm, with eyeless souls who scuttle between tall buildings hoping to find a bed, a bottle, a joint, a broad or even a loaf of bread. Streets filled with dark people, hunchbacked hobos, bums out of work, garbage of yesterday and tomorrow. (22–23)

22. According to Raymond A. Rocco, another important push/pull factor is the economic policy "pursued by the United States, particularly through its role in the International Monetary Fund and the World Bank" (371).

23. The term *cholo* is often used in Latin America as a racial slur against people of pre-Columbian descent, although it can also be used as a term of endearment. Peruvian psychoanalysts Jorge Bruce (in his book *Nos habíamos choleado tanto: Psicoanálisis y racismo* [2007]) and Walter Twanama (in his essay "Racismo peruano, ni calco ni copia") have studied the racist connotations of the term. In addition, as it frequently happens with these derogative terms, the word *cholo* has also been used, without stigmas, as a banner of ethnic pride in both the United States and Latin America.

24. As Michael Dear explains, the Great Wall of Los Angeles "tells California's popular history in an extended sequence along the walls of the Tujunga Wash. Under the direction of Judy Baca, large numbers of community artists were enrolled in the mural-making process" (*Postmodern* 254).

25. Balderrama and Rodríguez have investigated the circumstances around the mural that Siqueiros dedicated to the local Mexican community in 1932: "The Olvera Street merchants commissioned the famous artist David Alfaro Siqueiros to paint the America Tropical mural. But his portrayal of the Americas was deemed too controversial and bad for business" (105). And, later, they explain that "'America Tropical' portrayed a Native American impaled on a crucifix with a screaming American eagle covering on top" (161).

26. "Lo que me llamaba la atención era la constancia con que los muralistas mexicanos en los E.E.U.U. eran objeto de censura, controversia y obliteración" (592).

27. This was echoed in Laura del Fuego's *Maravilla* (2006) when the protagonist's grandmother loses her mind: "Back to the time when the government had bulldozed the rambling old Victorian [house] where she had lived for forty years to make way for the first L.A. freeway. 'The house was built in 1898,' my father said, 'solid as a rock.' The whole neighborhood was gone now" (163).

28. Danny Santiago writes accent marks on some English words, presumably to make them closer to the Mexican American pronunciation of English words.

29. This controversial bildungsroman has been the subject of numerous footnotes and academic studies focusing on the topics of authenticity and "ethnic imposture." The novel, which is narrated from a first-person perspective by a fourteen-year-old Chicano boy, initially received high praise from critics. Surprisingly (at least for me), when it was revealed that the author was not a Chicano, some critics dismissed it as a fraud. Instead, in my view, it should be considered more of an achievement precisely because of the successful "passing" (from Euro-American to Chicano) of someone outside the culture who was able to penetrate successfully the psychology of a displaced Chicano teenager. In this sense, Laura Browder claims that the narratives of the "genre of the ethnic impostor autobiography," as she terms it, stand

> as monuments to the tradition of American self-invention, the notion that it is possible to remake oneself in a chosen image, as well as testaments to the porousness of ethnic identity . . . fake ethnic autobiographies both point up the limitations of cultural nationalism and remind us of how strongly racial and ethnic expectations shape the mainstream acceptance of these narratives. While impostor ethnic memoirs may give the lie to "one-drop" and similarly essentialist theories of ethnicity, their positive reception seems to underscore the extent to which many members of the dominant culture subscribe to such ideas ("Under Cover" n.p.).

Before his first novel, *Famous All Over Town* (which won the 1982 Richard and Hilda Rosenthal Foundation Award as well as an award for fiction from the American Academy and Institute of Arts and Letters in 1984), Daniel James had published several books and was known as a playwright and screenwriter. He collaborated with Charlie Chaplin on the film *The Great Dictator* (1940). As a former member of the Communist Party, James was blacklisted by Hollywood in the 1950s. The author has explained that his knowledge of the Mexican American culture represented in the novel is the result of the volunteer social work he did during the 1950s and 1960s in Mexican American districts of Los Angeles.

30. The same nostalgia is evident in a Web site dedicated to Lincoln Heights, which has a page dedicated specifically to Clover Street: "The houses on Clover St. have been demolished. The land was converted to parking lots for the Piggy Back trailers of the Union Pacific railroad that bought out the Espee. Later, this land was sold to The United Parcel Service, which built a distribution center for their growing delivery service. The Golden State Freeway now borders the east side of the community. The aroma of frijoles de holla and tortillas de harina are gone. But on a quiet evening in the summer, if you listen very carefully, you could hear the sea breeze funneling through the space between the buildings and trucks hauntingly whispering a faint call, 'Paco Paco ven a casa, vamos a comer!'" (cloverstreet.net; R.G.).

31. *Costumbrismo* is a literary and artistic movement that offers a somewhat superficial and romanticized portrait of local everyday life, mannerisms, folklore, social customs, and traditions. It was created in nineteenth-century Spain and later exported to the Americas.

32. Although there are several opinions about what the Chicano expression "con safos" means, most people understand it as a warning that any insult toward what has just been written will slip off, or that the writer does not care if the reader does not like what has just been written. Others claim that it means "with respect." The novel *Famous All Over Town* also offers an explanation: "There were plenty Con Safos too, meaning that if you add something to the signer's name like Fuck you, it will bounce back double on your private reputation" (79).

33. The other factor they list is the increase of the urban underclass since 1980 (Maxson and Klein 261).

34. In *Two Badges,* Mona Ruiz explains that in the 1990s the culture of taggers became increasingly visible. Although they were usually not gangbangers, they shared the same fashion and language: "Tagging attracted a lot of kids who were enamored by the gang scene but did not want to plunge into the violence of banging. They figured that writing on a wall with spray paint and running away was enough of a criminal thrill" (266).

35. Luis Javier Rodríguez was born in El Paso, Texas, and lived in Ciudad Juárez, Mexico. In 1956, his family moved to Watts and the San Gabriel Valley, in the Los Angeles area. He is a poet, journalist, and critic, and lives in San Fernando, California. Rodríguez has written for *The Nation, Grand Street, Los Angeles Weekly,* and *Americas Review,* among others, and is the author of the three collections of poems: *Poems across the Pavement* (1989; Poetry Center Book Award from San Francisco State University); *The Concrete River* (1991; 1991 PEN USA West/Josephine Miles Award for Literary Excellence); and *Trochemoche: Poems* (1998). In addition, he has published *Always Running/La Vida Loca: Gang Days in L.A.* (1993; Sandburg Literary Award for nonfiction in 1993; *Chicago Sun-Times* Book Award for nonfiction in 1994; Notable Book by the *New York Times Book Review* in 1993), and *The Republic of East L.A.* (2002). Finally, he has also published two books for young children, *América Is Her Name* (1998) and *It Doesn't Have to Be This Way: A Barrio Story* (1999), and a study on gang violence titled *Hearts & Hands: Creating Community in Violent Times (2001).* In 1998, Rodríguez received the Hispanic Heritage Award for literature, presented at the John F. Kennedy Center for the Performing Arts in Washington, D.C. He is the founder of Tía Chucha Press and has won a National Book Award, a Lannan Foundation Fellowship, and an Illinois Arts Council Fellowship for poetry.

Helena María Viramontes was born in East Los Angeles to a Mexican American family. She took classes at California State University, Los Angeles and, in 1975, she received a bachelor of arts degree in English literature from Immaculate Heart

College. In 1994, she earned a master of fine arts degree from the University of California, Irvine. She is currently a professor of creative writing in the Department of English at Cornell University and lives in Ithaca, New York. Viramontes has won the John Dos Passos Prize for Literature, a Sundance Institute Fellowship, and the Luis Leal Award for Distinction in Chicano/Latino Literature, and she was named a 2007 USA Ford Fellow by United States Artists. She has been a contributor to *Cuentos: Stories by Latinas* (1983), *Woman of Her Word* (1984), *Beyond Stereotypes: A Critical Analysis of Chicana Literature* (1985), *Breaking Boundaries: Latina Writings and Critical Readings* (1989), and *New Chicana/Chicano Writing* (1992). She was also a contributor to and coedited *Chicana Creativity and Criticism* (1988) and *Chicana (W)Rites: On Word and Film* (1995) with María Herrera-Sobek, and has published the collection of short stories *The Moths and Other Stories* (1995), and the novels *Under the Feet of Jesus* (1995) and *Their Dogs Came with Them* (2007).

36. Mario Acevedo was born in El Paso, Texas, but spent most of his childhood in Las Cruces, New Mexico. He often visited his family in Chihuahua, Mexico, and in Pacoima, California, where part of *X-Rated Bloodsuckers* takes place. He lives in Denver, Colorado, and is a former infantry and aviation officer, military helicopter pilot, engineer, and art teacher. He is also the author of *The Nymphos of Rocky Flats* (2008), *The Undead Kamasutra* (2008), and *Jailbait Zombie* (2009).

John Rechy also made an incursion in the world of gothic fiction with his novel *The Vampires* (1971).

37. Joining a long tradition of denunciation of police corruption in Latino Los Angeles writing, *X-Rated Bloodsuckers* portrays an LAPD that is not only corrupt but also populated by vampires! Julius Paxton, the deputy chief of its Foothills Division, is actually a vampire who works for Cragnow Vissom, the entrepreneur of the porn industry who is behind the corrupt Project Eleven operation. Paxton and his vampire cops try to kill the protagonist, Félix Gómez, and his vampire friend, Coyote. The corrupt police officers, human and undead, hide the evidence of Roxy Bronze's murder and all the other crimes committed by the politicians who support Project Eleven.

38. Díaz also mentions the industrial pollution that has direct negative health consequences in four cities of the San Gabriel Valley, to the east of Los Angeles: La Puente, Baldwin Park, Industry, and Irwindale (215). Likewise, George Lipsitz explains, "In the Los Angeles area today, only 34 percent of whites inhabit areas with the most polluted air, but 71 percent of African Americans and 50 percent of Latinos live in neighborhoods with the highest levels of air pollution" (9). He also points out that "Latinos in East Los Angeles encounter some of the worst smog and the highest concentration of air toxins in southern California because of prevailing wind patterns and the concentration of polluting industries, freeways, and toxic waste dumps" (10).

39. Morales has published the following books: *Barrio on the Edge* (*Caras viejas y vino nuevo*, 1975), *Death of an Anglo* (*La verdad sin voz*, 1979), *The Brick People* (1988), *The Rag Doll Plagues* (1992), *Reto en el paraíso* (1993), and *Pequeña nación* (2005).

40. The navy, however, denies that these diseases have anything to do with the toxic waste they left behind in the eastern side of the island and refuses to clean it up.

41. Like *The Rag Doll Plagues,* the novel *Atomik Aztek* (2005) by the Japanese American Sesshu Foster offers an alternate history in which the Aztecs won the war against the Spanish invaders, and, in the 1940s, the "Aztek Socialist Imperium" became a world power after beating the Nazis in Stalingrad and then colonizing the rest of Europe. The story, which also shares elements of the science fiction genre, is told from the point of view of the protagonist, an Aztec commando named Zenzontli, who, in other chapters, becomes an undocumented immigrant working at a slaughterhouse in East Los Angeles.

42. In the introduction to the Grove Press edition, John Francisco Rechy-Flores states that this novel, which took him three years to write, is one of his best. He is also the author of the documentary *The Sexual Outlaw* (1977), the plays *Momma as She Became—but Not as She Was* and *Rushes* (1979), the collection of essays *Beneath the Skin* (2004), and the novels *City of Night* (1963), *Numbers* (1967), *This Day's Death* (1969), *The Vampires* (1971), *The Fourth Angel* (1972), *The Miraculous Day of Amalia Gómez* (1991), *Our Lady of Babylon* (1996), *Marilyn's Daughter* (1998), *The Coming of Night* (1999), and *The Life and Adventures of Lyle Clemens* (2003). He is a professor of creative writing at the University of Southern California and has also taught at the University of California and Occidental College. Rechy was awarded the Longview Foundation Prize in 1961, and a National Endowment for the Arts fellowship in 1976, and he is the first novelist to receive the PEN USA West Lifetime Achievement Award.

43. This last sentence makes reference to an actual sheik whose taste for decorating his Beverly Hills home outraged his neighbors.

44. Formerly called Arroyo Seco Parkway, the Pasadena Freeway was finished on December 30, 1940, and was the first freeway built in the United States. It connects Pasadena (formerly known as Indiana Colony) with Los Angeles.

45. Mortuaries also appear in *Numbers,* another novel by Rechy.

46. As Rechy himself has pointed out, death is the main metaphor in his novel *Numbers* as well.

47. Griffith Park also has a central presence in *Numbers.*

48. John Carpenter's film *Escape from L.A.* (1996) also mocks Los Angeles's perceived shallowness and its cult of physical appearance in a scene in which the protagonist is taken to a Beverly Hills building that is full of "surgical failures." These people have had too many implants and facelifts through the years and now have to survive by having fresh body parts transplanted over and over again.

49. David E. Johnson has also studied the exclusion of his oeuvre from studies about the Chicano novel: "No doubt one reason for a certain ignorance of Rechy was his early 'failure' to thematize Mexican-American concerns. His reluctance to do so resulted in his dismissal not only from current multicultural debates, but from earlier debates constitutive of the field of Chicano studies" (449). In response, the author proudly states: "I was writing about 'Mexican-Americans,' and identifying myself as such, in *The Nation, Evergreen Review, Saturday Review*. In virtually all my novels, the protagonist's mother is Mexican, like mine" (Castillo 113).

50. In the introduction to the Grove Press edition, Rechy declares the *intentio operis:* "I intended to explore beneath the clichés too often expressed about Los Angeles: its spurious obsession with artifice, not substance, its lack of defining center, its courtship of extremity, its mindless narcissism—that is, its want of profundity, of soul." He also wanted to present the city as "the place of exile chosen by banished angels after expulsion from Heaven for disobedience, angels still restive."

51. The protagonist of *City of Night* sexualizes nature as well: "Orange and yellow poppies like just-lit matches sputtering in the breeze. Birds of paradise with long pointed tongues; blue and purple lupines; joshua trees with incredible bunches of flowers held high like torches—along long, long rows of phallic palm-trees with sunbleached pubic hair . . ." (87). Overall, in *City of Night* Southern California is described as an area where people move to heal their soul aches, aided by the exuberance of the surrounding vegetation: "And what you came hoping to be cured with (which is, importantly, what someone else came to be cured *of*—your sickness being someone else's cure) is certainly here (although you may not find it): all here, among the flowers and the grass, the palmtrees" (177).

52. Johnny compares Los Angeles's aging theaters to hideously decaying mouths with missing teeth. This same metaphor is used in the description of a New York theater in *City of Night*.

53. *The Miraculous Day of Amalia Gómez* emphasizes the male chauvinism of Latino characters, both males and females. Thus, the protagonist who lends her name to the novel's title is raped repeatedly by her father (at age fourteen), by her boyfriend, and by her husband. When she tells her mother about these sexual abuses, the latter only blames her. In a case of homosocial relationship, Amalia's father and that of her rapist boyfriend, who happen to be *compadres* (a relationship between a father and the godfather of his sibling that creates a lifelong bond), decide that the youngsters should get married. Amalia is not the only victim of male violence, however: her mother always forgives her father every time he beats her, and Amalia's previous boyfriend, Raynaldo, sexually abuses her daughter as well. These episodes suggest that the worst enemies of Mexican American women are their own men.

54. In Michael Nava's *Rag and Bone,* Henry Ríos describes the sharp contrasts between the appearance and demeanor of Ortega, a Latino reverend who also works as a janitor in a "sleek Westside shopping mall," and the rest of the shoppers: "There were no children or old people among the hundreds of well-dressed shoppers; just sleek, well-groomed youngish white people whose eyes seemed to register nothing but the next purchase. The only conversations going on were into cell phones. . . . He was not simply of a different ethnicity than most of them, he was of a different species" (273). In contrast, in "Transmission to Los Angeles #5" of her "accidental memoir" *Frantic Transmissions,* Kate Braverman conceives of shopping malls in a completely different way: "The malls of Los Angeles are utterly egalitarian" (127). In fact, she confesses that they are one of the things she misses the most from Los Angeles: "They assure a known and protected environment with a recognizable purpose. They are our form of a sanctified public area, a commons or town square. And you don't need permission, don't have to show your ID, visa, or pay for admission. In a shopping mall there is the promise of discovery and reinvention" (125).

55. Environmental racism is also a matter of concern for the autobiographical protagonist of Luis J. Rodríguez's *Always Running* (1993), who shows awareness of the victimization of underprivileged communities: "Most of Watts and a large section of East Los Angeles were unincorporated country territory. Sometimes they had no sewage system or paved roads. They included hills, ravines and hollows" (38). Along with the denunciation, he recalls his personal contribution to consciousness-raising: as a young boy, he wrote a play in which local government officials were planning to uproot his community to build freeways and malls, something that would become a reality a few years later. By the same token, the author recalls in the epilogue how "a radio broadcast stated that in a three-mile radius of South Central, there were some 640 liquor stores, although not one movie house or community center!" (248).

Chapter 2

1. James R. Curtis has devised a four-stage barrio typology in the Hispanization of Los Angeles:

(1) (Barrio type): Plaza-based; (Phase and Spatial Process): Inception/ Constriction; (Time Period): 1781–1910; (Dependency-Orientation): Independent, Inward-oriented. (2) Urban *colonias;* Transition/Nodality; 1911–mid 1950s; Dependent; Outward-oriented. (3) Hierarchical; Maturity/Primacy; Mid-1950s–mid 1980s; Dependent, Inward-oriented. (4) Metropolitan Realms; Emergent/Expansion; Mid-1980s–present; Independent, Inward- and Outward-oriented. (131)

2. After reading *Decade of Betrayal,* explain Balderrama and Rodríguez, state senator Joseph Dunn "introduced two bills, one to provide a window of opportunity for repatriates who wished to file for redress of the injustice and the second to create a commission to study the issue and propose recommendations. The governor vetoed both bills" (339). *Decade of Betrayal* includes copies of veto message bill 933 by then–California governor Gray Davis and two other veto message bills (37 and 42) by California governor Arnold Schwarzenegger.

3. "Un *clown* impasible y siniestro, que no intenta hacer reír y que procura aterrorizar" (18).

4. The Broadway production debuted at the Winter Garden Theater and had forty-one performances. In 1981, a filmed version of the Broadway play, also directed by Luis Valdez, was released. It featured music by Daniel Valdez and Lalo Guerrero, and the cast included Daniel Valdez, Edward James Olmos, and Tyne Daly. As Tatum points out, "*Zoot Suit* represented an important step forward for popular Chicano theater because, for the first time, a contemporary play by a Chicano had successfully made the transition from the barrio and the university campus to commercial theater. Valdez and his troupe were able to carry their hard-hitting message to a wider audience" (129).

5. Mike Davis has also criticized the racism of the Los Angeles press in an article covering a Malibu fire: "The *Malibu Times* [11 November 1993] celebrated the case of two intrepid housewives from the Big Rock area who loaded their dogs into kayaks and took to the sea, where they were eventually rescued by Baywatch Redondo. Only the fine print revealed that, in saving their pets, they had left the Latina maids behind" (*Ecology* 128).

6. Over six hundred young Chicanos were arrested after the killing of José Díaz in an alleged brawl between rival Mexican American gangs at the Sleepy Lagoon reservoir. Twenty-two young Mexican American men were tried, but the convictions were reversed on appeal in October 1944. The sensationalist coverage of the case by the *Los Angeles Times* and the *Herald-Express* instigated the massive arrests and the criminal trial.

7. Including Allen L. Woll's *The Latin Image in American Film* (1977); the volume *Chicano Cinema: Research, Reviews, and Resources* (1985), edited by Gary D. Keller; George Hadley-García's *Hispanic Hollywood* (1990); the volume of essays *Chicanos and Film: Representation and Resistance* (1992), edited by Chon A. Noriega; Rosa-Linda Fregoso's *The Bronze Screen: Chicana and Chicano Film Culture* (1993); Gary D. Keller's *Hispanics and United States Film: An Overview and Handbook* (1994); the collection of essays *The Ethnic Eye: Latino Media Arts* (1996), edited by Chon Noriega and Ana López; Christine List's *Chicano Images: Refiguring Ethnicity in Mainstream Film* (1996); Chon Noriega's *Shot in America: Television, the State, and the Rise of Chicano Cinema* (2000); Charles Ramírez Berg's *Latino Images in Film* (2002); and Clara E. Rodríguez's *Heroes, Lovers, and Others: The Story of Latinos in Hollywood* (2004).

8. Among these exceptions, we may include *Border Incident* (1949), *Right Cross* (1950), *Touch of Evil* (1958), *Zoot Suit* (1981), *La Bamba* (1987), *Born in East L.A.* (1987), *The Milagro Beanfield War* (1988), *Stand and Deliver* (1988), and *American Me* (1992).

9. Fortunately, the situation is changing. Thus, in the extra features of Edward James Olmos's film *Walkout,* the producer, Moctesuma Esparza, celebrates the presence of young Latino actors in Hollywood: "We couldn't have done it five years ago or ten years ago. We didn't have all these beautiful, talented actors. . . . People under thirty in the United States, 28 percent are Latino. Hollywood, our industry, where we work, is a youth industry, and we're still only—what? 2 percent?—but we now have a beautiful group of actors and actresses, and so we were so blessed that we could make this movie now."

10. As Chon Noriega explains, *Born in East L.A.* won "the best script award in Havana, speaking to such oppositional standards as the Hollywood box office and the 'aesthetics of hunger' of New Latin American Cinema" ("Between" 146). In a humorous scene, the protagonist, Rudy (Cheech Marín), teaches a group of Asian immigrants how to be Chicano: they get tattoos and learn barrio handshakes, to walk with an attitude, and to use East L.A. jargon (*órale vato,* what's happening?, *simón, suave, ahí te watcho*). By embracing the stereotype and ridiculing it, Christine List argues, these films counter the derogatory effects of Chicano stereotypes: "Since all ethnic groups, including Anglos, are typed in equally absurd ways, Marín's broadly drawn comic technique forces the audience to consider that ethnic stereotypes are overgeneralizations" ("Self-directed" 192). Charles M. Tatum contends that "the film focuses on differing and contested definitions of foreignness and thereby captures some of the U.S. political xenophobia, which in its most extreme and virulent form would seek to rid the United States of all foreigners, including Chicanos and Asian Americans who were also considered to be foreign (i.e., nonwhite)" (80). However, one may argue that *Born in East L.A.* is also a problematic testimony of the stereotypes that some Chicanos have of Mexico and of Mexicans, as we see in the caricatured Mexican character played by Paul Rodríguez.

11. This particular way of combating mainstream ethnic stereotypes and ethnocentrism through humor has also been used by comedian, writer, and actor Carlos Mencía (1967–), host of the half-hour comedy show *Mind of Mencía* on the cable channel Comedy Central. In his stand-up act, sketches, and parodic segments, Mencía offers his own version of East Los Angeles and gets by with using racial slurs and ethnic stereotypes by including frequent racist epithets against himself and his own ethnic group. Following these self-stereotyping tactics, his comedy show portrays Latinos as undocumented migrant workers and gardeners, and Latinas as domestic workers and pregnant teenagers. Like Cheech Marín in *Born in East L.A.,* Mencía often uses the topic of undocumented immigration as a source of comedy. While his act is comedy and therefore should not

be taken seriously, his discourse is nonetheless political and has a darker side. He is well aware—and even mentions it in his show—that most of his audience is Euro-American, and perhaps for this reason, in recent episodes he has decided to emphasize his exaggerated American patriotism, while denigrating the image of Mexico; he even justifies Manifest Destiny as a rationale for the conquest of Mexican territories by the United States.

12. I viewed the episodes of *Gangland* under discussion on March 27 and 28, 2008, and on April 3 and 4, 2008. See Bibliography for individual episode titles and the original airdates.

13. A list compiled by Morgan Quitno Press, which bases the rankings on FBI figures released in June 2006, included only Compton among the most dangerous cities in the United States, after Saint Louis, Detroit, and Flint (Michigan).

14. The name "Crips" is believed to have originated from the nickname "Cripples," allegedly given to them by a neighbor who mocked their habit of walking with canes during the 1970s. Organizations such as FACES (Family and Children Enrollment System) and NOGUNS (Networks Organized for Gang Unity and Neighborhood Safety), among numerous others, have also tried to unite Bloods and Crips simply to end black-on-black violence.

15. According to the Los Angeles city attorney's office and the LAPD, in 2007 Los Angeles officials listed the most violent street gangs in Los Angeles, which include approximately eight hundred members and were responsible for 6 percent of the city's violent crimes in 2006: Black P-Stones (African American), Mara Salvatrucha (MS-13) (Latino), Rollin' 40s (African American), Rollin' 30s (African American), Rollin' 60s (African American), 18th Street Westside (Latino), 204th Street (Latino), Avenues (Latino), Canoga Park Alabama (Latino), Grape Street Crips (African American), and La Mirada Locos (Latino) ("L.A's most violent" n.p.). The 18th Street gang is believed to be the first Latino street gang to have actively recruited members of other ethnic groups.

16. Actually, Maxson and Klein estimate that only 5 percent of resident youth participate in gang activities in East Los Angeles, and 6 percent in South Central Los Angeles. Yet they were "warned by an experienced gang 'expert' in the police department that 'every kid down in there is a gang member—every one'" (249).

17. Homi Bhabha has also focused on the importance of respect in interethnic conflicts: "Conflicts in South Central Los Angeles between Koreans, Mexican-Americans and African-Americans focus on the concept of 'disrespect'—a term forged on the borderlines of ethnic deprivation that is, at once, the sign of racialized violence and the symptom of social victimage" (2).

18. The prison gang Mexican Mafia, or La Eme, was created in 1957 by Mexican American street gang members from East Los Angeles imprisoned at the Deuel Vocational Institution in Tracy, California. Their members, known as *sureños,* typically wear red clothing. One of their main symbols is *la mano negra*

(the black hand), modeled, like their name, after the Italian Mafia. La Eme claims the Southern Californian territory from Bakersfield to the international border with Mexico. Their main rival gang is Nuestra Familia (Our Family), whose members are usually known as *norteños,* since they come from Northern California. They usually wear blue clothing, and they use, among other symbols, the eagle that Richard Chávez designed for the United Farm Workers, and a sombrero with a bloody machete. The rivalry between La Eme and Nuestra Familia began in California's prisons, where their headquarters are still located.

19. This motto, "Blood in, blood out," basically means that the only way to join the gang is to shed blood, while the only way to leave is death.

20. The Chicano term *carnalismo* is generally used to refer to the love and loyalty one feels for his or her friends.

21. In these narratives and films, gangbangers are often referred to with alternative names such as *vatos, cholas, pandilleros,* or *locas.*

22. In an interview, Morales explained to me that the novel originated from a collection of autobiographical notes, poems, and short stories that he wrote while still in high school. All of them reflect a reality that he lived in the Simons barrio of Montebello where he was raised, not far from downtown Los Angeles. Using a more realist approach, he describes the origins of his barrio in *The Brick People* (1988), his first novel written in English.

23. We find a very negative description of the Latino barrio in *The Revolt of the Cockroach People,* where Acosta's autobiographical protagonist states: "We swell through streets of dogs and cats and trash, narrow jungle paths of garbage cans, beat-up jalopies, mudholes and dogshit. A thousand kids streaming through a barrio of palm trees and Mexicatessens" (41). He describes Tooner Flats and other barrios as hopeless war zones controlled by gangs, where boys learn to write by spraying graffiti on walls. Genaro Padilla (1987) has summarized Acosta's contradictory feelings toward the barrio: "there are numerous occasions during which Acosta feels a swell of cooperation and love throughout the barrio, but just as often, and usually for inexplicable reasons, there is confusion of motive, senseless faction, distrust for all Chicano outsiders, all of which leaves Acosta distraught, even disillusioned with the barrio" (165). Acosta's criticism of the metropolis, on the other hand, is quite conventional if we place it in the context of Los Angeles literature. What sets him apart from other authors, according to Paredes, is "the linkage he establishes between the unsavoriness of the city and its long-standing abuse of its Mexican-American population" (251).

24. Likewise, in the first pages of *Two Badges* Mona Ruiz links overpopulation and the environmental deterioration of the barrio with the increasingly high level of criminality: "Santa Ana was a small quiet town, rows of wood-frame houses dotted by orange groves and surrounded by clear skies when I was born, but by the 1980s, whole strips of the city looked like a Third World country. Crime was a daily part of life and the gangs were a problem in nearly

every school" (12). The realization that there is a Third World (often referred to as a Fourth World) within the economically wealthiest country in the world seems to evoke the idea of "internal colonialism," one of the most commonly used paradigms in Chicano studies. Likewise, Miguel Durán begins his novel *Don't Spit on My Corner* by establishing a connection between the deplorable state of his barrio and the city authorities' neglect: "T-Flats got its name from the book, *Tortilla Flats* [*sic*], which was written by John Steinbeck. There was a gully called Bernal Street, which was unpaved but lined with houses which were really ramshackle. For sure, no building inspector had okayed any house down here. Nobody seemed to give a damn" (15).

In *Hearts and Hands: Creating Community in Violent Times* (2001), Rodríguez proposes new ways to end gang violence. This book is now part of the curriculum in the staff training program for State of California juvenile detention centers, halls, and camps.

25. His friend Mateo, for example, recalls how, although Julián belonged in the third grade, the school board told his mother that he could not be promoted, because there weren't enough chairs in the classroom. He was also unfairly expelled after an older Euro-American boy started a fight with him. Even though the other boy confessed his guilt, the expulsion was never lifted.

26. This passage is reminiscent of Richard's adviser in José Antonio Villarreal's *Pocho* (1959), who recommends that he take auto mechanics or welding instead of going to college (108).

27. This metaphoric use of the Los Angeles River is commonplace in several films set in Los Angeles. As we can see in Maroon 5's 2007 video clip "Wake Up Call" (from the album *It Won't Be Soon Before Long*), even pop/rock bands use images of the Los Angeles river to toughen up their own image.

28. This film, which won the Audience Award (Dramatic) at the Sundance festival, was based on a play by Josefina López.

29. Even in James L. Brooks's *Spanglish* (2004), which shows an awareness of political correctness, one of the main characters, Flor (played by Spanish actor Paz Vega), is still a beautiful Mexican housekeeper for an affluent Los Angeles family. Furthermore, she is somewhat of a stereotypical "spitfire." In the words of film critic Andre Soares, "*Spanglish* pretends to be open minded about cultural differences and relations while reinforcing every old stereotype in the book" (n.p.).

30. According to Edward James Olmos, "At the height of the walkout there were over twenty-two thousand kids that stood up and walked out of their classes in the L.A. County area" ("Interview" n. p.).

31. Although they also protested the disproportionate death toll of Latinos in the Vietnam War, as Edward James Olmos posits in an interview, the "key issue for the 1968 walkouts was that there was a real lack of cultural history being taught in the East L.A. schools" ("Interview" n.p.).

32. Emulating the Black Panthers, young Chicanos in the Chicano Movement formed, in the late 1960s, the Brown Berets, a Chicano nationalist and activist group determined to combat police brutality, fight for educational equality, and protest the Vietnam War. They published the newspaper *La Causa* and claimed the Southwest of the United States as Aztlán, the original homeland of their Aztec ancestors.

33. Harry Gamboa Jr. came up with the term "Walkout" and suggested using this strategy.

34. The civil unrest of the 1992 Los Angeles Uprising left more than forty persons dead and approximately a billion dollars worth of damage. When asked about the Rodney King beating, LAPD Chief Daryl Gates lamented the excessive violence used by the cops but provided the following explanation: "That's the impression that was given, but a totally false impression, because there was nothing racist about it. No one knew what Rodney King had done beforehand to be stopped. No one realized that he was a parolee and that he was violating his parole" (Boyer n.p.). As to the nearly all-white suburban jury's verdict of "not guilty" for the four LAPD officers in the Rodney King case, Gates answered: "So I said, 'Hey, that's good, justice has been served.' And then, of course, the rioting began, which, quite frankly, surprised me. . . . And we were slow to react, there was no question about it. Slow to react" (Boyer n.p.). Michael Nava's *Rag and Bone* echoes the political consequences of this scandal: He "[District attorney Anthony Earl] was also black, and he fell victim to the silent racial civil war going on in post–Rodney King, post–O.J. Simpson L.A. One of the battlegrounds was the polling booth, where whites voted in greater and more consistent numbers than any of the city's other major ethnic groups" (152–53).

35. Puerto Rican officer Rafael Pérez exposed the widespread and systematic corruption in the Rampart antigang CRASH unit, which included robbing banks, selling narcotics, making bogus arrests, falsifying evidence, imprisoning innocent people, and working part-time as bodyguards for rappers from the Death Row label. However, he failed five lie detector tests about his accusations. Regarding the Rampart scandal, LAPD Chief Daryl Gates argued, "Two things are happening with Rafael Pérez. One, he wants a better deal, and two, he doesn't want to look like the bad guy, so he makes other police officers look like bad guys, because he doesn't want to look like a bad guy. It's his own self-esteem. 'It's not just me, it's those other guys, too. I wasn't the only one, those other guys did it too.' So he puts a finger on a whole bunch of people, and right from the very beginning, I would have had a hard time believing anything that guy said. I know Internal Affairs has done a lot of investigating, but who are you investigating, gang members? Are you going to listen to what they have to say, too?" (Boyer n.p.). Incidentally, in Michael Nava's *Rag and Bones,* the lawyer Henry Ríos turns the Rampart scandal into political capital: "There will be black and brown jurors. All I need to do is breathe the word 'Ramparts' while he's

on the stand and I'll hang the jury" (224). Incidentally, the assassination of star rappers Tupac Shakur and Biggie Smalls in 1996 and 1997 respectively has been linked with the Rampart scandal.

36. The film's title alludes to the blue and red colors used by the Crips and Bloods respectively.

37. According to Charles Ramírez Berg, other Latino stereotypes in American film include the *bandido,* the dark lady, the female clown, the harlot, the Latin lover, and the Latino male buffoon.

38. Taking a big step down as far as aesthetic quality is concerned, Chris Fisher's *Nightstalker* (2002) includes two Latino officers among its cast of characters, even though in 1980 80 percent of LAPD officers were still Euro-American. The East Los Angeles depicted in this film features a Chicano drug addict and satanic serial killer, played by Bret Roberts and modeled after the real-life Richard Ramírez (nicknamed "The Night Stalker" by the press), who terrorized the Los Angeles and San Francisco metropolitan areas during the 1980s. Perhaps to balance this very negative Chicano figure who suffers from schizophrenia and appears to obey a bald, white, and diabolic figure, the rookie Cuban Officer Gabrielle Martínez (Roselyn Sánchez) is portrayed as a dignified, religious, and educated character who has abandoned her teaching position in the East to help her senile mother in Los Angeles. Officer Frank Luis (Danny Trejo), the Latino who works with the protagonist, is also dignified (although he uses cocaine and is somewhat of a womanizer), and before being shot, he generously helps his partner to succeed professionally.

39. The LAPD has the second-largest civilian air force in the world.

40. We find a similar example in Durán's *Don't Spit on My Corner,* where, after a fraudulent arrest, the police officers make the pachucos walk back home through hostile territory, thus potentially instigating a confrontation between pachuco gangs.

41. "Se sabía que el sindicato de policías y guardias había contratado la agencia más grande de especialistas de influencia para proteger sus intereses en el gobierno estatal y nacional" (60).

42. As to the other enemies of the barrio, when Micaela finds out about the city's plans to displace Latino families to build two new stadiums, she organizes the neighborhood and manages to stop the project. The federation also expels from the barrio all parents who neglect their children. In this regard, the story seems to condone some of the extreme measures taken by Los Angeles politicians: "In Spring of 1989 (Year Two of the HAMMER)," Mike Davis reminds us, "[Los Angeles mayor] Hahn's office tested STEP's 'bad parent' provision with the sensationalized arrest of a 37-year-old Southcentral woman whose 15-year-old son had earlier been arraigned for participation in gang rape" (*City* 283).

43. This is not the case with the autobiographical Chicano lawyer, Buffalo Zeta Brown, in Óscar Zeta Acosta's *The Revolt of the Cockroach People* (1998),

a sequel to the road trip work *Autobiography of a Brown Buffalo* (1972). The protagonist's fictional participation in the bombing of the Hall of Justice symbolizes his relentless defiance against mainstream society's rules and "his lack of respect for the racism of the court system" (Calderón 92). In real life, during the 1969 trial proceedings where Acosta defended four Mexican American activists accused of having set nine fires in the Biltmore Hotel while Governor Ronald Reagan was giving a speech inside, "presiding judge Arthur L. Alarcon jailed Acosta along with fellow attorneys Beth Livesey and Joan Anderson for contempt of court after a verbal encounter with him" (Calderón 93). During the trial, Acosta "maintained that the fires had been set by a Los Angeles Police Department infiltrator and informant, Fernando Sumaya" (Calderón 92). In 1970, Acosta unsuccessfully ran for sheriff of Los Angeles County. One of the points in his platform was "the immediate withdrawal of sheriffs from the barrios and ghettos" (Calderón 93).

44. Contradicting this improved image of the LAPD, Latino characters blame the National Immigration Agency for the closure of most businesses in the formerly prosperous César Chávez Avenue, after its officers raid the downtown garment district and arrest almost one hundred undocumented Mexicans.

45. As Ruiz explains, when the gang veterans were incarcerated, they made connections with the most powerful prison gang in Southern California, the Mexican Mafia, and became drug dealers or even killers: "The guys who went to prison always came back different—harder and more desperate. I've heard people say the prisons are like a college for criminals, a place that will turn you into a hardened criminal if you aren't one when you go in. Guys that went in as robbers and burglars came out as killers. Others, who weren't strong enough to protect themselves, had to sell themselves sexually to keep alive inside" (60).

Chapter 3

1. "Su ideal es, realmente, ser hombres, pero para ellos, ser hombres es la contradicción en que siempre estuvieron y cuya superación no tienen clara, equivale a ser opresores" (35).

2. Kate Braverman was born in Philadelphia, but when she was eight years old, her parents moved to Los Angeles. Seven years later, she ran away to San Francisco and Berkeley, later moving back to Los Angeles, where she lived from 1971 to 1995. She currently lives in San Francisco. She has published three other novels: *Lithium for Medea* (1979), *Wonders of the West* (1993), and *The Incarnation of Frida K.* (2001); four books of poetry: *Milk Run* (1977), *Lullaby for Sinners* (1980), *Hurricane Warnings* (1987), and *Postcard from August* (1990); and two collections of short stories: *Squandering the Blue* (1990) and *Small Craft Warnings* (1997). She has won the O. Henry Award for her short story "Tall Tales from the Mekong Delta"; the Best American Short Stories award; the Carver

Short Story Award; the Economist Prize; a Christopher Isherwood Foundation Fellowship for lifetime recognition of achievement; the Pushcart Prize for her short story "Cocktail Hour"; the 2005 Mississippi Review Prize; and the Editor's Choice Raymond Carver Short Story Award for "Mrs. Jordan's Summer Vacation." She is also the first recipient of Graywolf Press's Creative Nonfiction Award, for *Frantic Transmissions to and from Los Angeles: An Accidental Memoir* (2006), and has been nominated for four Pulitzer prizes for her poetry. Her works have been translated into Turkish, French, Italian, and Spanish. Although Braverman finished *Palm Latitudes* in 1984, she was unable to find a publisher for four years.

3. Braverman, on the other hand, has commented sarcastically on this kind of reception—a common one—of what she considers her best work: "Most people have never read *Palm Latitudes* (it's so literary) but it is my Big Book and product of a fusion of the Spanish [*sic*] winds blowing in from Neruda, Paz, García Márquez and the revolutionary genre-busting work of the '70s writers and the edgy power of Punk" (Block n.p.).

4. Judith Butler, in *Gender Trouble: Feminism and the Subversion of Identity* (1990), has explained how problematic the traditional association of women with nature is: "reason and mind are associated with masculinity and agency, while the body and nature are considered to be mute facticity of the feminine, awaiting signification from an opposing masculine subject" (48). In *Palm Latitudes,* however, the female body is commonly associated with cityscapes rather than with natural landscapes.

5. Braverman coincides with John Rechy in her numerous descriptions of bougainvilleas, a South American woody shrub or vine that represents the city of Los Angeles in their novels.

6. As mentioned in the introduction, among the works with apocalyptic overtones are Rechy's *Bodies and Souls,* Nava's *The Burning Plain,* Acevedo's *X-Rated Bloodsuckers,* Hopper's film *Colors,* and a long list of novels and films by Euro-American writers and directors included in the sixth chapter of Mike Davis's *Ecology of Fear.*

7. Mike Davis has studied this ecologic tragedy of the river that Spanish explorers named Porciúncula: "The opposing solution was to deepen and 'armor'—that is, pave—a narrow width of the river's channel in order to flush storm runoff out of the city as efficiently as possible, and thus allow extensive industrial development within the floodplain. Beneficial to large landowners, this strategy would force the natural river into a concrete straitjacket—destroying the riparian ecology and precluding use of the riverway as a greenbelt. . . . The Los Angeles River—the defining landscape of the nineteenth-century city—was sacrificed for the sake of emergency work relief, the preservation of industrial land values, and a temporary abatement of the flood problem" (*Ecology* 69–71).

8. Abandonment is also a central topic in both of Braverman's collections of short stories.

9. Likewise, the novel portrays the Catholic Church as an accomplice in the subjugation of Latinas. Not only does a misogynous priest, Padre Pérez, forbid women from abandoning their husbands, but according to a curandera, the entire church has misrepresented biblical women: "God is a man and therefore severe with his judgments. Remember this. María Magdalena was no less a saint than La Virgen de Guadalupe" (43).

10. Incidentally, "Money, Power and Respect" (1998) is the title of a hit single included in an eponymous album by rappers The Lox and Little Kim. As they explained in interviews, these are, in their view, the three central values for youth urban subculture.

11. Two famously male-chauvinistic texts that reflect the mindset of the times are Óscar Zeta Acosta's memoirs, *Autobiography of a Brown Buffalo* (1972) and *The Revolt of the Cockroach People*. In these two works, the author's concern for justice for the Latino community is sometimes overshadowed by his disregard for gender inequality. Although in *The Revolt* Brown tells his friend Gilbert that women have the right to participate in the Movement ("Isn't the revolution for all people?" [120]), in the remainder of the story the first-person narrator constantly sexualizes and objectifies women and uses sexist language to describe his fellow female militants, even in scenes where they are in the middle of a fight: "Girls with long mascara-eyes, long black hair done up *chola* style, with tight asses and full blouses bursting out with song" (12). Again, in a passage where the narrator wonders about his own double consciousness, he refers to prostitutes in a disparaging manner: "All through schools, jobs and bumming, I haven't even held the hand of a Mexican woman, excepting whores who are all the same anyhow" (29). Overall, it is evident that women are left outside Acosta's nationalist plans. As Rafael Pérez-Torres has observed, "mestizo consciousness is tied directly to a masculinist desire and affirmation of mestizo agency at the cost of a liberated *mestiza* subjectivity" (54). In his Gonzo style, Brown at times presents the social struggle as a way for male militants to show their manliness and to obtain sexual rewards for it: "How many times have I shouted 'Viva la Raza!' waiting for a score? . . . thanks to the revolution, at last I have a brown babe for my hurts. Three of them under the same blanket!" (86–87). His lowest point in *Autobiography* comes when he fantasizes about stabbing and raping his girlfriend after their breakup. The struggle against the racialization and discrimination of Chicano people does not prevent the protagonist from using homophobic language, essentializing other ethnic groups, or referring to them in racist terms. In this regard, Juan Bruce-Novoa has tried to explain Acosta's choice of vocabulary: "the liberal use of obscenities, racial and ethnic insults, and slander" is, according to him, part of the "Gonzo style" invented by Hunter S. Thompson ("Fear" 42). Incidentally, as Hames-García points out, in a

"1973 letter Acosta claimed to be the co-creator of this style" (4). Likewise, referring to Acosta's racist and sexist vocabulary, Héctor Calderón argues, "Although not in good taste, these words refer not so much to racist language but to obscenity of racism that Acosta has endured throughout his life" (109–110).

12. Sexist vocabulary and questionable (in)action are recurrent in *Always Running,* Luis J. Rodríguez's memoir of his gang life. In chapter 5, for example, when the young Luis J. Rodríguez (according to the preface, this work is not fiction) realizes that a young, naked girl who is drugged out is to be raped by several of his peers, he leaves without trying to prevent the act: "Yuk Yuk by then had thrown the girl to the ground. I knew what they were going to do, and wandered off" (123). According to the author, sexual violence against females was a common occurrence, part of "a way of life" in the barrio (121). He mentions that one barrio boy raped seventeen girls in a summer. On different occasions, Rodríguez's peers invite him to participate in the gang rapes of drugged young girls; he always refuses. Monica Brown has analyzed these appalling scenes: "Rodríguez takes the role of silent (and in his silence, complicit) witness to violence against women, but this time the stakes are higher—he witnesses his homeboys rape young girls and describes these scenes in graphic detail. He is invited to join these gang rapes but declines. In a world where women are not treated as individuals with agency, women exist primarily as a medium to communicate men's desire for power and each other" (69–70).

13. Laura del Fuego received a Literature Fellowship from the California Arts Council and has published her poetry, essays, and stories in the *Haight Ashbury Literary Journal* and in other journals and anthologies. She has also published *Carmen García Was Here 'c/s'* (A. Figueroa Press). She is also a screenwriter and works as an editor for Sonoma County *Women's Voices.*

14. Yxta Maya Murray was born in California and lives in Los Angeles. She is an associate professor at Loyola Law School in Los Angeles and has written fiction and nonfiction for publications such as *Buzz, Glamour,* and *Zyzzyva.* She has published four other novels: *What It Takes to Get to Vegas* (1999), *The Conquest* (Winner of the 1999 Whiting Writers' Award for fiction), *The Queen Jade* (2005), and *The Good Girl's Guide to Getting Kidnapped* (2010).

15. Throughout *The Revolt of the Cockroach People,* examples abound of what might be considered internalized self-hatred and racism, even if it is used as a rhetorical device for shocking purposes or to heighten the countercultural context in the written text. For example, the narrator mimics his antagonists by referring to his people as "greasers," "savages," and "cockroaches." He then exposes his negative self-image by constantly pointing out his dark complexion and corpulence. The ostensibly self-hating remarks increase up to the last chapter, where, switching to fiction, the protagonist states, "We've got seven big ones to blow a hole in this cement-concrete-steel building, right under that motherfucking greaser" (254). While it may be argued that the use of racial slurs against

himself and his people mitigates their offensiveness, new questions arise when the protagonist realizes that he has never had a true relationship with a woman of Mexican descent and wonders whether he is marked by alienation and false consciousness: "*Am* I ashamed of my race?" (31). Pérez-Torres would answer affirmatively: "Although there is within both Mexican and Chicano nationalist discourses a clear affirmation of the indigenous, one need not search hard to encounter social values that often reject the autochthonous. Acosta's memoir *The Autobiography of a Brown Buffalo* (1972) dwells at length on the devaluation of his indigenous identity" (63). Similarly, in *Autobiography of a Brown Buffalo*, the autobiographical protagonist stands before the mirror several times and describes himself as an overweight man with pig eyes, a small penis, knock-knees, peasant hands, and other derogatory terms: "I could see myself in the mirror. I was the original Cro-Magnon Man from the profile. The beast they found in the tar pits was my grandfather" (50). We learn further on that this negative self-perception began with his mother's unflattering descriptions of his physique and her disdain for Indians.

16. In Mexican slang, "gabacho" is a term used to refer to foreigners. It is sometimes a synonym of "gringo," and it can be derogatory.

17. Luis J. Rodríguez states, "I've talked to enough gang members and low-level dope dealers to know they would quit today if they had a productive, livable-wage job. You'll find people who don't care about who they hurt, but nobody I know *wants* to sell death to their children, their neighbors and friends" (*Always Running* 251).

18. Lucía, in turn, also wonders about Manny's motivations: "I can't tell what they want more, to make a man bleed or to get his money" (34). In *Two Badges,* Mona Ruiz argues that despite other factors such as self-protection, joining a gang is a personal choice: "Too often when I was young, I took the wrong road. I could try to blame it on a lot of factors, I suppose, like economics or foolish youth or the influence of the people in my neighborhood and schools, but really it all comes down to me. Everyone is responsible for their own actions" (279).

19. The East Los Angeles 18th Street gang, according to the aforementioned series *Gangland,* was also known as the "Children's Army," for their notorious recruitment of elementary and middle-school kids. The show also claims that MS-13 recruits children as young as eight or nine years old.

20. Anders lived for some time in Echo Park.

21. This story about sisterhood is linked with several others that are narrated from different perspectives. For instance, in one of three separate vignettes we find a precedent for Lucía's character in Murray's novel *Locas,* in the blonde Whisper (Nélida López), who learns about drug dealing from Ernesto. Although Whisper considers "starting her own operation," she instead chooses to teach the narcotics business to her young brother. In another intercalated story, Sad

Girl's sister, La Blue Eyes (Magali Alvarado), becomes interested in El Durán, a prison inmate who writes romantic letters to her.

22. The following passage from John Rechy's *The Miraculous Day of Amalia Gómez* (1991) also condemns the masculinism of graffiti iconography:

> There was a wall painting that fascinated and puzzled her, and she went there often to look at it: A muscular Aztec prince, amber-gold-faced, in lordly feathers, stood with others as proud as he. They gazed toward the distance. . . .
>
> . . . an old Mexican man who had been sitting nearby on a bench came up to her and explained: "The *conquistadores* are about to subdue the Indians with weapons, as they did, but over there"—he pointed to the band of muslin-clad men—"are the *revolucionarios,* who will triumph and bring about *Aztlán,* our promised land of justice."
>
> Amalia thanked him for his explanation. She continued to study the mural. There were no women. Where were they? Had *they* survived? (45)

Indeed, as Gloria Anzaldúa and other Mexican American feminist critics have pointed out, the rhetoric of the Chicano Movement, as contained in the "Plan Espiritual de Aztlán" (Spiritual Plan of Aztlán) as well as in "Yo soy Joaquín," a foundational poem by Rodolfo "Corky" Gonzales (1928–2005), presented the Chicano militant as male, thus preventing women from being part of the nationalist imagery.

The "Plan Espiritual de Aztlán" was a manifesto proposed in 1969 by the First National Chicano Liberation Youth Conference, which advocated Chicano nationalism and self-determination. "Corky" Gonzales read the poem "Yo soy Joaquín" at this conference.

23. At any rate, as Aihwa Ong has explained, we must question the popular idea that the nation-state is becoming obsolete because of the increasing circulation of transnational capital and labor: "we sometimes overlook complicated accommodations, alliances, and creative tensions between the nation-state and mobile capital, between diaspora and nationalism, and between the influx of immigrants and the multicultural state. Attention to specific histories and geopolitical situations will reveal that such simple oppositions between transnational forces and the nation-state cannot be universally sustained" (16).

24. See the introduction to my book *Imaging the Chinese in Cuban Literature and Culture* (Gainesville: University Press of Florida, 2008).

25. A concrete reflection of these new times is the (at times controversial) change of nomenclature of some Chicana/o studies departments to Latina/o studies departments.

26. See my essay "The Spanish-Language *Crónica* in Los Angeles: Francisco P. Ramírez and Ricardo Flores Magón" (2008).

27. This novel received Boston's Gustavus Myers Outstanding Book Award. Graciela Limón was born in Los Angeles and lives in Montebello, California.

She is professor emeritus of Loyola Marymount University in Los Angeles, where she taught U.S. Latina/o Literature and chaired the Chicana and Chicano Studies Department. She is also the author of these novels: *In Search of Bernabé* (1993; translated into Spanish in 1997 as *En busca de Bernabé*; *New York Times* Notable Book of the Year in 1993 and American Book Award in 1994; a third-place winner of the University of California, Irvine, Chicano/Latino literary competition); *The Memories of Ana Calderón* (1994); *Song of the Hummingbird* (1996); *The Day of the Moon* (1999); *Left Alive* (2005); and *The River Flows North* (2009).

28. The Zapatistas' assumptions seem to have been prophetic. In a *New York Times* article entitled "Report Finds Few Benefits for Mexico in NAFTA" (November 19, 2003), Celia W. Dugger quotes a study by the Carnegie Endowment for International Peace, which concludes that "the pact failed to generate substantial job growth in Mexico, hurt hundreds of thousands of subsistence farmers there" (1).

29. Zapatismo has inspired José Ramírez, a Chicano graphic artist from Los Angeles's El Sereno, and several Chicano music bands, including Quetzal, Rage against the Machine, Ozomatli, Revelations, and Aztlán Underground.

In the acknowledgments of *Erased Faces,* Graciela Limón thanks her colleague Roberto Flores, a Chicano activist from Los Angeles who has conducted research on the role of women leaders (particularly senior women) in creating and sustaining the Zapatista movement. He is currently trying to adapt the Zapatista autonomous community to the structural rebuilding of his community in Los Angeles. He plans to follow the Zapatista structure of participatory democracy and intersubjectivity (a "process of sharing and learning across cultures in which no one culture dominates" [McLaren 12]) in the development of a long-term strategy for social justice and self-determination. According to Flores, this infrastructural development should bring about the organized participation of the vast majority of civil society, that is, "non-government, non-corporate, non-military force" (McLaren 4): "Because of vast and growing similarities between the socioeconomic situation of indigenous people in Mexico and the Chicano Mexicano Latino pluriethnic communities within the U.S. (Latinos are now the poorest of the poor), I believe that the Zapatista Autonomy process has invaluable revolutionary resources and should be looked at as a possible model for structural empowerment. I am here proposing that a thorough study of the Autonomy model as it is being carried out in Chiapas be made to enrich and enhance the efforts for democracy and justice in the U.S. Autonomy" ("Autonomy" 3).

30. Most Zapatistas belong to eleven ethnic groups, including Tojolabales (the core Zapatista indigenous group), Tzetzales, Tzotziles, Choles, Lacandones, Kachiqueles, and Mams.

31. Limón has explained that, although she had initially planned to make Orlando and Juana lovers, the characters themselves decided their own destiny ("Zapatistas" n.p.).

32. The nationalist stance, according to Flores, is understandable as a reaction to being marginalized but can become a weakness ("Zapatista" n.p.). Likewise, Anna Sampaio states, "Traditional formations of Chicana/o and Latina/o subjectivity inscribed in the context of a nation-state analysis have become increasingly obsolete with the changes to their daily lives introduced by globalization and increasingly supplanted by the emergence of binational and transnational communities" (50).

33. Limón also explains that some details in the novel, such as the episode where Juana Galván's father exchanges her for a mule, are based on facts: "As we speak, right now—this is not last century—right now, young girls of twelve and thirteen are being bartered off for a handful of pesos, a mule, a donkey, whatever. And this, of course, is a huge injustice to any human being. And this is one of the reasons why in that huge rebellion the women have a big invested voice in saying 'Look, we're human beings'" ("Expanding" 2).

34. Comandanta Ramona died in January 2006 of cancer. In 1993, she drew up, along with Mayor Ana María, the Ley Revolucionaria de Mujeres (The Zapatista Women's Revolutionary Law) to stop the exploitation of indigenous women. The following are the ten parts of that law:

1. Women, regardless of their race, creed, color or political affiliation, have a right to participate in the revolutionary struggle in any way that their desire and capacity determine.
2. Women have the right to work and receive a just salary.
3. Women have the right to decide the number of children they have and care for.
4. Women have the right to participate in the matters of the community and to take charge if they are freely and democratically elected.
5. Women and their children have the right to primary attention in their health and nutrition.
6. Women have the right to education.
7. Women have the right to choose their partner and are not obliged to enter into marriage.
8. Women have the right to be free of violence from both relatives and strangers. Rape and attempted rape will be severely punished.
9. Women will be able to occupy positions of leadership in the organization and hold military ranks in the revolutionary armed forces.
10. Women will have all the rights and obligations which the revolutionary laws and regulations give. (Translated by Matt Miscreant)

35. *Hutizitzilín* means "hummingbird" in English. The pre-Columbian world also plays an important role in Limón's previous novel *Song of the Hummingbird* (1996).

36. In real life, Samuel Ruiz, the bishop of San Cristóbal (now forcibly retired), is widely considered one of the main supporters of the rebellion. In a

1999 interview with Sylvia Marcos for *Ixtus,* he explains some of the premises of his *Teología India,* or Indian Theology: "Indian Christian Theology presupposes the recognition of a revelation of God in all cultures—what Vatican II called Seeds of the Word . . . fortunately, Christopher Columbus did not bring God in his three caravels, since God was already present among the Indian communities" (n.p.).

37. According to Flores, the Zapatistas use these masks with the dual purpose of anonymity to defend themselves from the thousands of governmental troops that surround them and to symbolize that they "are all the same" ("Zapatista" n.p.). Incidentally, this new use of the mask in Mexican literature and culture should provide additional nuances to the study of its symbolic role in Octavio Paz's chapter, "Mexican Masks," included in *The Labyrinth of Solitude.*

38. Rufino's main role as a character is to demonstrate how a particular society, corrupted by centuries of racial inequalities, can easily turn an innocent boy into a merciless oppressor.

39. In a foreshadowing scene in chapter 12, don Absolón Mayorga strikes his younger sister, tears off her clothes, has her whipped in public until she faints, and later abandons her in the jungle for being a lesbian. Afterward, we see in Juana's thoughts how different types of oppression across class, ethnicity, gender, and sexual orientation become entangled: "I also see that to the men who want to be our masters, being *una india* or *un indio,* being poor and forced to scratch a life out of a piece of dry dirt, being a *manflora* or a man who loves men, being anyone contrary, is all the same. In their eyes, we share a common destiny in which we are hated, persecuted, tortured and condemned because we threaten their way of life" (100–101).

40. The protagonist's surname, Mora, evokes another different and remote culture, that of the Moors (*moros* in Spanish), whose presence in the Iberian Peninsula from 711 to 1492 could have been part of her ethnic heritage.

41. Likewise, in her short story "The Cariboo Café," featured in the collection *The Moths and Other Stories* (1995), Chicana author Helena María Viramontes connects the suffering of Central American women living under authoritarian regimes to the ordeal of undocumented immigrants in the United States, who struggle to survive in an unknown world and under constant fear of the Immigration and Naturalization Service. The story, which mixes different narrative perspectives, focuses on a Central American washerwoman whose son disappears and who, years later, delusional under so much grief, believes that she has found him in the United States. When at the start of her search she reminds authorities that her son Geraldo is only five years old, they answer: "Anyone who so willfully supports the Contras in any form must be arrested and punished without delay" (73). United in common suffering, this Central American woman and an undocumented Latina in the United States seem to become the same woman. Their female subjectivities overlap, in spite of their different backgrounds, and make them one.

We find another example of this broadening approach in the extra features of Edward James Olmos's film *Walkout,* where the producer, Moctesuma Esparza, reveals that many students in leadership positions within the Chicano Movement belonged to other Latino ethnicities:

So this was a broad, broad movement, even though the identity was Chicano. As an example, the editor of *La Raza* newspaper was Cuban American, Eliezer Risco, and he was one of the key strategists to our efforts in the movement. And, later, one of the chairs of UCLA MEChA was a Puerto Rican girl, and several of the key members were Puerto Rican. So, I think this is a key moment in that here [referring to Paola's character in the film] we have a leader who is half Filipino, half Mexican in descent and completely adopts the Chicano identity because of its power at liberating all of us at that time.

42. On account of this Bracero Program initiated in 1942,

Mexicans were once again actively recruited to come and work in the United States. With 16,000,000 men and 350,000 women in the armed forces, a source of dependable labor was sorely needed. In 1942, only 4,203 Braceros were brought in, but by 1944, the number had swelled to 67,860. Although it began as a temporary measure, the Bracero Program lasted until 1964. Ironically, some of the Braceros had been among those who were repatriated a few years earlier. (Balderrama and Rodríguez 287)

43. The seven novels are the following: *The Little Death* (1986), *Goldenboy* (1988), *Howtown* (1990), *Hidden Law* (1992), *The Death of Friends* (1996), *The Burning Plain* (1997), and *Rag and Bone* (2001), supposedly Nava's last Henry Ríos book. A third-generation Mexican American, Nava was born in Stockton, California, and grew up in Sacramento. He received a BA from Colorado College, and in 1981 he graduated with a law degree from Stanford University. He is currently employed by an appellate court judge in Los Angeles as a research attorney (Klawitter 291). He is the winner of the Lambda Award for best mystery for five of his Henry Ríos novels: *Goldenboy, Howtown, Hidden Law, The Death of Friends,* and *Rag and Bone.* Nava is the author of the novel *Unlived Lives* (1999), the co-author, along with Robert Dawidoff, of the nonfiction book *Created Equal: Why Gay Rights Matter to America* (1994), and has also edited the anthology *Finale: Short Stories of Mystery and Suspense* (1997).

44. The darkest side of the Hollywood district again takes center stage in Rechy's *City of Night* and *The Miraculous Day of Amalia Gómez.* In the latter, the protagonist, Amalia Gómez, hears an old *veterano* lecturing children about the "old days" in East L.A. gangs and realizes that, in her new barrio, gangbanging has spread like a disease; it is now part of a proud tradition that goes back to the pachucos and the Zoot Suit Riots. After her son Manny becomes a gang leader and is later imprisoned for attempted murder, Amalia decides that it is time to

move elsewhere. Soon, she learns the reason she can afford living in the supposedly glittery Hollywood: the legendary heart of the American film industry is now populated by impoverished minorities and infested by gangs. The pervasive gang graffiti, the presence of prostitutes, and the annoying echo of police sirens all foreshadow the assassination of a boy by the Seventh Street gang that she will witness a few days later. To make matters worse, her other two children become involved in gangs, drug trafficking, and gay hustling, but the optimistic protagonist discovers signs of hope in nature: a rosebush in her backyard and a prophetic silver cross in the sky over the Hollywood Hills. The sharp contrast between Amalia's dreams and the harsh reality she finds in Hollywood is first highlighted by the wealth of other districts that she visits, such as Beverly Hills and Hancock Park. Later, however, the dystopian world of unfettered violence and ominous decay that she discovers during a visit to her friend Milagros in the garment district eclipses the suffering in East Los Angeles and Hollywood. These sewing sweatshops, or *maquiladoras,* located only a few blocks from glassy highrises in downtown and central Los Angeles, illustrate the broken dreams of other Latina immigrants, who live and work in subhuman conditions. Hollywood is also recreated in a negative light in Luis J. Rodríguez's *The Republic of East L.A.* Although Cruz Blancarte, the protagonist and first-person narrator of the short story "My Ride, My Revolution," criticizes the rest of the nation's contempt for Los Angeles, he still describes Hollywood (or "Hollow-wood," as he calls it) as a depressed and ordinary district that has little to do with the glamorous image most of the world has of it. Instead of movie stars, he explains, one will find only adult bookstores and peepshows, drug addicts, gang members, and homeless people there.

45. West Hollywood has a central position in John Rechy's works as well. However, Rechy also locates several of his scenes in Griffith Park and in the beaches of Santa Monica and Venice West. As to the other Hollywood (the film industry), it is briefly cast in a good light in Luis Valdez's play *Zoot Suit.* Mirroring actual events, Jewish lawyer Alice informs Henry: "Rita Hayworth lent your sister Lupe a ball gown for the occasion. She got dressed at Cecil B. DeMille's house, and she looked terrific. Her escort was Anthony Quinn, and Orson Welles said . . ." (82).

46. Ralph E. Rodríguez's study, however, focuses on the articulation of the idea of "family" in Nava's works.

47. Although, as it is widely known, Hollywood never employed many Mexicans, Lupe Vélez, a Mexican actor from the 1940s known as "The Mexican Spitfire" is briefly mentioned, when her death is compared to that of one of the characters.

48. Both Rechy's and Nava's oeuvres have autobiographical overtones. As George Klawitter points out, "Although Nava denies he is Ríos, readers cannot help but note the similarities: Hispanic origin, law degree, gay life-style, and, as

Zonana notes, recovering alcoholic" (296). Likewise, Bruce-Novoa argues, "In Rechy's case this inversion is compounded by the supposed, and to a large degree admitted, autobiographical quality of his work" ("In search" 37). Ricardo L. Ortiz agrees with them when he states that Johnny Río is "a copy, an echo of both 'John' the author and the 'john'-like reader of porn" ("John Rechy" 63).

49. There are also references to Agatha Christie's *The A.B.C. Murders,* Jorge Luis Borges's "The Babylon Lottery," and Jean Paul Sartre's *Huis clos* (the intertextuality with *Huis clos* appears when the sentence "hell is other people" ["l'enfer c'est les autres"] is quoted). Incidentally, the title of Nava's novel is identical to that of Juan Rulfo's novel *El llano en llamas* (1953).

50. A similar scene appears in Michael Nava's *Rag and Bone,* albeit this time all Angelenos described are of Mexican origin. Henry Ríos explains that, in a Mexican restaurant named María's Ramada, the clientele "seemed about equally divided between *mexicanos* in straw hats playing Javier Solis on the jukebox and would-be Anglo bohemians from nearby Silverlake, complaining to the waiters about the loudness of the music and anxious over whether the refried beans were vegetarian or not" (55).

51. Again, there are echoes of this description of Los Angeles's socioeconomic contrasts in Nava's *Rag and Bone:*

> Mount Washington was one of those neighborhoods that tourists to L.A. never see and that even most residents would have been unable to find on the map. . . . walls were scarred by gang graffiti, and the few businesses had bars on the windows and closed when the sun went down. This was Third World L.A., populated by Central American immigrants. The men could be found standing on street corners hoping to be hired for a day's work as cut-rate gardeners or painters. . . . Rather the hills seemed inhabited by old-fashioned L.A. bohemians, the kind of people who had always given the city its reputation for benign looniness—health cultists, guru followers, past-life regressionists, mediums and spiritualists of every stripe. (110)

52. We find the same type of contrast between the glamorous Anglo past of a district and the dilapidated appearance under the new Latino majority in *Rag and Bone:*

> La Iglesia de Cristo Triunfante was located in a storefront on a stretch on Beverly Boulevard known as Little Tegucigalpa because of all the Central American restaurants and travel agencies that had set up shop in the crumbling, ornate one- and two-story buildings that dated back to the 1910s, when it had been the heart of a prosperous Jewish neighborhood. The buildings were now painted blue and lime and pink, but they retained their original Art Deco zigzags and chevrons. . . . On the sidewalk, a squat, dark man with a broad, impassive Indian face pushed a cart with an ear of corn painted on it and cried out, '*Elote, elote.*' (241–42)

Mike Davis has also described the deplorable deterioration of this park: "once the jewel in the crown of the city's park system, [MacArthur Park] is now a free-fire zone where crack dealers and street gangs settle their scores with shotguns and uzis" (*Ecology* 378).

53. Robert Dawidoff has indicated the point in the Henry Ríos series when he ponders his Mexican background: "In *Hidden Law* (1992) Henry begins to make the connection between himself and his ethnicity. It isn't that he ever denied his ethnicity any more than he did his homosexuality, but it begins to matter to him more, although that culture's homophobia and religiosity and his own family history keep him at a distance" (n.p.).

54. In *Rag and Bone*, Ríos explains the sources of this resentment: "My father's drinking and violence had made for an unpredictable and terrifying childhood" (9). As to his mother, who was the daughter of Mexican immigrants, he recalls her "making excuses for him, admonishing me to stay out of his way, denying the reality of his brutality by pretending he was no more than an average disciplinarian even when he left me black and blue. The time he broke my arm, it was my mother who took me to the emergency room and told the doctor that I had fallen from a tree. My hatred of my father kept him vivid in my memory for decades after I had left home, but my mother had faded away, leaving only the faint residue of contempt" (49).

55. The protagonist provides additional cultural translations for the Euro-American reader while confessing that the comfort foods of his childhood have suddenly turned sour: "The chocolate burned my tongue while the *pan dulce,* a little mound of bread topped with squares of crumbly sugar, was flavorless" (102).

Conclusion

1. The following are some of the most recent popular publications: *Mambo Montage: The Latinization of New York,* edited by Agustín Laó-Montes and Arlene M. Dávila (2001); Frances Negrón-Muntaner's *Boricua Pop: Puerto Ricans and the Latinization of American Culture* (2004); Jorge Ramos's *The Latino Wave: How Hispanics Are Transforming Politics in America* (2005); Cristina Benítez's *Latinization: How Latino Culture Is Transforming the U.S.* (2007); Geraldo Rivera's *His Panic: Why Americans Fear Hispanics in the U.S.* (2008); and, from an anti-Latino perspective, Patrick "Pat" Buchanan's *The Death of the West: How Dying Populations and Immigrant Invasions Imperil Our Country and Civilization* (2002) and *State of Emergency: The Third World Invasion and Conquest of America* (2006).

Bibliography

"ABC7 vs. LAPD—Race a Factor in Violence?" *Laist.* 6 March 2008. http://laist .com/2008/03/06/abc7_vs_lapd.php. Accessed 29 March 2008.

Acevedo, Mario. *X-Rated Bloodsuckers.* New York: Rayo Harper Collins, 2007.

Acosta, Óscar Zeta. *Autobiography of a Brown Buffalo.* New York: Vintage, 1989.

———. *The Revolt of the Cockroach People.* Ed. Hunter Thompson and Marco Acosta. New York: Vintage, 1989.

Aguirre Beltrán, Gonzalo. Introducción. *Ricardo Flores Magón: Antología.* Ed. Gonzalo Aguirre Beltrán. Mexico City: Universidad Nacional Autónoma de México, 1970.

Ahouse, John. Introduction. *Literary L.A.* By Lionel Rolfe. Los Angeles: California Classics Books, 2002. 7–10.

Ahrens, Ruüdiger, et al., eds. *Violence and Transgression in World Minority Literatures.* Heidelberg: Universitätsverlag, 2005.

The American Heritage Dictionary of the English Language. United States: Houghton Mifflin, 1996.

American Me. Dir. Edward James Olmos. Perf. Edward James Olmos, William Forsythe, Daniel A Haro, Pepe Serna. Universal Pictures, 1992.

Anaya, Rudolfo. *Bless Me, Última.* Berkeley: Quinto Sol Publications, 1972.

———. *Curse of the Chupacabra.* Albuquerque: University of New Mexico Press, 2006.

Anderson, Benedict. *Imagined Communities: Reflections on the Origin and Spread of Nationalism.* London: Verso, 1983.

Anzaldúa, Gloria. *Borderlands/La Frontera: The New Mestiza.* San Francisco: Aunt Lute, 1999.

"Aryan Brotherhood." *Gangland.* History (formerly known as The History Channel). A&E Television Networks, New York. 1 Nov. 2007.

Ávila, Eric. *Popular Culture in the Age of White Flight: Fear and Fantasy in Suburban Los Angeles.* Berkeley and Los Angeles: University of California Press, 2004.

Balderrama, Francisco E., and Raymond Rodríguez. *Decade of Betrayal: Mexican Repatriation in the 1930s.* Albuquerque: University of New Mexico Press, 2006.

Banham, Reyner. *Los Angeles: The Architecture of Four Ecologies*. London: Allen Lane, 1971.

"Behind Enemy Lines." *Gangland*. History (formerly known as The History Channel). A&E Television Networks, New York. 28 Nov. 2007.

Benítez, Cristina. *Latinization: How Latino Culture Is Transforming the U.S.* New York: Paramount Market, 2007.

Bhabha, Homi. *The Location of Culture*. London: Routledge, 2004.

Block, Elizabeth. "An Interview with Kate Braverman." *Bookslut* (February 2006): n.p. http://www.bookslut.com/features/2006_02_007804.php. Accessed 24 June 2007.

Blood In Blood Out (also known as *Bound by Honor*). Dir. Taylor Hackford. Perf. Jesse Borrego, Benjamin Bratt, Enrique Castillo, Damian Chapa, Billy Bob Thornton. Hollywood Pictures, 1993.

"Blood In, Blood Out." *Gangland*. History (formerly known as The History Channel). A&E Television Networks, New York. 10 Jan. 2008.

Born in East L.A. Dir. and written by Richard "Cheech" Marín. Perf. Cheech Marín, Paul Rodríguez, Daniel Stern, Jan-Michael Vincent, Kamala López, Tony Plana, and Lupe Ontiveros. Universal Studios, 1987.

Bourdieu, Pierre. *Language and Symbolic Power*. Cambridge: Harvard University Press, 2001.

Bourgois, Philippe. *In Search of Respect: Selling Crack in El Barrio*. Cambridge: Cambridge University Press, 1995.

Boyer, Peter J. "LAPD Blues." Interview with Daryl Gates. PBS *Frontline*. Interviews. http://www.pbs.org/wgbh/pages/frontline/shows/lapd/interviews/gates.html. Accessed 29 March 2008.

Boyle, T. Coraghessan. *The Tortilla Curtain*. New York: Viking, 1995.

Las braceras. Dir. Fernando Durán Rojas. Perf. Lyn May, Maritza Olivares, and Patricia Rivera. Mexico City: Producciones Fílmicas Agrasánchez, 1981.

Brady, Mary Pat. *Extinct Lands, Temporal Geographies: Chicana Literature and the Urgency of Space*. Durham, NC: Duke University Press, 2002.

Braverman, Kate. *Frantic Transmissions to and from Los Angeles: An Accidental Memoir*. Saint Paul: Graywolf Press, 2006.

———. *Lithium for Medea*. New York: Harper and Row, 1979.

———. *Palm Latitudes*. New York: Linden Press/Simon and Schuster, 1988.

Browder, Laura. *Slippery Characters. Ethnic Impersonators and American Identities*. Chapel Hill: University of North Carolina Press, 2000.

———. "Under Cover: Ethnic Imposture and the Construction of American Identities." http://www.has.vcu.edu/eng/symp/p_o.htm. Accessed 25 Apr. 2005.

Brown, Monica. *Gang Nation: Delinquent Citizens in Puerto Rican, Chicano, and Chicana Narratives*. Minneapolis: University of Minnesota Press, 2002.

Bruce, Jorge. *Nos habíamos choleado tanto: Psicoanálisis y racismo*. Lima: Universidad de San Martín de Porres, 2007.

Bruce-Novoa, Juan. "Fear and Loathing on the Buffalo Trail." *Melus* 6.4 (Winter 1979): 39–50.

———. "In Search of the Honest Outlaw: John Rechy." *Minority Voices* 3.1 (1979): 37–45.

Bruhn, Kathleen. "Zapatistas, Literature, and the Chicano Experience." Symposium. *Voices.* Ed. and dir. Todd Gillespie. 89 min. University of California, Santa Barbara. 14 Feb. 2003. http://www.uctv.ucsb.edu/more/voices/m37841imon.html. Accessed 22 March 2004.

Buchanan, Patrick Joseph. *The Death of the West: How Dying Populations and Immigrant Invasions Imperil Our Country and Civilization.* New York: St. Martin's Press, 2002.

———. *State of Emergency: The Third World Invasion and Conquest of America.* New York: Macmillan, 2006.

Buell, Lawrence. *The Environmental Imagination.* Cambridge: Harvard University Press, 1995.

Butler, Judith. *Gender Trouble: Feminism and the Subversion of Identity.* New York: Routledge, 1990.

Calderón, Héctor. *Narratives of Greater Mexico: Essays on Chicano Literary History, Genre, and Borders.* Austin: University of Texas Press, 2004.

Cantú, Roberto. Rev. of *Rewriting North American Borders in Chicano and Chicana Narrative,* by Monika Kaup. *Modern Language Quarterly* 64.4 (Dec. 2003): 508–13.

Castillo, Debra. Interview with John Rechy. *Diacritics* 25.1 (Spring 1995): 113–25.

Castro, Juan de. *The Spaces of Latin American Literature: Tradition, Globalization and Markets.* New York: Palgrave Macmillan, 2008.

Chang, Justin. *Entertainment News.* 6 Oct. 2004. http://www.entertainment-news.org/breaking/9279/gang-warz.html. Accessed 24 Oct. 2007.

Chesney-Lind, Meda, and John M. Hagedorn, eds. *Female Gangs in America: Essays on Girls, Gangs, and Gender.* Chicago: Lakeview Press, 1999.

Chicano! History of the Mexican American Civil Rights Movement. Dir. Héctor Galán. Los Angeles: National Latino Communications Center. Distributed by NLCC Educational Media, 1996.

Ciotti, Paul. "Palm Latitudes, Tropical Depressions and Cocaine Highs." *Los Angeles Times.* 29 June 1985. http://www.katebraverman.com/palmlatitudes3.html. Accessed 24 June 2007.

"Code of Conduct." *Gangland.* History (formerly known as The History Channel). A&E Television Networks, New York. 15 Nov. 2007.

Coleman, Alexander. "English Hurt Her Lips." *New York Times.* 21 August 1988. http://www.katebraverman.com/palmlatitudes.html. Accessed 24 June 2007.

Colors. Dir. Dennis Hopper. Perf. María Conchita Alonso, Don Cheadle, Robert Duvall, Sean Penn, and Damon Wayans. Orion Pictures Corporation, 1988.

Curtis, James R. "Barrio Space and Place in Southeast Los Angeles, California." *Hispanic Spaces, Latino Places. Community and Cultural Diversity in Contemporary America*. Ed. Daniel D. Arreola. Austin: University of Texas Press, 2004. 125–41.

Davis, Mike. *City of Quartz: Excavating the Future in Los Angeles*. London: Verso, 2006.

———. *Ecology of Fear: Los Angeles and the Imagination of Disaster*. New York: Vintage, 1999.

———. *Magical Urbanism: Latinos Reinvent the U.S. City*. London: Verso, 2001.

Dawidoff, Robert. "The Education of Henry Ríos: Why Michael Nava's Seven-Volume Bildungsroman Is a New American Classic." *San Francisco Bay Guardian* 39.28 (April 14–20, 2005). http://www.sfbg.com/lit/apro1/. Accessed 4 March 2004.

A Day without a Mexican. Dir. Sergio Arau. Perf. Yareli Arizmendi, María Beck, Yeniffer Behrens, Todd Babcock. Eye on the Ball Films, 2004.

Dear, Michael J. *The Postmodern Urban Condition*. Oxford: Blackwell, 2000.

Díaz, David R. *Barrio Urbanismo: Chicanos, Planning, and American Cities*. New York: Routledge, 2005.

Díaz del Castillo, Bernal. *The Conquest of New Spain*. Trans. J. M. Cohen. New York: Penguin Classics, 1963.

Dugger, Celia W. "Reports Finds Few Benefits for Mexico in NAFTA." *New York Times*. International ed. 19 Nov. 2003. 1–4. http://www.nytimes .com/2003/11/19/international/americas/19NAFT.html?th. Accessed 2 Feb. 2004.

Durán, Miguel. *Don't Spit on My Corner*. Houston: Arte Público Press, 1992.

Escape from L.A. Dir. John Carpenter. Perf. Kurt Russell, Steve Buscemi, Peter Fonda, Pam Grier, Stacy Keach, Cliff Robertson, Georges Corraface. Paramount Pictures, 1996.

Escobar Ulloa, Ernesto. "Estados Unidos es un país latinoamericano. Entrevista con Alberto Fuguet." *Barcelona Review* 42 (May–June 2004). http://www .barcelonareview.com/42/s_af_int.htm. Accessed 20 Aug. 2007.

Estok, Simon C. "A Report Card on Ecocriticism." *AUMLA: The Journal of the Australasian Universities Language and Literature Association* 96 (Nov. 2001): 220–38.

Figueroa, María P. "Resisting 'Beauty' and *Real Women Have Curves*." *Velvet Barrios: Popular Culture and Chicana/o Sexualities*. Ed. Alicia Gaspar de Alba. Foreword by Tomás Ybarra-Fraustro. New York: Palgrave MacMillan, 2003.

Fine, David. *Imagining Los Angeles: A City in Fiction*. Albuquerque: University of New Mexico Press, 2000.

———, ed. *Los Angeles in Fiction: A Collection of Original Essays*. Albuquerque: University of New Mexico Press, 1984.

Flores, Roberto. "Autonomy: Empowerment for Profound Structural Change." *In Motion Magazine.* 22 Nov. 2003. 1–4. http://inmotionmagazine.com/. Accessed 23 Nov. 2004.

———. "Zapatista Influence on the Chicano Movement." Presentation at California State University. Los Angeles, California. 20 Nov. 2003.

Flores Magón, Ricardo. "A la mujer." *Ricardo Flores Magón.* Ed. Reggie Rodríguez. http://dwardmac.pitzer.edu/Anarchist_Archives/bright/magon/works/regen/mujer.html. Accessed 20 March 2007.

———. *Ricardo Flores Magón: Antología.* Ed. Gonzalo Aguirre Beltrán. Mexico City: Universidad Nacional Autónoma de México, 1970.

———. "To Women." *Ricardo Flores Magón.* Ed. Reggie Rodríguez. http://dwardmac.pitzer.edu/Anarchist_Archives/bright/magon/works/regen/mujer.html. Accessed 20 March 2007.

Foster, David W. *El ambiente nuestro: Chicano/Latino Homoerotic Writing.* Tempe, AZ: Bilingual Press/Editorial Bilingue, 2004.

Foster, Sesshu. *Atomik Aztek.* San Francisco: City Lights, 2005.

Fregoso, Rosa-Linda. *The Bronze Screen: Chicana and Chicano Film Culture.* Minneapolis: University of Minnesota Press, 1993.

———. "Hanging Out with the Homegirls? Allison Anders's 'Mi Vida Loca.'" (Race in Contemporary American Cinema: Part 4) *Cineaste* 21.3 (Summer 1995): 36. http://www.lib.berkeley.edu/MRC/MiVidaLoca.html. Accessed 26 Aug. 2007.

———. "Re-Imaging Chicana Urban Identities in the Public Sphere, *Cool Chuca Style.*" *Between Woman and Nation: Nationalisms, Transnational Feminisms, and the State.* Ed. Caren Kaplan, Norma Alarcón, and Minoo Moallem. Durham, NC: Duke University Press, 1999. 72–91.

Freire, Paulo. *Pedagogía del oprimido.* Mexico City: Siglo XXI, 1990.

———. *Pedagogy of the Oppressed.* Trans. Myra Bergman Ramos. New York: Seabury Press, 1970.

Frémont, John Charles. *Memoirs of My Life.* New York: Cooper Square Press, 2001.

Frías, Gus. *Barrio Warriors.* Los Angeles: Díaz, 1982.

Fuego, Laura del. *Maravilla.* Mountain View, CA: Floricanto Press, 2006.

Fuentes, Carlos. *Los años con Laura Díaz.* Mexico City: Alfaguara, 1999.

———. *The Years with Laura Díaz.* Trans. Alfred Mac Adam. New York: Farrar, Straus and Giroux, 2000.

Fuguet, Alberto. *The Movies of My Life.* Trans. Ezra E. Fitz. New York: Rayo, 2003.

Gang Warz. Dir. Chris T. McIntyre. Perf. Chino XL, Coolio, Reni Santoni, Robert Vaughn. Pittsburgh Pictures, 2004.

García, Isela Alexandra. "Yxta Maya Murray's *Locas:* A Failed Vision of Latina Cholas." *Berkeley McNair Research Journal* 7.0 (Winter 1999): 59–69.

García Canclini, Néstor. *Transforming Modernity: Popular Culture in Mexico*. Trans. Lidia Lozano. Austin: University of Texas Press, 2000.

García-Corales, Guillermo. *Dieciséis entrevistas con autores chilenos contemporáneos: La emergencia de una nueva narrativa*. New York: Mellen Press, 2005.

Gómez-Quiñones, Juan. *Las ideas políticas de Ricardo Flores Magón*. Trans. Roberto Gómez Ciriza. Mexico City: Era, 1977.

———. *Roots of Chicano Politics, 1600–1940*. Albuquerque: University of New Mexico Press, 1994.

Griswold del Castillo, Richard. *The Los Angeles Barrio 1850–1890: A Social History*. Berkeley and Los Angeles: University of California Press, 1979.

———. "The Mexican Revolution and the Spanish-Language Press in the Borderlands." *Journalism History* 4.2 (Summer 1977): 42–47.

Grosfoguel, Ramón, Nelson Maldonado-Torres, and José David Saldívar, eds. *Latino/as in the World-System: Decolonization Struggles in the 21st Century U.S. Empire*. New York: Paradigm 2005.

Guthmann, Edward. "In Los Angeles, Kate Braverman Starved for Culture until S.F. Called Her Back Home." *San Francisco Chronicle*. 30 Jan. 2006. http://www.sfgate.com/cgi-bin/article.cgi?f=/c/a/2006/01/30/DDGEDGTL1O55.DTL&hw=kate+braverman&sn=001&sc=1000. Accessed 24 June 2007.

Gutiérrez, Félix. "Francisco P. Ramírez. Californio editor and Yanqui conquest." *Courage: Media Studies Journal* 14.2 (Spring/Summer 2000): 16–23. http://www.freedomforum.org/publications/msj/courage.summer2000/y03.html 1–12. Accessed 23 Dec. 2004.

Gutiérrez, Ramón A. "Nationalism and Literary Production: The Hispanic and Chicano Experience." *Recovering the U.S. Hispanic Literary Heritage*. Ed. Ramón A. Gutiérrez and Genaro Padilla. Houston: Arte Público, 1993. 241–64.

Hadley-García, George. *Hispanic Hollywood: The Latins in Motion Pictures*. New York: Citadel Press, 1990.

Hames-García, Michael. "Dr. Gonzo's Carnival: The Testimonial Satires of Óscar Zeta Acosta." *American Literature* 72.3 (2000): 463–93.

Hamilton, Nora, and Norma Stoltz Chinchilla. *Seeking Community in a Global City: Guatemalans and Salvadorans in Los Angeles*. Philadelphia: Temple University Press, 2001.

Harris, Jennifer. "Helena María Viramontes Biography." *Brief Biographies*. http://biography.jrank.org/pages/4804/Viramontes-Helena-Maria.html. Accessed 16 Aug. 2008.

Harsh Times. Dir. David Ayer. Perf. Christian Bale, Eva Longoria, and Freddy Rodríguez. Andrea Sperling Productions, 2005.

Hayden, Dolores. *The Power of Place: Urban Landscapes as Public History*. Cambridge: MIT Press, 1995.

Hayes-Bautista, David E. *La Nueva California: Latinos in the Golden State*. Berkeley: University of California Press, 2004.

Heise, Ursula K. Letter. *PMLA* 114.5 (Oct. 1999): 1096–97.

Hernández, David Manuel. "Review of *Locas* by Yxta Maya Murray." *Aztlán* 23.1 (Spring 1998): 153.

Hoffman, Stanton. "The Cities of Night: John Rechy's *City of Night* and the American Literature of Homosexuality." *Chicago Review* 17.2–3 (1964): 195–206.

Holmes, Amanda. *City Fictions: Language, Body, and Spanish American Urban Space*. Lewisburg, PA: Bucknell University Press, 2007.

"Interview with Edward James Olmos." http://www.hbo.com/films/walkout/interviews/. Accessed 25 Oct. 2008.

Johnson, David E. "Intolerance, the Body, Community." *American Literary History* 10.3 (Autumn 1998): 446–70.

Kakutani, Michiko. "Books of the Times; an Insolent Sun Heats the Passions." 25 June 1988. http://www.katebraverman.com/palmlatitudes2.html. Accessed 24 June 2007.

Kanellos, Nicolás. Introduction. *The Adventures of Don Chipote, or, When Parrots Breast-Feed*. By Daniel Venegas. Ed. Nicolás Kanellos. Trans. Ethriam Cash Brammer. Houston: Arte Público Press, 2000. 1–11.

———. "A Socio-Historic Study of Hispanic Newspapers in the United States." *Recovering the U.S. Hispanic Literary Heritage*. Vol. 2. Ed. Ramón Gutiérrez and Genaro Padilla. Houston: Arte Público Press, 1993. 107–28.

Keller, Gary D. *Hispanics and United States Film: An Overview and Handbook*. Tempe, Arizona: Bilingual Review/Press, 1994.

Kettle, Martin. "Clinton Apology to Guatemala." 12 March 1999. *Guardian*. http://www.guardian.co.uk/world/1999/mar/12/jeremylennard.martinkettle. Accessed 6 Aug. 2008.

"Kings of New York." *Gangland*. History (formerly known as The History Channel). A&E Television Networks, New York. 13 Dec. 2007.

Klawitter, George. "Michael Nava (1954–)." *Contemporary Gay American Novelists: A Bio-Bibliographical Critical Sourcebook*. Westport, CT: Greenwood Press, 1993. 291–97.

Knickerbocker, Brad. "A 'Hostile' Takeover Bid at the Sierra Club." *Christian Science Monitor*. 20 Feb. 2004. http://www.csmonitor.com/2004/0220/p01s04-ussc.html. Accessed 6 Aug. 2008.

Kyung-Jin Lee, James. *Urban Triage: Race and the Fictions of Multiculturalism*. Minneapolis: University of Minnesota Press, 2004.

"L.A.'s Most Violent Gangs." 9 February 2007. http://www.streetgangs.com/topics/2007/020907mostv.html. Accessed 20 April 2008.

LAHSA. Los Angeles Homeless Service Authority. "2007 Greater Los Angeles Homeless Count." 2007. http://www.lahsa.org/docs/homelesscount/2007/LAHSA.pdf. Accessed 18 April 2008.

Laó-Montes, Agustín, and Arlene M. Dávila. *Mambo Montage: The Latinization of New York*. New York: Columbia University Press, 2001.

Leal, Luis. "The First American Epic: Villagrá's *History of New Mexico*." *Pasó por Aquí: Critical Essays on the New Mexican Literary Tradition, 1542–1988*. Ed. Erlinda Gonzáles-Berry. Albuquerque: University of New Mexico Press, 1989. 47–62.

Lefebvre, Henri. *The Production of Space*. Trans. Donald Nicholson-Smith. Oxford: Blackwell, 1991.

Limón, Graciela. *The Day of the Moon*. Houston: Arte Público Press, 1999.

———. *Erased Faces*. Houston: Arte Público Press, 2001.

———. "Expanding Canon: Teaching Multicultural Literature. Authors and Literary Works." 1–4. http://www.learner.org/channel/workshops/hslit/session5/aw/work2.htm. Accessed 3 Feb. 2004.

———. *In Search of Bernabé*. Houston: Arte Público Press, 1993.

———. "Zapatistas, Literature, and the Chicano Experience." Symposium. *Voices*. Ed. and director Todd Gillespie. 89 min. University of California, Santa Barbara. 14 Feb. 2003. www.uctv.ucsb.edu/more/voices/m37841imon.html. Accessed 2 April 2004.

Lipsitz, George. *The Possessive Investment in Whiteness: How White People Profit from Identity Politics*. Philadelphia: Temple University Press, 2006.

List, Christine. *Chicano Images: Refiguring Ethnicity in Mainstream Film*. New York: Garland, 1996.

———. "Self-Directed Stereotyping in the Films of Cheech Marín." *Chicanos and Film. Representation and Resistance*. Ed. Chon A. Noriega. Minneapolis: University of Minnesota Press, 1992. 183–94.

Lomelí, Francisco A. Introduction. Alejandro Morales. *Barrio on the Edge/Caras viejas y vino nuevo*. Trans. Francisco A. Lomelí. Tempe, AZ: Bilingual Press, 1998.

———, and Clark A. Colahan, eds. and trans. *Defying the Inquisition in Colonial New Mexico: Miguel de Quintana's Life and Writings*. Albuquerque: University of New Mexico Press, 2006.

———, Victor Alejandro Sorell, and Genaro M. Padilla, eds. *Nuevomexicano Cultural Legacy: Forms, Agencies, and Discourse*. Albuquerque: University of New Mexico Press, 2002.

López-Calvo, Ignacio. "The Spanish-Language *Crónica* in Los Angeles: Francisco P. Ramírez and Ricardo Flores Magón." *Journal of Spanish Language Media* 1 (2008): 125–38. http://www.spanishmedia.unt.edu. Accessed 2 April 2009.

Maxson, Cheryl L., and Malcolm W. Klein. "'Play Groups' No Longer. Urban Street Gangs in the Los Angeles Region." *From Chicago to L.A.: Making Sense of Urban Theory*. Ed. Michael J. Dear. Thousand Oaks, CA: Sage, 2002. 239–66.

McLaren, Peter. "Autonomy and Participatory Democracy: An Ongoing Discussion on the Application of Zapatista Autonomy in the United States."

(Interview of Roberto Flores and Greg Tanaka by Peter McLaren.) *Journal of Educational Reform* 10.2 (Spring 2001): 130–44.

Menchú, Rigoberta, and Elizabeth Burgos-Debray. *I, Rigoberta Menchú: An Indian Woman in Guatemala*. London: Verso, 1984.

Mi vida loca. Dir. Allison Anders. Perf. Ángel Avilés, Seidy López, Jacob Vargas, Devine, Mónica Lutton, and Christina Solís. Channel 4 Films, 1993.

Monahan, Torin. "Los Angeles Studies: The Emergence of a Specialty Field." *City and Society* 14.2 (2002): 167.

Monroy, Douglas. *Rebirth: Mexican Los Angeles from the Great Migration to the Great Depression*. Berkeley and Los Angeles: University of California Press, 1999.

Montero-Sieburth, Martha, and Edwin Meléndez. *Latinos in a Changing Society*. New York: Greenwood, 2007.

Morales, Alejandro. *Barrio on the Edge/Caras viejas y vino nuevo*. Trans. Francisco A. Lomelí. Tempe, AZ: Bilingual Press, 1998.

———. *The Brick People*. Houston: Arte Público Press, 1988.

———. "Pequeña nación." *Pequeña nación*. Phoenix: Orbis Press, 2005.

———. *The Rag Doll Plagues*. Houston: Arte Público Press, 1992.

Morgan Quitno Awards. "13 Annual America's Safest (and Most Dangerous) Cities." http://www.morganquitno.com/cit07pop.htm. Accessed 2 March 2008.

"Murder by Numbers." *Gangland*. History (formerly known as The History Channel). A&E Television Networks, New York. 8 May 2008.

Murphet, Julian. *Literature and Race in Los Angeles*. Cambridge: Cambridge University Press, 2001.

Murray, Yxta Maya. *Locas*. New York: Grove Press, 1997.

———. *What It Takes to Get to Vegas*. New York: Grove Press, 1999.

Natter, Wolfgang, and John Paul Jones III. "Identity, Space, and Other Uncertainties." *Space and Social Theory: Interpreting Modernity and Postmodernity*. Ed. Georges Benko and Ulf Strohmayer. Oxford: Blackwell, 1997. 141–61.

Nava, Michael. *The Burning Plain*. New York: Putnam's Sons, 1997.

———. *Rag and Bone*. New York: Putnam's Sons, 2001.

Navarro, J. L. *Blue Day on Main Street*. Berkeley: Quinto Sol, 1973.

Negrón-Muntaner, Frances. *Boricua Pop: Puerto Ricans and the Latinization of American Culture*. New York: New York University Press, 2004.

Noriega, Chon A. "Between a Weapon and a Formula: Chicano Cinema and Its Contexts." *Chicanos and Film. Representation and Resistance*. Ed. Chon A. Noriega. Minneapolis: University of Minnesota Press, 1992. 141–67.

———. *Shot in America: Television, the State, and the Rise of Chicano Cinema*. Minneapolis: University of Minnesota Press, 2000.

Noriega, Chon, and Ana López, eds. *The Ethnic Eye: Latino Media Arts*. Minneapolis: University of Minnesota Press, 1996.

Obregón Pagán, Eduardo. *Murder at the Sleepy Lagoon: Zoot Suits, Race, and Riot in Wartime L.A.* Chapel Hill: University of North Carolina Press, 2003.

Olivas, Daniel. "Interview with Helena María Viramontes." *La Bloga.* 2 April 2007. http://labloga.blogspot.com/2007/04/interview-with-helena-mara-viramontes .html. Accessed 16 Aug. 2008.

Ong, Aihwa. *Flexible Citizenship: The Cultural Logics of Transnationality.* Durham, NC: Duke University Press, 1999.

Ortiz, Ricardo L. "John Rechy and the Grammar of Ostentation." *Cruising the Performative: Interventions into the Representation of Ethnicity, Nationality, and Sexuality.* Ed. Sue-Ellen Case, Philip Brett, and Susan Leigh Foster. Bloomington: Indiana University Press, 1995. 59–70.

———. "Sexuality Degree Zero: Pleasure and Power in the Novels of John Rechy, Arturo Islas, and Michael Nava." *Critical Essays: Gay and Lesbian Writers of Color.* Ed. Emmanuel S. Nelson. Binghamton, NY: Haworth Press, 1993. 111–25.

Padilla, Genaro Miguel. "The Anti-Romantic City in Chicano Fiction." *Puerto del Sol* 23.1 (1987): 159–69.

———. "Discontinuous Continuities: Remapping the Terrain of Spanish Colonial Narrative." *Reconstructing a Chicano/a Literary Heritage: Hispanic Colonial Literature of the Southwest.* Ed. María Herrera-Sobek. Tucson: University of Arizona Press, 1993. 24–36.

Paredes, Raymund A. "Los Angeles from the Barrio: Óscar Zeta Acosta's *The Revolt of the Cockroach People.*" *Los Angeles in Fiction: A Collection of Essays.* Ed. David Fine. Albuquerque: University of New Mexico Press, 1984. 209–47.

Paz, Octavio. *The Labyrinth of Solitude: Life and Thought in Mexico.* Trans. Lysander Kemp. New York: Grove Press, 1961.

Pérez, Emma. *The Decolonial Imaginary: Writing Chicanas into History.* Bloomington: Indiana University Press, 1999.

Pérez-Torres, Rafael. *Mestizaje: Critical Issues of Race in Chicano Culture.* Minneapolis: University of Minnesota Press, 2006.

Poot-Herrera, Sara, Francisco Lomelí, and María Herrera-Sobek, eds. *Cien años de lealtad en honor a Luis Leal/One Hundred Years of Loyalty in Honor of Luis Leal.* Vols. 1 and 2. Mexico City: University of California, Santa Barbara, University of California Mexicanistas, Universidad Nacional Autónoma de México, Instituto Tecnológico de Monterrey, Universidad del Claustro de Sor Juana, 2007.

Priewe, Marc. "Bio-Politics and the ContamiNation of the Body in Alejandro Morales' *The Rag Doll Plagues.*" *MELUS* 29.3–4 (Autumn–Winter 2004): 397–412.

Quinceañera. Dir. Richard Glatzer and Wash Westmoreland. Perf. Emily Ríos, Jesse García, Chalo González, J. R. Cruz. Cinetic Media, 2006.

Raat, W. Dirk. *Mexico and the United States: Ambivalent Vistas.* Athens: University of Georgia Press, 1996.

Ramírez, Francisco P. "La doctrina de Monroe." *USC Digital Archive*. 3 March 2007. http://digarc.usc.edu:8089/cispubsearch/collectiondetails.jsp?collection=clamor& recordid=clamor-m235&issubcollection=false. Accessed 20 March 2007.

———. "Folleto notable." *USC Digital Archive*. 3 March 2007. http://digarc.usc .edu:8089/cispubsearch/collectiondetails.jsp?collection=clamor&recordid= clamor-m235&issubcollection=false. Accessed 1 Apr. 2007.

Ramírez Berg, Charles. *Latino Images in Film: Stereotypes, Subversion, Resistance.* Austin: University of Texas Press, 2002.

Ramos, Jorge. *The Latino Wave: How Hispanics Are Transforming Politics in America.* New York: Harper, 2005.

Real Women Have Curves. Dir. Patricia Cardoso. Perf. América Ferrera, Ingrid Oliú, Lupe Ontiveros. HBO Independent Productions, 2002.

Rechy, John. *Bodies and Souls*. New York: Carroll and Graf, 1983.

———. *City of Night*. New York: Grove, 1963.

———. Introduction. *Bodies and Souls*. New York: Grove, 2001.

———. *The Miraculous Day of Amalia Gómez*. New York: Grove, 1991.

———. *Numbers*. New York: Grove, 1967.

Rieff, David. *Los Angeles: Capital of the Third World*. New York: Simon and Schuster, 1991.

Right at Your Door. Dir. Chris Gorak. Perf. Rory Cochrane, Mary McCormack, Tony Pérez. Thousand Words, 2006.

Rivera, Geraldo. *His Panic: Why Americans Fear Hispanics in the U.S.* New York: Penguin, 2008.

Rocco, Raymond A. "Latino Los Angeles: Reframing Boundaries/Borders." *The City: Los Angeles and Urban Theory at the End of the Twentieth Century.* Ed. Allen J. Scott and Edward W. Soja. Berkeley and Los Angeles: University of California Press, 1996. 365–89.

Rodríguez, Ana Patricia. "Refugees of the South: Central Americans in the U.S. Latino Imaginary." *American Literature: A Journal of Literary History, Criticism, and Bibliography* 73.2 (June 2001): 387–412.

Rodríguez, Clara E. *Heroes, Lovers, and Others: The Story of Latinos in Hollywood.* Washington, DC: Smithsonian Books, 2004.

Rodríguez, Luis J. *Always Running/La Vida Loca: Gang Days in L.A.* New York: Touchstone, 1993.

———. *Hearts and Hands: Creating Community in Violent Times*. New York: Seven Stories Press, 2001.

———. *The Republic of East L.A.* New York: Rayo, 2002.

Rodríguez, Ralph E. *Brown Gumshoes: Detective Fiction and the Search for Chicana/o Identity.* Austin: University of Texas Press, 2005.

Rodríguez, Reggie. "Ricardo Flores Magón. Commentary." 28 Feb. 2007. http://dwardmac.pitzer.edu/Anarchist_Archives/bright/magon/comment/ inequality.html. Accessed 25 May 2005.

Rodríguez, Richard. *Days of Obligation: An Argument with My Mexican Father.* New York: Penguin Books, 1993.

Rolfe, Lionel. *Literary L.A.* Los Angeles: California Classics Books, 2002.

Ruiz, Mona, with Geoff Boucher. *Two Badges: The Lives of Mona Ruiz.* Houston: Arte Público Press, 1997.

"Runaways." *Oracle ThinkQuest.* http://library.thinkquest.org/3354/Resource _Center/Virtual_Library/Runaways/runaways.htm. Accessed 18 Oct. 2008.

Saldívar, José. *Border Matters: Remapping American Cultural Studies.* Berkeley and Los Angeles: University of California Press, 1997.

Saldívar, Ramón. *Chicano Narrative: The Dialectics of Difference.* Madison: University of Wisconsin Press, 1990.

Sampaio, Anna. "Transforming Chicana/o and Latina/o Politics: Globalization and the Formation of Transnational Resistance in the United States and Chiapas." *Transnational Latina/o Communities: Politics, Processes, and Cultures.* Lanham, MD: Rowman and Littlefied, 2002. 47–71.

Sánchez, George J. *Becoming Mexican American: Ethnicity, Culture and Identity in Chicano Los Angeles, 1900–1945.* New York: Oxford University Press, 1993.

Sánchez, Thomas. *Zoot-Suit Murders.* New York: Vintage Books, 1991.

Sandoval, Chela. "U.S. Third World Feminism: The Theory and the Method of Oppositional Consciousness in the Postmodern World." *Genders* 10 (1991): 1–24.

Santiago, Danny. *Famous All Over Town.* New York: Plume, 1984.

Saragoza, Alex M. "Cinematic Orphans: Mexican Immigrants in the United States since the 1950s." *Chicanos and Film: Representation and Resistance.* Ed. Chon A. Noriega. Minneapolis: University of Minnesota Press, 1992. 114–26.

Scheib, Richard. "Nightstalker." *Moria: The Science Fiction, Horror, and Fantasy Film Review,* 2005. http://www.moria.co.nz/horror/nightstalker02.htm. Accessed 9 March 2008.

Shields, Rob. "Spatial Stress and Resistance: Social Meanings of Spatialization." *Space and Social Theory: Interpreting Modernity and Postmodernity.* Ed. Georges Benko and Ulf Strohmayer. Oxford: Blackwell, 1997. 186–202.

Sircello, Guy. "How Is a Theory of the Sublime Possible?" *Journal of Aesthetics and Art Criticism* 51.4 (Autumn 1993): 541–50.

Smethurst, James. "The Figure of the *Vato Loco* and the Representation of Ethnicity in the Narratives of Óscar Z. Acosta." *Melus* 20.2 (Summer 1995): 119–32.

Soja, Edward. "Taking Los Angeles Apart: Towards a Postmodern Geography." *The City Reader.* Ed. Richard T. LeGates and Frederic Stout. London: Routledge, 2005. 189–200.

Spivak, Gayatri Chakravorty. "Can the Subaltern Speak?" *The Postcolonial Studies Reader.* Ed. Bill Ashcroft, Gareth Griffiths, and Helen Tiffin. London: Routledge, 1997. 24–28.

————. "The Trajectory of the Subaltern in My Work." Lecture at the University of California, Santa Barbara. http://www.youtube.com/watch?v=2ZHH4ALRFHw. Accessed 1 Sept. 2008.

Stand and Deliver. Dir. Ramón Menéndez. Perf. Edward James Olmos, Andy García, Rosana De Soto. American Playhouse, 1988.

Stavans, Ilan. "The Latin Phallus." *Transition* 65 (1995): 48–68.

"Stone to the Bone." *Gangland.* History (formerly known as The History Channel). A&E Television Networks, New York. 20 Dec. 2007.

Stoner, Madeleine R. "The Globalization of Urban Homelessness." *From Chicago to L.A.: Making Sense of Urban Theory.* Ed. Michael J. Dear. Thousand Oaks, CA: Sage, 2002. 213–34.

Sullivan, Felicia C. "Felicia C. Sullivan interviews Kate Braverman, author of most recently, *Frantic Transmissions to and from Los Angeles.*" *Small Spiral Notebook* 4.4 (Spring 2006): n.p. http://www.smallspiralnotebook.com/fa1105/katebravermaninterview.shtml. Accessed 24 June 2007.

Tatum, Charles M. *Chicano Popular Culture: Que hable el pueblo.* Tucson: University of Arizona Press, 2001.

Tayee Mohajer, Shaya. "FBI: Los Angeles Hospitals Used Homeless in Medical Fraud." EMSresponder.com. http://www.emsresponder.com/online/article.jsp?siteSection=1&id08026. Accessed 12 Aug. 2008.

"Teología India." *Ethnoscope.* http://www.docfilm.com/mexfilms/di/Indiantheology.htm. Accessed 9 June 2004.

Tobar, Héctor. "Héctor Tobar's homepage." www.hectortobar.com. Accessed 19 Oct. 2007.

————. *The Tattooed Soldier.* Harrison, NY: Delphinium Books, 1998.

————. *Translation Nation: Defining a New American Identity in the Spanish-Speaking United States.* New York: Riverhead Books, 2005.

Trevino, Roberto R. "Becoming Mexican American: The Spanish-Language Press and the Biculturation of Californio Elites, 1852–1870." Center for Comparative Studies in Race and Ethnicity Working Paper Series. Stanford University. http://ccsre.stanford.edu/pdfs/wps27.pdf. Accessed 5 March 2007.

Twanama, Walter. "Racismo peruano, ni calco ni copia." Revista *Quehacer* 170 (Apr.–June 2008). http://209.85.141.104/search?q=cache:jdVYQxmiglIJ:www.desco.org.pe/apc-aa-files/6172746963756c6f735f5f5f5f5f5f5f/qh170wt.doc+Walter+Twanama&hl=en&ct=clnk&cd=4&gl=us. Accessed 22 Aug. 2008.

Ulin, David L., ed. *Writing Los Angeles: A Literary Anthology.* New York: Literary Classics of the United States, 2002.

Valdez, Luis. *Zoot Suit and Other Plays.* Houston: Arte Público Press, 1992.

Valle, Víctor. "Chicano Reporter in 'Hispanic Hollywood.'" *Chicanos and Film: Representation and Resistance.* Ed. Chon Noriega. Minneapolis: University of Minnesota Press, 1992.

Valle, Víctor M., and Rodolfo D. Torres. *Latino Metropolis*. Minneapolis: University of Minnesota Press, 2000.

Vásquez, Richard. *Chicano*. Garden City, NY: Doubleday, 1970.

Véa, Alfredo. *Gods Go Begging*. New York: Dutton, 1999.

Venegas, Daniel. *The Adventures of Don Chipote, or, When Parrots Breast-Feed*. Ed. Nicolás Kanellos. Trans. Ethriam Cash Brammer. Houston: Arte Público Press, 2000.

Villa, Raúl Homero. *Barrio-Logos: Space and Place in Urban Chicano Literature and Culture*. Austin: University of Texas Press, 2001.

———. "Ghosts in the Growth Machine: Critical Spatial Consciousness in Los Angeles Chicano Writing." *Social Text* 58 (Spring 1999): 111–31.

Villarreal, José Antonio. *Pocho*. New York: Anchor Books, 1959.

Viramontes, Helena María. "The Cariboo Café." *The Moths and Other Stories*. Houston: Arte Público Press, 1995.

———. "Neighbors." *The Moths and Other Stories*. Houston: Arte Público Press, 1995.

———. *Their Dogs Came with Them*. New York: Atria Books, 2007.

Walkout. Dir. Edward James Olmos. Perf. Alexa Vega, Michael Peña, Yancey Arias, Efrén Ramírez, Tonantzín Esparza, Bodie Olmos, and A. Verónica Díaz. HBO Films, 2006.

Weaver, Frederick Stirton. *Inside the Volcano: The History and Political Economy of Central America*. Boulder, CO: Westview Press, 1994.

Weinraub, Bernard. "Film on Hollywood's Underbelly: How Success Lures Runaways." *New York Times*. "Movies." 23 July 1992. http://query.nytimes.com/gst/fullpage.html?res=9E0CE2DF1130F930A15754C0A964958260. Accessed 28 Oct. 2008.

Where the Day Takes You. Dir. Marc Rocco. Perf. Kyle MacLachlan, Dermot Mulroney, Sean Astin, Lara Flynn Boyle, Balthazar Getty, Ricki Lake, Christian Slater, Laura San Giacomo, Nancy McKeon, and Will Smith. United States: Sony Pictures, 1992.

Wilson, Clint C. II, Félix Gutiérrez, and Lena M. Chao. *Racism, Sexism, and the Media: The Rise of Class Communications in Multicultural America*. Thousand Oaks, CA: Sage, 2003.

Wolch, Jennifer. "From Global to Local: The Rise of Homelessness in Los Angeles during the 1980s." *The City: Los Angeles and Urban Theory at the End of the Twentieth Century*. Ed. Allen J. Scott and Edward W. Soja. Berkeley and Los Angeles: University of California Press, 1996. 390–425.

Wolch, Jennifer, Stephanie Pincetl, and Laura Pulido. "Urban Nature and the Nature of Urbanism." *From Chicago to L.A.: Making Sense of Urban Theory*. Ed. Michael J. Dear. Thousand Oaks, CA: Sage, 2002. 367–402.

Woll, Allen L. *The Latin Image in American Film*. Los Angeles: UCLA Latin American Center Publications, 1977.

"You Rat, You Die." *Gangland*. History (formerly known as The History Channel). A&E Television Networks, New York. 8 Nov. 2007.

Zahniser, David. "Welcome to Gentrification City. Teardowns. Evictions. Investment. Rebirth. And the Significance of That New Gelato Stand. The Perils and Pleasures of Gentrification." *Los Angeles Weekly*. 26 August, 2006. 1–9. http://www.laweekly.com/news/features/welcome-to-gentrification-city/14285/. Accessed 13 March 2008.

Zukin, Sharon. "Whose Culture? Whose City?" *The City Reader*. Ed. Richard T. LeGates and Frederic Stout. London: Routledge, 2005. 137–46.

Zulkey.com. "The Kate Braverman Interview: Just Under Twenty Questions," 9 June 2006. www.zulkey.com http://www.zulkey.com/diary_archive_060906 .html. Accessed 24 June 2007.

Index

About the Author

Ignacio López-Calvo is Professor of Latin American literature at the University of California, Merced. He is the author of four books on Latin American and U.S. Latino literature and culture: *Written in Exile: Chilean Fiction from 1973–Present* (Routledge, 2001); *Religión y militarismo en la obra de Marcos Aguinis 1963–2000* (Mellen, 2002); *"Trujillo and God": Literary and Cultural Representations of the Dominican Dictator* (University Press of Florida, 2005); and *Imaging the Chinese in Cuban Literature and Culture* (University Press of Florida, 2007). In addition, he has edited the books *Alternative Orientalisms in Latin America and Beyond* (Cambridge Scholars, 2007) and *One World Periphery Reads the Other: Knowing the "Oriental" in the Americas and the Iberian Peninsula* (Cambridge Scholars, 2009), and coedited *Caminos para la paz: literatura israelí y árabe en castellano* (2008).